CAPTAIN PAT

COMETH THE HOUR, CUMMINS THE MAN

RON REED

Published by Wilkinson Publishing Pty Ltd
ACN 006 042 173
PO Box 24135, Melbourne, VIC 3001, Australia
Ph: +61 3 9654 5446
enquiries@wilkinsonpublishing.com.au
www.wilkinsonpublishing.com.au

Follow Wilkinson Publishing on social media.

WilkinsonPublishing
wilkinsonpublishinghouse
WPBooks

ISBN: 9781925927993
eBook ISBN: 9781922810175
A catalogue record for this book is available from the National Library of Australia.

Design by Jo Hunt.

Printed and bound in Australia by Ligare Pty Ltd.

CONTENTS

INTRODUCTION

One wall of my home office is completely taken up with shelves full of cricket books—hundreds of them (books that is, not shelves), maybe one thousand. Ancient Wisdens by the dozens, at least 20 on the life and times of Don Bradman, captains' diaries, biographies, encyclopedias and lists, joke books and umpiring manuals, and even the history of a bush club I played for as a teenager.

Cricket tragic, much? You bet.

I've often wanted to add one more—a cricket book I have written myself. Now, here it is—and not before time. I have been writing professionally about the noble old game for well over 50 years, travelling the world to do so. It has been the definition of a labour of love.

Why it has taken so long for this to translate into book form, I don't rightly know. I've written seven others, and contributed to several more, but they've all been about other sports—footy, tennis, cycling and the Olympics. And it got to the stage where I was just about ready to leave it at that.

Then, along came Pat Cummins.

Well, not just Pat Cummins—but Captain Pat Cummins.

To me, there was a big difference. The NCO—non-commissioned officer—version had been around for a decade, half of which had been spent in the Test match wilderness because of constant injury.

Once he emerged from that, he quickly became a star, the best fast bowler in the world—but he was still just one of the troops, with only

30-odd Tests behind him, and a huge future still ahead of him. It just seemed to me that making him the subject of a book might be a tad premature, so when first asked to do so by publisher Michael Wilkinson I declined. Not once but several times.

That all changed when, without warning, the captaincy of the Test team became vacant late in 2021 in highly controversial circumstances and the most obvious choice—the only one, really, given all the circumstances—was the incumbent vice-captain and all-round golden boy, Patrick James Cummins, 28, from the outskirts of Sydney.

Not only that, his first assignment as the holder of the most prestigious sporting office in the land was to defend The Ashes against England, the oldest and most important contest on the Australian sporting calendar.

While nobody could predict precisely how that would play out, one thing was beyond certain—it was going to capture the imagination of the Australian public big-time, major talking points were guaranteed, the headline writers and talking heads would be earning their money double-time for the next two months.

And if Australia won, so much the better—a new king of Australian cricket would have been crowned to unstinting applause.

That's how it panned out—professional scriptwriters couldn't have improved on it, as captain Pat led from the front, took the most wickets, changed the image of the team for the better and guaranteed himself a level of fame and fortune rarely seen before in Australian cricket.

It hasn't been an altogether straightforward task pulling the story together. Nothing about cricket or any other sport these days is, thanks to the covid pandemic.

In my case it meant watching it all play out mostly from afar, glued to the TV every day, poring through the newspapers and tuning into talkback sports shows in search of information, insights and talking points, which were always plentiful—not the least because of the high standard of cricket journalism in this country these days, and of course in England.

Inevitably one must be careful about crossing the line between what is acceptable in terms of referencing other people's work and what is not, and I hope I have been able to do that in good faith. With a project of this sort and given the inherent difficulties with working remotely, that is not always easy. But where it seems most appropriate, I have included acknowledgements.

I want to particularly thank Captain Pat himself who made time after the Ashes to provide substantial and helpful input after the final Test, even though he said he was so busy "I haven't had time to scratch myself." A captain's work—like a woman's, as they say—is never done apparently. He also politely thanked me for dedicating such a project to him, to which I could only reply "my pleasure".

My gratitude goes to my long-time mate Steve Crawley, who runs Fox Sports, for his permission to mine their excellent documentary, *The Making of Pat Cummins*, for information, quotes and insights.

I also thank other old mates and one-time close colleagues Malcolm Conn and Robert Craddock for their help, as well as my old boss at News Corp Peter Blunden. Chris McLeod, another old colleague and mate, has been invaluable with his research, statistical input and editing, while publisher Michael Wilkinson was right in the first place—yes, we should do a book on Pat Cummins.

This won't be the last book about him, or by him, nothing surer than that, but I'm pleased I eventually agreed to do the first one. I just hope I can find room in the bookcase for it.

CHAPTER 1

NEW KING ASCENDS TO THE THRONE

Life has a habit sometimes of putting the foot down on the accelerator just when you're not really expecting it—and leaving it there, while you cling to the wheel and see where and how far the wild ride is going to take you. That's been the case for Patrick James Cummins for most of his relatively young life, most notably from the day—November 17, 2011—when in South Africa he achieved the dream of countless thousands of young Australian men (and, these days, a lot of women as well) and became a Test cricketer, the 423rd man to wear the baggy green cap that distinguishes this proud and privileged cohort from every other exponent of the nation's most popular and important international sport. And he was just a boy of 18 years and 193 days, the second youngest ever to wear the iconic headwear behind Ian Craig, the precocious Sydney batsman who debuted, also against South Africa, in Melbourne in 1953, aged 17 and 239 days.

Ten years later, almost to the very day, November 26, 2021, now 28, Cummins was appointed Australia's 47th Test captain, another huge achievement that neither he nor anybody else associated with the noble old game was expecting to happen, not at that particular juncture anyway. In the not-too-distant future, perhaps—but not yet.

And most certainly not in the dramatic circumstances that brought it about.

A week earlier his predecessor Tim Paine had resigned in tears—in disgrace, in the eyes of many—when it was revealed that he had been guilty of sending lewd text messages, including what is colloquially known as a "dick pic", to a female workmate three years earlier.

This ticking timebomb exploded more or less on the eve of what is always the most important fixture on the cricket calendar, an Ashes series against England. For all concerned, the timing couldn't have been worse—with the possible exception of the English team who were already in the country, preparing, and who would hardly be dismayed at their opposition suddenly being confronted with a massive and embarrassing internal distraction inside and outside the dressing room.

But it is an ill wind that blows nobody any good and Cummins was the most obvious beneficiary.

He wasn't necessarily the only one. Australian cricket—indeed, the game at large—was being confronted by issues of image and culture in various ways and Cummins' arrival in a position of such power and influence on and off the field of play had a lot going for it.

True, he had next to no experience in such a hot seat but that was balanced by enormous respect, from the Cricket Australia administration to his teammates and, crucially, the sporting public.

It is hard to think of any Australian captain who has come to the post with so much goodwill.

Long before this life-changing development, he had become—to employ a cliché that does not sit comfortably with his own self-estimation—the Golden Boy of the Australian game.

There were multiple reasons for that.

Not only was he a brilliant player in all three forms of the game—officially recognised as the world's best fast bowler for the past two years—but he was also highly intelligent, and, not to be underestimated, blessed with the good looks of a film star. Tall, dark and handsome seems an understatement.

As a package, it was beyond pleasing—impossible to dislike, in fact.

He had never been involved in any lurid behaviour or trouble-making, unless you wanted to count that he was a member of the team that was responsible for the ball-tampering scandal that brought the Australian team to its knees in South Africa in 2018 and saw then captain Steve Smith, senior batsman David Warner and rookie Cameron Bancroft stripped of leadership roles and suspended for long periods.

There was never any suggestion that Cummins, or the other fast bowlers, Mitchell Starc and Josh Hazlewood, were involved in illegally sandpapering the ball—cheating, in other words. If it ever emerges that they were—and a lot of people are waiting with great interest if not trepidation on the book that Warner, the accused mastermind, is expected to write as soon as he retires—that will be something that has to be dealt with then.

Unless and until that happens, Cummins' charisma, charm and common-sense will be assets almost as important as his bowling, batting and fielding skills.

In the way that he meets the eye he has often been compared— certainly, by me—with Keith Miller, the legendary all-rounder who was such a powerful force in the post-war years, especially when Don Bradman led the 1948 Invincibles throughout a long tour of England without losing a match, a feat never repeated.

Miller was a great bowler but Cummins already had him covered, with 164 wickets at 21.59 in the 34 Tests he had played before his promotion, compared to Miller's 170 at 22.97 from 21 more games. Cummins was about to sail straight past him with another 21 in the upcoming battle. But Miller averaged 36.97 with the bat, more than double Cummings' 16.46.

Miller, also a League footballer good enough to play for Victoria and a fighter pilot during the war, and also the perfect physical specimen that made him irresistible to women everywhere, even Royalty in the case of Princess Margaret, was an incorrigible playboy with little regard for authority. Even his own leadership at state level was never embraced all that seriously, all of which almost certainly explains why he was never entrusted with the Test captaincy.

Much the same can be said about another great playboy champion with charisma and talent to burn—and a lot more ambition than

Miller—in the late, great Shane Warne, who was overlooked in favour of the much more uncontroversial Steve Waugh when Mark Taylor passed the baton in 1999.

The champion leg-spinner—the best Australian cricketer of his time—had his ample share of flaws and foibles, but when he died suddenly of a heart attack at just 52, a few weeks after the Ashes, they had been well and truly submerged by reflections on how good he had been for the game in every respect.

Would he have been a good captain? Almost certainly. In the outpouring of grief after his death, many of his fans suggested the administration might have missed a trick by overlooking him, even if they did have their very valid reasons.

But that is unfair to Waugh, who brought no baggage to the table and did the job superbly for a long period of Australian Test domination.

Personality has always been regarded as a crucial component whenever the Cricket Australia directors have to decide on a new figurehead, every bit as important as playing ability.

That's because they jealously protect the long-held public assertion that there is no more prestigious post in all of Australian sport, and very few in any area of public life.

There has always been a sort of urban myth that it ranks only a single rung behind the Prime Ministership, which may or may not have been true in days gone by. Bradman, for instance, was more revered than any politician—but the comparison is probably more romantic than rational these days.

Nonetheless, when the day arrived to assess Cummins' suitability for the role, this concept mattered enormously.

The previous two captains, Smith and Paine, had both departed in tears, having been seen to have feet of clay in very different ways.

Paine's painful exit was beyond ironic, given that he was hurriedly appointed mid-match when Smith's tenure ended so traumatically.

The veteran wicketkeeper was designated as a safe pair of hands in every respect as the powers that be set out to try to restore badly shattered public confidence and respect, a process that saw several senior administrators, the incumbent coach and the team's operational manager also depart one after the other.

Responsibility for the rehab was accepted by Paine and the new coach Justin Langer, along with white-ball captain Aaron Finch, while Smith and Warner paid their penance in exile, pledging to return better men for the experience.

Although results on the scoreboard were mixed, the repair job was seen to have been largely successful, with Paine widely praised for his calm demeanour and emphasis on integrity, pride and respect for the game's image and traditions.

But for most of that time, he—and an increasing number of other people, not all of them in official positions—were aware that it could all blow up in his face, which it inevitably did. And in a few other faces, as well.

So where to next? And how? There could be no wriggle room for getting the next move wrong. And it was far from a straightforward decision.

There were only two logical candidates, Cummins and Smith—and there were authentic issues with both, although one much less so than the other.

Cummins was vice-captain and therefore the front-runner, but his only experience was a handful of games in charge of the New South Wales limited overs team a few months earlier, an assignment given to him for this very contingency—that he might need the experience at the highest level in due course.

He didn't lead under-age teams as most obviously gifted juniors do because he was such a prodigy that he would always be the youngest player in the team.

And of course, he was a specialist fast bowler, and no one of that ilk had ever been entrusted with the Test captaincy, with the exception of Ray Lindwall who stepped in for one match in India in 1956 as a temporary replacement for the injured Ian Johnson.

Yes, there are obviously reasons why on-field decision-making is more easily handled by batsmen who do not have the added mental strain of bowling themselves, but it has nevertheless always seemed to be an anachronism—not to mention an insult to some very good people who have specialised in that demanding skill for long periods.

It hasn't stopped players from other countries, such as Pakistan's Imran Khan and Wasim Akram, England's Bob Willis, India's Kapil Dev, West Indies' Courtney Walsh and South Africa's Shaun Pollock, among others, making a reasonably successful fist of it.

Besides, the captaincy extends well beyond the boundary rope and the designated hours of play. The job requires skills in man management, diplomacy, media interaction and public relations—"smarts" of all sorts.

There is no good reason to believe that fast bowlers should be any less capable of this than the blokes who bat—Cummins certainly no exception.

Smith was keen to take back the job that he inherited from Michael Clarke in 2014 and held for 34 matches, of which he won 18, lost 10 and drew six, for a winning percentage of 52.94.

But that was never going to sit well with large sections of the public, many of whom continued to believe that he should not even be welcome back in the team as a player, and certainly never as the captain.

It would have been a potentially explosive decision to put him back in charge.

Still, that didn't mean Cummins was a walk-up start. Normally, any new captain is recommended by the selectors, and then approved—or not, in Warne's case—by the CA board of directors.

But this time they went the extra mile, requiring two of the selectors—the chairman George Bailey and the recent appointment Tony Dodemaide, but not the third one, coach Justin Langer—to join the interim chairman Richard Freudenstein, the chief executive Nick Hockley and board member Mel Jones on a panel to interview both men.

The full board was then required to vote, as usual, with Cummins getting the nod and Smith appointed vice-captain.

That meant that Smith could still potentially take charge if anything, such as injury was to happen to Cummins, which remained a highly controversial contingency with talkback radio and the letters columns of newspapers making it clear that there had never been a vice-captain with less general approval.

But there had also never been one with more responsibility.

Cummins was in furious agreement with the popular opinion that his best chance of making a success of the gig, especially in the searing heat of his first campaign, was to have plenty of experienced hands to back him up, Smith the most obvious example.

In fact, Cummins insisted on the appointment, not only for that pragmatic reason but because they are firm friends with a history of having each other's back.

The new boss assured the world that he would be captain collaborative, not just accepting plenty of assistance from Smith and other old hands of the dressing room but insisting on it.

Some, notably Michael Clarke, who had an uneasy relationship with the main man when he was deputy to Ricky Ponting for three years, were sceptical about the proposed arrangement. "There can only be one captain," declared Clarke, whose own winning record from 18 matches in charge was an impressive 66.67 per cent.

A slightly different but very relevant take on it came from Ian Botham—that's Sir Ian, or Lord Botham to you and to me, even though I once played a few games of park cricket with him the first time he ever came to Australia as a 20-year-old holder of a now long defunct cricket scholarship—who was a close mate of Willis when he led England between 1982 and 1984.

Sir Ian, who had a brief and unsuccessful crack at the captaincy himself as an all-rounder who bowled often enough to take 383 Test wickets, then a record for an Englishman, was sceptical about the chances of Cummins or any other fast bowler succeeding.

Shortly after arriving in Australia to do TV commentary on the series, he said: "You've got a new captain coming in. I wish him all the very best but it's going to be a difficult baptism.

"A fast bowler historically doesn't really work. I mean, when my great friend Bobby Willis, when he was captain, we virtually set the fields for him between balls because he was so focused running in quick and getting everything right at his end. The captaincy becomes, if anything, secondary in a bowler's thinking and planning."

None of that was in any way likely to daunt Cummins, for whom having his senior teammates—especially Smith—assist with the technical aspects of on-field strategy was precisely the plan, for better or for worse.

If it worked he would happily take the credit, if it didn't he would accept the blame, which is precisely how it should always be, according to the late great Richie Benaud, one of Australia's most astute and successful skippers and an analyst and commentator with very few equals.

Cummins accepted his promotion with a measured equanimity, probably well aware that in the circumstances gleeful celebration— not his style anyway—might come across as unseemly, which wouldn't be in anyone's interests.

"Pride cometh before a fall" is always a cautionary aphorism well worth bearing in mind.

At his first press conference, he was at pains to present himself as "not perfect" but said he was not daunted by the powerful public scrutiny that had played such a big role in the downfall of his two predecessors.

He guaranteed that he would never rest from Test cricket while he held the reins. "I've never rested from a game of Test cricket and I doubt I'll start now," he said. Other formats, he said, were a bridge he would cross when he came to it.

He said he did not see himself as a captain until retirement and envisaged a time when he could hand the mantle back and play out the final years of his career as a foot soldier, not that such a regression has ever really happened voluntarily.

He left no doubt about his commitment to the double act with Smith, saying there would be times when the arrangement—with Smith moving fieldsmen and making bowling changes—might look different to past captains "and that's great".

Having witnessed the public humiliations of Smith and Paine first-hand, he admitted that he was "not overly comfortable" with being labelled some sort of golden boy but would not shy away from the high expectations that came with the role.

"I think a lot of the pressure and responsibility of being perfect is unreasonable," he said. "When it comes to moral character, I'm probably my own harshest critic and judge. That doesn't worry me too much."

In every way, it was a pitch-perfect presentation that was music to the ears of the nervous men at Cricket Australia, who were under plenty of pressure themselves to ensure the game's reputation was not threatened again.

Time was going to be the judge of that—and not very much time at that, as it transpired.

Cummins' year could scarcely have been any bigger or busier already and now it was about to go into overdrive.

It had begun with an unexpected defeat on home soil by India, who clinched it, 2–1, by winning at the Gabba fortress in Brisbane where Australia had not been beaten for 32 years.

That was followed by a period of tension after it was revealed that some senior players were unhappy with coach Justin Langer's management style. Few, if any, names were mentioned, but journalists with their ear to the ground as it became a major talking point correctly arrived at the conclusion that Cummins was one of them, a weighty factor if true given that he was vice-captain of the Test and white-ball teams.

It meant that he had to participate in an investigation in which the then chairman of the CA board, Earl Eddings, and the Chief Executive, Nick Hockley, quizzed him and white-ball captain Aaron Finch about the allegations of unrest. Langer was given the thumbs up to carry on, but the uneasiness lingered.

In fact, it never quite went away.

Cummins also had a commitment to the Indian Premier League, the world's biggest Twenty20 tournament, where he was on a massive salary of $3.1m to represent the Kolkata Knight Riders, $50,000 of which he donated to a charity dealing with the covid pandemic. He withdrew from the second half of the competition after it was suspended because of the pandemic and transferred to the Middle East.

More importantly than any of this, on October 8 he became a father for the first time, his fiancée Becky Boston giving birth to their son Albie.

Four days later, he was back at work, on the plane to the Middle East for the T20 World Cup, where he was a key performer as the Australians claimed the trophy for the first time in seven attempts—a huge achievement in its own right, but also a welcome morale boost ahead of the main event, the Ashes. No one was more pleased about it than the under-siege Langer.

For Cummins, all was well in the world—until the Paine drama meant that he was, with little warning, more in the spotlight than ever before as the debate over the captaincy succession took its place high on the national news agenda.

His eventual appointment meant that regardless of the veracity of the old line about the job being second to the Prime Minister, it was certainly true that he was suddenly being written and talked about more than anybody in the land other than Scott Morrison, and even that would have been a close-run thing.

This book was immediately commissioned and embarked upon, and it won't be the last one.

Within a week, he was on the cover of the glossy magazine *Good Weekend*, which is published with the *Sydney Morning Herald* and

The Age in Melbourne, one of the headlines proclaiming him to be Australian cricket's big hope. Another labelled him Mr Congeniality, the copy suggesting that his sophisticated, stress-free attitudes to life and uncomplicated personality would go a long way to ensuring he would be a success.

The next day, he was featuring in the general news pages with the announcement that he had become the first male Australian cricketer to be appointed the national ambassador to the United Nations children's charity, UNICEF, with which he had become involved when contributing to the covid fight in India.

What the rest of the year, and the remainder of the summer, was destined to bring was anybody's guess—including his own.

But pretty much the entire country was deeply interested in finding out.

CHAPTER 2

WHY THE CAPTAIN AND THE COACH HAD TO PART WAYS

Pat Cummins' first summer at the helm of the men's Test cricket team couldn't have been more triumphant, for him and for his troops, thrashing England 4–0 and defending the Ashes in double-quick time.

As an enjoyable experience, it was a ten out of ten, he said in an interview specifically for this book.

And yet, it descended three weeks later into bitterness and acrimony, with a former teammate accusing him of gutlessness and his team of reducing the mystique and pride of the famed baggy green cap to a symbol of selfishness.

The noble old game's governors, Cricket Australia, who should have been celebrating one of the most successful summers ever, were left to soak up public disdain for what the vast majority of fans—and a substantial cohort of former players and other closely linked observers—felt was a shambolically unprofessional handling of the biggest controversy of their tenure, in most cases.

That, of course, was the highly contentious removal of head coach Justin Langer.

It was the first time in his career, not just his captaincy, that Cummins had encountered any significant public criticism for anything he had said or done on or off the field, and it was, in his own estimation, a really good learning experience.

His response to it proved one thing beyond any reasonable doubt.

At a time when Australian cricket in general was in desperate need of strong leadership, Cummins confirmed that his appointment—made necessary in unfortunate circumstances but far from a foregone conclusion—was a masterstroke by an administration with very little about which to, er, pat itself on the back in recent times.

He navigated what amounted to a public crisis of confidence with candour and confidence, defusing it with both his trademark smile and an iron-clad commitment to standing up for what he believed needed to happen, even if it meant staring down some of the biggest names in the game's history.

This was such a messy affair with so many competing emotions and viewpoints, so much hidden from plain sight, that it was never going to be possible to reach a complete consensus on who was to blame for what, and Cummins might perhaps have lost a certain amount of skin—but not much, and not permanently.

To most—this observer no exception—it was the most meaningful off-field performance of his brief reign, mainly because he opted to tell it like it was without sacrificing any respect or admiration for the other man in the middle of it, his long-time coach.

The summer of 2021–22 will be remembered in posterity for two distinctly different reasons, each of them momentous.

As uplifting as it was on the field, it was bookended by embarrassment for the men and women who run the game, starting with the incumbent captain Tim Paine having to be cut loose over a scandal of his own making and finishing with the Langer debacle, in which he chose to resign rather than accept a token extension to his expiring contract.

Paine and Langer were the biggest individual losers, the ex-captain far more so than the ex-coach.

In one important sense Langer wasn't a loser at all—yes, he forfeited the job he so loved, but he emerged with his dignity, integrity and respect intact, with the general public, not just cricket fans, believing that he had been harshly treated. He conducted himself with impressive restraint, declining to fire any angry bullets on his way through the door.

And within days, he had been inundated with offers of new employment, inside and outside of cricket, some to continue coaching, some to explore other roles.

Worse damage was self-inflicted on Cricket Australia, who took far too long to come to grips with a situation that had been simmering for at least a year, and when they finally did they found what came across as a devious way of making Langer resign rather than looking him in the eye and telling him his time was up.

It created uproar, wiping away much of the goodwill regained— thanks largely to Langer—since the infamous ball-tampering cheating scandal three years earlier, which sabotaged Australian cricket's brand like never before.

One newspaper survey revealed that 90 per cent of the public were in favour of Langer keeping his job and could not understand why he would not, given what a dominant few months he had overseen.

That said, moving him on wasn't necessarily the wrong decision— all coaches in all sports have their use-by dates and often outstay their welcome especially if their rapport with their players becomes frayed, as Langer's undoubtedly had.

And what has always worked in the past is often not necessarily the right option for the future.

It is also true that the public do not appoint, or unappoint, the coach of any elite sports team—or the captain. That's why you have administrations, who hopefully know what they're doing.

But the way Cricket Australia went about it was "a public relations exercise that failed in almost every measure", according to a newspaper column by crisis communications expert Jason Gregory.

When the dust began to clear, this was officially acknowledged when the board finally got around to appointing a permanent chairman' to succeed Richard Freudenberg, who had overseen both the Paine and Langer imbroglios in an "interim" capacity following the departure of Earl Eddings, who had been shown the door by the state associations.

The board looked at a range of outsiders before opting for one of their own, West Australian Dr Lachlan Henderson, who admitted as soon as he took over that the Langer saga had "got messy in terms of it playing out in the media".

Interestingly, he also said the appointment of an ethics commissioner—a hitherto unheard-of job in Australian cricket—was imminent, in itself a comment on the unedifying events of the summer and, really, all the way back to Cape Town.

Recovery from the Langer PR disaster was likely to take a long time.

The Board were lucky they had a Test captain with so much popularity, goodwill, respect and authority to "calm the waters", to employ one of his own favourite expressions.

Coach sackings have long been a staple of Australian sport, especially in the football codes. "There are only two sorts of coaches, those who have been sacked and those who are about to be" is a favourite aphorism of the media.

They are less common in cricket because the Test team hasn't had them for very long, with one former captain, Ian Chappell, famously ranting for years that the only use his teams would have had for a coach was to transport them from the hotel to the ground.

It changed in 1986 when another former captain Bob Simpson became the first appointee, doing the job for a decade, before being replaced by Geoff Marsh and then John Buchanan, Tim Neilsen, Mickey Arthur and Darren Lehmann, with Langer making it only seven in more than two decades.

They were all moved on for various reasons, none harder to reconcile with their results than Langer, who had just overseen an historic first win in the Twenty20 World Cup in November 2021, and then the walloping of England in the Ashes.

How it came to that is a long and complex saga that ended up becoming a bigger media fixation than almost anything that happened during the Ashes, an event that is normally hard to upstage whenever and wherever it is being played.

It dated all the way back to the sandpaper catastrophe that led to the axing of the then captain and vice-captain, Steve Smith and David Warner, and in due course the resignation of coach Lehmann.

There has never been a more damaging blow to the image and reputation of Australian cricket and repairing it was going to require some extremely strong leadership.

Paine seemed a good choice to take over the captaincy, nobody suspecting he was already burdened with a guilty secret that would one day come back to bring him undone, and until that sad day did arrive he did a very good job of navigating the stormy waters.

Langer was deemed just the man to succeed Lehmann, for several reasons.

Of the six previous coaches only Simpson rivalled him as a player. He was a future inductee into the Australian cricket Hall of Fame for his 102 Tests between 1993 and 2007 in which he scored 7696 runs at 45.3—numbers that earn automatic respect.

More than that, he was a cricketer of great courage and commitment, making the most of what was not necessarily the abundant talent of many of his contemporaries, and once having to be restrained by captain Ricky Ponting from risking his life by returning to the crease after being badly concussed.

He was already a successful career coach with the West Australian State team and the Perth Scorchers in the Big Bash, basing his methods on discipline, effort and integrity.

He was appointed on a four-year contract that was to expire in June 2022.

For the first couple of years he and Paine made a good combination in restoring pride, culture and public confidence, even if it was never explicitly clear who was calling the shots—although the coach usually had at least as much media exposure as the captain did, the louder voice.

This was not particularly surprising given that in the unusually fragile environment he was shouldering more responsibility than any previous coaches.

He had come into the job with the team in disgrace and the nation's most popular international sport having had its brand trashed and its support base angry and disillusioned, so he was not only a cricket coach but a cultural influencer, working not only for the team but for the good name of the entire country.

Never before had a coaching tenure been quite so complex in its demands. Or a captaincy, for that matter.

The cracks started to appear in early 2021 when the Channel Nine newspapers, the *Sydney Morning Herald* and *The Age*, were leaked information that the dressing room collectively wasn't seeing eye to eye with the coach whose methods they were finding to be overbearing and intense.

On a short and disappointing tour of Bangladesh that year Langer berated a team staffer about a minor matter, which did not go down well with some players and it, too, quickly found its way into the media.

In hindsight, that may have been a pivotal moment—the stretching of the elastic to breaking point, or close to it.

Within a month, the whispering campaign was so loud that Cricket Australia (CA) was forced to step in, with then chairman Earl Eddings and CEO Nick Hockley meeting with the captains, Paine and Aaron Finch and vice-captain Cummins.

At the time, Hockley released a statement voicing appreciation for the job Langer had performed in "raising the culture, values and behaviours" of the team. But it did nothing to defuse the issue. It was just an uneasy truce in the overly optimistic hope that the smoke would clear.

It had been made clear that the players were increasingly uncomfortable with Langer's micro-management style and volatile mood swings and that he needed to adjust it accordingly.

That he did, taking more of a back seat—delegating more responsibility to assistant coaches Andrew McDonald and Michael de Venuto during the T20 World Cup and the Ashes—and tweaking his "bedside manner" with the players.

From that point, the team lost only one match—early in the World Cup—a success rate that would have most coaches knocking on their boss's door demanding a pay rise, not wondering, as Langer was forced to do, whether he would even keep his job.

Despite celebrating win after win, the players—Cummins included—were unconvinced that Langer was capable of sustaining his new methodology if the good times stopped rolling. Nothing had changed, and wasn't likely to.

There was nothing personal against him—he was liked and admired, at least by most—but they wanted him gone.

They just couldn't say so publicly—which, of course, did not mean they could not or would not do so privately to media contacts, thereby ensuring that the coach's predicament would be a live topic.

Every time Cummins (and to a lesser extent Finch, given his teams weren't playing) were asked, they pointedly declined to endorse his re-appointment, which Langer had made abundantly clear he would be seeking.

That was fair enough. As Cummins repeatedly said, it wasn't his or his team's call to make, and until it was made, until due process was carried out, anything they said—for or against—had the potential to inflame a delicate and uncertain situation.

CA, meanwhile, straight-batted every media inquiry by stating that the appropriate conversations would begin "after the Ashes" without specifying what that meant, exactly.

And so it dragged on—and on.

More and more past players—really heavy hitters, including Steve Waugh, Adam Gilchrist, Ricky Ponting, Shane Warne, Matthew Hayden and Mark Taylor—were going into bat for their old mate, saying they couldn't fathom why his reappointment wouldn't be a no-brainer, given his on-field results.

They were getting stuck into not only CA but the current players Cummins included, who they were accusing of not offering their coach the support he deserved, and helping hang him out to dry.

This created a gulf between the contemporary players and their celebrated predecessors that had seldom been seen before and which served only to heighten an impression that the game was in danger of going to war with itself.

The situation took an awkward turn when CA announced that they were inducting Langer into their Hall of Fame—lauding him for his career on one hand, but still not cutting to the chase.

Finally, on Friday, February 4—19 days after the last ball had been bowled in the Ashes—CA's full board met in Melbourne, only to break up several hours later without making any announcement.

Their decision was to offer Langer a six-month extension which, they said, would provide him with the opportunity to defend the T20 title when the next World Cup was held in Australia at the end of the year. A chance to go out on a high, they told him.

The nine directors—interim chairman Freudenberg, Mike Baird, Mel Jones, Greg Rowell, Paul Green, John Harnden, Dr Vanessa Guthrie, Dr Henderson and Michelle Tredenick—plus their CEO must have known that no self-respecting coach was likely to accept that.

If so—if it was a deliberate ploy—they were correct.

Recognising it as the tokenism that it was—an insult, really—Langer slept on it before ringing CEO Hockley the next morning and telling him, politely, where he could stick the offer—and then flew home to Perth for the first time in almost five months to be with his family, who were as dismayed as he was by this unwelcome outcome.

In a lengthy and uncomfortable press conference, Hockley defended the decision, saying it wasn't just a matter of wins and losses—but that unity was a key criterion, which confirmed that the players views had been taken on board.

"The decision to start a process of transition is what we believe is in the best interests of the men's team for unity and future success," he said.

"In the middle of the year we did have some challenging conversations, and some issues. It was well-documented that we had some pretty robust conversations after coming back from Bangladesh, which was actually a really constructive process that led to role clarity.

"We recognised that the team had evolved and the requirements and needs of the head coach have also evolved.

"We are now evolving to the next phase of a more shared leadership model."

Hockley said that while Cummins and Finch were among the individuals consulted as part of the evaluation process the discussion was also broadened to include other members of team staff as well as selectors.

He said it had been made "pretty clear" to Langer that he was being offered a period of transition.

"It was a very lengthy discussion by the board but ultimately there was consensus this was the right way forward. We really would have loved JL to stay on and defend the T20 World Cup but the thinking was now is the time to look forward to the next phase. He has been an outstanding coach. His impact has been fundamental in restoring trust and respect in the team."

Langer responded by releasing his letter of resignation—which, poignantly, included an apology.

"There has been a great deal of media speculation on my future which has taken an enormous toll on my family," he wrote. "I hope through this time and through my tenure, I have held myself with integrity and dignity. Last night I was offered a short-term contract until the end of the T20 World Cup in Australia with the sentiment of going out on a high.

"After careful consideration I have decided not to accept this contract renewal and as a result I believe it is in everyone's best interests for the Australian cricket team to begin the next chapter immediately.

"If media reports are correct several senior players and a couple of support staff don't support me moving forward and it's now apparent the CA board, and you Nick, are also keen to see the team move in another direction. I respect that decision.

"My life has been built on values of honesty, respect, trust, truth and performance and if that comes across as 'too intense' then I apologise."

He said he was proud of what he had achieved. "It is said in any venture. If you leave things in a better place than when you started, then you have done your job.

"Whilst it is not up to me to judge, I hope Australians respect what has been achieved over this last four years. From day one I believed it was possible to both win and play the game in the spirit that is now expected from our supporters.

"For the last four years it has been proven this can be achieved and I am very proud of the team for their efforts on and off the field.

"I hope we have made Australians proud and earned respect from countries around the world.

"In terms of 'going out on a high' I am blessed to have been part of a T20 World Cup-winning squad, watched the Test team rise to No. 1 ranked in the world, been selected as the Wisden coach of the year and been elevated to the Australian cricket Hall of Fame, all this in the last five months.

"I am grateful that today I am going out on a high. Australian cricket means the world to me. It has since I was a kid and I am grateful for the opportunity to play for, and coach, our national team.

"I will take with me many cherished memories and friendships from the last four years. Hopefully a good job has been done and I wish the team every success in the future."

It is difficult to imagine how an exit statement could be couched in more conciliatory terms—in a word, it was classy.

The Old Mates Club stepped up their howls of protest at his treatment, accusing both CA and the players—including Cummins— of shafting him.

Ponting said it was "poor and embarrassing", Gilchrist called it pathetic, Hayden said it was hurtful and Mitchell Johnson went right over the top.

The former fast bowler—a teammate when Cummins played his first Test—wrote a savagely vitriolic column in his home-town newspaper, the *West Australian*.

"Pat Cummins has been lauded as some type of cricketing saint since his elevation to the top job this summer. Cummins might have delivered with the ball during the Ashes series but he has failed his first big test as captain pretty miserably," Johnson ranted.

"He's had plenty of public opportunities to endorse an extension for Langer. So when he let it through to the keeper every time it was pretty obvious he didn't want it to happen.

"Cummins holds a lot of power and must have been central to what's happened. He's clearly had an agenda to get in a coach he wants. His recent interviews have been gutless by not respecting his coach when he could have been upfront from the start.

"The baggy green is hyped as the most revered symbol in Australian sport. But what does it stand for now? In the wake of the disgraceful white-anting of Langer as coach, it stands for selfishness."

If there was a prize for the most unfair—not to say the most stupid—commentary of the summer, Johnson would have won hands down, and should have apologised.

Cummins hadn't failed any test or been gutless, he had simply waited until the decision that wasn't his to make was made before explaining where he and his troops stood.

After a brief hiatus, he did so comprehensively, first releasing a lengthy written statement and then fronting a press conference where he answered every question candidly.

His statement, almost certainly crafted with professional help but no less credible for that, is worth recalling in its entirety.

"There has been much public comment since Justin Langer's resignation," he wrote. "For good reason I haven't made public comment. To speak about a decision which was yet to be made and which is for Cricket Australia to make, would have put CA and the team in an impossible position.

"I'd never do that. I believe in respecting the sanctity of the changeroom and proper process.

"Now that a decision has been made by Justin to resign and give his own public comments and others by CA, I can provide some clarity. Justin has acknowledged that his style was intense, and it was. He has apologised to players and staff for his intensity. I think the apology was unnecessary. Because the players were OK with JL's intensity.

"It came from a good place—his fierce love of Australia and the baggy green—something which has served Australian cricket well for three decades. It's what makes him a legend of the sport. And Justin's intensity drove a better team culture and higher team standards. These are significant Justin Langer legacies. And on behalf of the players, I thank Justin.

"More than that we owe him a lot and Justin will be a welcome face in the dressing room in the future. So, his intensity was not the issue for players and staff. The question is: what is the best style of coaching for the future, given how the team has evolved? We have been very well schooled in how to play cricket the right way—in the correct Australian way. We understand the importance of always playing to the highest ethical standards. And the players need no motivation as I've never played with more motivated cricketers. To be better players for Australia, from this solid foundation, we need a new style of coaching and skill set.

"This was the feedback the players gave to Cricket Australia. And it's the feedback I understand staff also gave. We welcome that CA invited the players and staff to contribute to its evaluation.

"I add that as professional sportspeople we would have accepted any decision CA were to make because that's what professionals do. CA have made a brave call to transition, given the team has been winning.

"Finally, we are custodians of cricket, with one very big thing in common: our first duty is to Australian cricket, which is bigger than any one of us. I take this responsibility seriously. I live and breathe it.

We also have a duty to our mates. Many former players have reached out to me and silently offered me their advice, which is welcome. Some others have spoken in the media which is also welcome and comes from a love of the game and their support of a mate.

"To all past players, I want to say this: Just as you have always stuck up for your mates, I'm sticking up for mine."

Pretty straightforward, all of that. And the message to Johnson was unmissable.

There was nothing to be gained by spelling out Langer's idiosyncrasies chapter and verse so Cummins didn't.

What he did do was express gratitude and respect, while making it abundantly clear that he believed change was needed—there was no sugar-coating that, no watering it down, no euphemisms employed.

Elaborating later, he said: "It's a difference of opinions and if you can't resolve those difference in opinions, unfortunately you need change.

"That's happened. I don't think he should be surprised by it, it's been two years of evaluations.

"We felt the players would benefit from a more collaborative approach. A big theme for the summer has been keeping more calm, more composed and that's been really clear in the feedback from the players, support staff and CA and that's the direction we want to take the team."

Cummins rejected assertions that player power had got out of control. "We're all professionals here, so if we didn't get the coach we wanted, that's fine, we'd keep playing, there's no stress."

He agreed Langer deserved better than the way the saga played out in public. "He felt at the end of it, he hasn't been fairly treated. That's not on, and I hope we can learn from that," he said.

"I've just got huge respect for the man. I love what he's done. I owe him a lot. He's been brilliant, not only for this team but me individually.

"He's given me a lot of opportunities and backed me in a lot. He's someone I'm sure I'll be leaning on in the future because he gives a lot."

It is difficult to understand the angst in some quarters over the players being given a say in determining whether the coach stays or goes. Why shouldn't the people best-placed to understand the dynamics of the dressing room not be entitled to have an opinion and to have it listened to—not necessarily acted upon, but acknowledged and considered—when the road forward is being charted?

They would have a better handle on that than most of the board members who were actually making the decisions, with only Rowell, who represented three states at first class level but not Australia, and Jones, who played for the national women's team, boasting any significant, elite playing experience.

That applies to nobody more than the captain, who is usually the most experienced and who is—or should be—more in charge, more responsible for results, than the coach.

As many observers pointed out, running a cricket team is very different from a football team in any code, where the coach is clearly the main man who dictates tactics and assigns roles to players. It is the footy coach who speaks to the media before and after games, not the captain, in most circumstances.

The cricket captain shoulders most of those responsibilities and is the spokesman for the team.

Perhaps it took Langer too long to fully come to grips with that reality and by the time he did the horse had bolted. In hindsight, it might have been better if he had read the room more perceptively and departed on his own terms, at least publicly, after the Ashes, which would have been "going out on a high".

But he was a bare-knuckle fighter in his playing days and walking away from a challenge had never been his style so he saw no reason to start now.

Nor did his many old comrades believe that he should have to do that.

If Cummins lost any sleep when they started plotting him, it did not show when he was asked about it.

"I actually haven't really had much of it (criticism) before so it's actually been good to get it out of the way early in my captaincy," he said, laughing. "I knew when I took on the job it was going to come with added scrutiny so the last week has been good to know that I'll cop it—but I'm absolutely fine with it."

In a much later interview with News Corp cricket writer Ben Horne, he said the lesson he had learned—and he is by no means the first to come to this conclusion—was that "if you try and spend your life pleasing everyone, you end up pleasing no one. It gave me clarity on what my role is and that it to try to do what's best for our team and our environment, but also what I think is best for Australian cricket. It really strengthened my beliefs in what I thinks is right and who I should listen to and it made me think of where my responsibilities lie."

One of his key mentors, life coach Ben Crowe, added the astute observation that there had been a second lesson. "You don't want to be disliked but you've got to have the courage to be disliked," he said.

Johnson's outburst was a case in point. "Look, he's just standing up for his mates. I absolutely disagree with what he said. He hasn't reached out (to square off) but that's fine," Cummins said. "He's entitled to his opinion but I can hold my head up so I'm fine.

"My responsibility as captain is to my teammates, to the environment and to Australian cricket. So as part of the feedback process, I canvassed as many thoughts as I could and I know being captain carries a bit more weight and a bit more voice than perhaps others do. I'm sticking up for them, making sure they're heard. And I hope in some regards I am keeping the sanctity of the changing room and not overstepping my mark.

"There's been a lot of emotion flying around and you've got to take it in that kind of context. (Past players) are all people I really respect so I listen to them, for sure, and I'd welcome chatting to any of them directly about feedback and thoughts that I have.

"We're custodians of the Australian cricket team, it's not forever.

We just want to do what's best. Me as captain, it's a responsibility I've been given and I take that really seriously."

In which case, the game is in good hands. But we pretty much already knew that.

CHAPTER 3

PAINFUL END FOR CAPTAIN WHO DID A LOT RIGHT

They say a week is a long time in politics, but the seven days of public humiliation that one of Australia's most popular and important sportsmen, Tim Paine, endured as his cricket career came crashing down around him must have felt like a lifetime in Hell.

This unprecedented drama had a massive impact on the build-up to the eagerly-anticipated Ashes campaign, delivering the Test captaincy to Pat Cummins, which was central to everything else that was to happen for the rest of a tumultuous summer.

There had been plenty of scandals in Australian cricket over the past 150 years or so, but this one was both bizarre and unique with ramifications more far-reaching than most.

For cricket in general, wrestling with a range of cultural and behavioural issues, it was an uncomfortable period, with the visiting English team in no position to claim occupation of the moral high ground as it was confronted with a racism uproar at least indirectly involving its captain Joe Root.

None of the various issues in play were more personally painful—pardon the pun—than the Paine affair.

It was his own fault, no doubt about that, but whether he deserved the level of condemnation that a great many people thought appropriate, and weren't slow to say so, or the embarrassment and anguish that he had to confront within the four walls of his own home is just one of several questions that may never be answered to everyone's satisfaction.

Another one is how much of the blame should be shared by the heavy-hitters, past and current, who run the game at Cricket Australia and Cricket Tasmania? Even the media's role did not sit comfortably with many onlookers, although shooting the messenger is rarely a useful solution to anything.

What is for certain is that no other captain of the Australian cricket team has ever lost this prestigious job in quite this way—although his predecessor Steve Smith did so in a different set of scandalous circumstances—and it is a huge price that Paine has had to pay, one that will haunt him for the rest of his life.

His offence was sending lewd text messages to a woman who was not his wife and following up with a photograph of his genitals, a "dick pic" as it is colloquially known.

This was not a crime or even a breach of any written rules of the game, including codes of conduct, just a monumental error of judgment, extremely stupid but far from uncommon in society generally in this, the 21st century.

Against that, though, cricket more than most sports has made a conscious effort to promote respect and opportunity for women, a factor that has to be part of the response to any plea for sympathy. It has not been a simple consideration.

All sportsmen have no shortage of ways to bring into disrepute the games—the industries, really—that provide such generous livelihoods for many of them, and cricketers have been guilty of plenty of them in recent and not so recent times, from match-fixing to gambling to racism to verbal abuse to straight-out cheating, you name it. You are welcome to decide which is more egregious than the other.

Even gender identification has become an issue with the governing body, the ICC, decreeing that the word batsman must be replaced by the neutral term batter, a policy that this book has not the slightest intention of observing. Batsmen is what the blokes have always been and still are, and if the girls wish to call themselves something else they are perfectly welcome to do so—but some of us old dinosaurs see no good reason to submit to new-age woke-ism just for the sake of it.

In any case, that's the least of the game's worries.

The inescapable irony of Paine's predicament, of course, is that he was thrust into the captaincy mid-match when the Australian team was sprung using sandpaper to tamper with the ball—a form of cheating—during a Test in Cape Town, South Africa, in 2018, which saw Smith stripped of the leadership and he, senior batsman David Warner and rookie Cameron Bancroft were hit with long suspensions amid a national uproar.

Paine got the job because he was seen as a cleanskin with no dubious negative history who could help oversee an urgently-needed makeover of the dressing room culture and image and help restore public confidence and respect—which he and a new coach, Justin Langer, successfully achieved over the next two or three years.

And yet now here he was, like Smith, losing the prize gig in tears and disgrace—two captains in quick succession. This is the stuff of nightmares for administrators.

By the time Paine's indiscretions became public, the England party was in Australia and already on the back foot, psychologically, because of the embarrassment generated by multiple explosive investigations—eventually involving the Government—into the proud and famous Yorkshire County club, Root's home base.

This was sparked by Pakistan-born Azeem Rafiq claiming he had been the victim of institutionalised racism while playing there, which reduced him to tears and left him on the verge of suicide.

Former England captain Michael Vaughan was accused of being one of the perpetrators, which he denied, and it cost him some of his commentary roles in the upcoming campaign in Australia, although he still found plenty of work on various platforms and few commentators were more outspoken.

The upshot was that the club—a Test venue almost every year—was banned from staging international matches, while the chairman resigned, the director of cricket and the head coach were both removed and other officials walked away. Three months later the hosting ban was rescinded, which was unsurprising given the clout and seniority Yorkshire have always enjoyed within the England cricket family.

Whether this was a worse scandal than "Sandpapergate" was open to debate, but from any reasonable perspective it outranks the Paine affair on any shame file by a goodly margin.

However, that's not necessarily how the media machine works when it comes to the here and now.

From his new vantage point in a luxury quarantine hotel on the Gold Coast, Root wisely had nothing to add, advised no doubt that the issue would have faded into the background by the time the cricket started, which of course it did.

Paine made doubly sure of that.

His downfall will be remembered by posterity as the great dick pic debacle, and it is entirely possible that until this shot to the top of the national news agenda there would have been people of a certain age who would have needed it to be explained to them. What's a dick pic, exactly?

If so the answer wasn't long in being provided on every front page and news service.

Sometimes such behaviour is romantic, sometimes its harassment, sometimes its consensual, sometimes its offensive, sometimes it leads to legal redress. In Paine's case all/most of these elements seem to have been in play to some degree, making it all the more difficult to get a handle on the exact extent of his culpability.

His day of eternal regret was November 23, 2017, the start of the first Ashes Test at the Gabba in Brisbane, and all was well in Paine's world. Couldn't have been better, really.

He had been married for a year to Bonnie Maggs, the love of his life, was the father of infant daughter Milla—later to be joined by a son, Charlie—and was back in the Test team after a long absence, keeping wickets and batting in the lower middle order, a welcome development after having almost opted for retirement in the belief that his limited opportunities at the highest level had come and gone after just four Tests in an earlier incarnation.

The fateful day in Cape Town was still several weeks in the future.

All of which makes the brain fade that followed all the more difficult to rationalise.

Sitting in his hotel room about 7am, Paine began flirting by text with a workmate at Cricket Tasmania, Renee Ferguson, with whom he regularly engaged over organisational matters relating to his job as a professional cricketer, as did other state players.

The messages were far from the usual trivia about collecting bags and so on.

They have since been widely published, verbatim, but are now, perhaps, best left to the imagination, except to say that juvenile, puerile and crass have them covered, at least from his end. She is much less explicit, perhaps because she later claimed in court that the exchange was not consensual.

One exception needs to be made.

FERGUSON: A real woman would never kiss and tell... regardless neither of us are in a position of power... we are both fucked if this ever got out.

PAINE: True, so fucked.

FERGUSON: One thing I can guarantee you. I am a vault. Never repeat a thing.

PAINE: Same here.

"If this ever got out..." As famous last words go, they are pretty much 24-carat. But it took four years before it did get out, at least beyond the cricket bubble in which Paine lived and into the media, and all the while a time bomb ticked away in the back of his mind.

A lot happened in the interim, most notably his dramatic promotion to the Test captaincy.

You can tie yourself in knots attempting to accurately pin-point precisely what took place, how and when, at whose instigation, over the ensuing weeks, months and years until the time bomb exploded publicly in mid-November 2021, as it was always destined to do eventually.

But the most inflammatory development occurred just two months after his appointment, in May, when both Cricket Australia and Cricket Tasmania became aware of the matter and conducted parallel secret investigations, concluding that it had been a private, consensual exchange between adults that did not breach their official code of conduct.

That being the case, they saw no reason to say anything publicly because if they did so it would inevitably reflect badly on their captain even though he had been found to have no case to answer, not an unreasonable position to take—but nonetheless, still not silencing the ticking time-bomb.

Paine reportedly co-operated fully and did not attempt to deny or sugar-coat what he had done.

Officially not guilty of anything, he was allowed to continue to lead the team. Tick, tick, tick.

Ferguson resigned from her job at CA in less than amicable circumstances in 2018 but did not go away.

Some time after the investigation, she complained to her former employers that she was concerned about Paine's behaviour, that it was part of a wider pattern she had experienced in her time with the state association.

As a result Paine's brother-in-law and former State player Shannon Tubb also left the association's staff with a confidential settlement and was later reported to have also sent similar texts.

Ferguson became involved in two legal matters with Cricket Tasmania, one relating to the handling of her sexual harassment claim and the other to allegations linked to her employment. Both remained unresolved at the time of this publication. Paine was not a party to those actions.

According to a front-page investigation by *The Age* newspaper, discussions with Cricket Tasmania continued through the latter part of the year as Paine was leading his team in an unsuccessful series against India, with requests forthcoming for an apology and assistance with legal fees.

Cricket Australia decided not to intervene, no doubt hoping—for the second time—that the issue would go away. That was something bitter experience should have told them was highly unlikely.

The governing body had a dubious history of attempting to cover up embarrassing scandal, most notably when it was revealed in 1998 that star players Mark Waugh and Shane Warne had been heavily fined for accepting money from an Indian bookmaker for providing team information during a tour of Sri Lanka four years earlier.

It took three years for the media to expose the deception, but they eventually did, with highly-regarded newspaper journalist Malcolm Conn winning a Walkley Award for leading the way.

Paine was always resigned to the reality that this would happen to him too as much as he desperately hoped it would not.

After it did, he admitted: "I thought the issue was dealt with, but it always popped up around a big series or at the start of the cricket season. Over the last three years there have been numerous times where media agencies have put to us that they have evidence, yet they never chose to write it. As to why, I'm not sure, but I knew it was going to come out at some point."

That point arrived in mid-November 2021 when Australia's biggest-selling newspaper, Melbourne's *Herald Sun*, made Cricket Australia and Paine's manager James Henderson aware that it was in possession of the texts and was about to publish them—unless there was any overpowering reason why they should not.

No such response was provided to Peter Blunden, the News Corp group's national executive whose major responsibilities included sports matters, who had taken personal charge of the story.

This would have been an unfortunate development at any time to say the least, but with the Ashes only three weeks away, the timing was particularly alarming.

Over two or three days, CA had several crisis meetings after the paper first started asking hard questions, while Blunden negotiated with Henderson about precisely when and how the blockbuster would be published and senior reporter Stephen Drill and others began preparing the copy.

Blunden delayed hitting the "print" button because he believed it was important to give all concerned an opportunity to respond. "We gave them the chance to say no, it's all bullshit, but there was no denial, no valid reason, so we were fair to them. But we had it all," he said.

The story appeared online on a Friday morning, followed quickly by an update that Paine would be resigning the captaincy that afternoon— which he duly did in a tearful lone media conference, in which he said he did not want to become a distraction to his team or his family.

The texts, he said, "did not meet the standard of an Australian cricket captain or the wider community."

There was no CA representative by his side, just a carefully-worded statement that the decision had been accepted as his own without having been officially prompted to make it, and that his language and behaviour was "not condoned".

It was quickly and widely pointed out that it had, to all intents and purposes, condoned it when allowing him to keep his job after the initial investigation.

After his statement Paine took no questions and did not elaborate. But to the surprise of the rest of the media, he and his wife both bared their souls almost immediately in the same newspaper that had exposed him, the *Herald Sun*, the Sunday edition of which carried a three-page interview with them both, a strategy agreed upon by Blunden and Henderson.

It hopefully allowed Paine and his wife to avoid being confronted by a media frenzy every time either of them set foot outside their front door.

Conducted by well-known media all-rounder Hamish McLachlan, whose in-depth one-on-one interviews with celebrities had long been one of the paper's regular features, and who was also a presenter with Channel 7, the cricket broadcaster, the exchange was emotional but dignified.

Paine told McLachlan that he was distressed, upset, frustrated and embarrassed, and felt sick on his wife's behalf.

He could not explain why he had sent the messages. "Maybe it's as simple as stupidity? Or an inflated ego? Or feeling needed or wanted, being flattering. Or that it was dangerous or risqué. I don't know. I know I wish I hadn't and it will be a life of regret that I did," he said.

Bonnie said she had mixed emotions when she learned about it at the time of the investigation, betrayed, hurt, upset and pissed off, "but also feelings of gratitude because he was being so honest with me. I thought, 'OK, do I walk? Or forgive and rebuild?' I chose the latter.

"I learned that I could forgive someone. I never thought I was strong enough (to do that), to move past it and stick with them. I've learnt the skill of forgiveness, which is really difficult.

"My trust was a bit shattered and learning to try and trust again was a process. I had my doubts and there were times I wanted to leave, and there were times I wasn't sure what I wanted to do. It was very confusing."

Both agreed that as hurtful as the episode had been, their relationship was now stronger than it had been before—proving again that there is usually a silver lining to every cloud.

Paine had already said he wanted to retain his place in the team which quickly became a controversy all of its own.

If he had not been the captain he would have been no rolled-gold certainty to be selected anyway because he was coming off an operation on his neck that had prevented him playing any cricket, or even training properly, for most of the year.

And in any case, he was not far short of his 37th birthday—which fell on the first day of the first Test, his former teammates taking time out from their busy day to send him warm messages—and was expected to retire after the campaign against the Englishmen.

Other younger, in-form wicketkeeper-batsmen were jostling for his spot come what may.

CA raised no objections to him being selected, but they were under siege themselves, for at least two very different reasons.

There was a strong and predictable school of public opinion that they should have stripped him of the captaincy the moment they learned of his indiscretions, rather than attempt an ill-fated cover-up.

This grew legs when interim chairman Freudenstein stated that while neither he nor Chief Executive Hockley were in their roles back then, the current board would not have made the same decision "with the benefit of all the relevant information".

In other words, they would have been looking for a new captain.

That was seen as not only throwing Paine under the bus, but also discomforting the only two remaining directors who were on the board back then, John Harnden and Michelle Tredenick.

Another view was that by making no attempt to talk Paine out of his resignation, or even physically supporting him as he delivered it, they had hung him out to dry for an offence that many did not believe warranted such a devastating outcome.

The previous CA chairman David Peever weighed in with an angry formal statement blasting Freudenstein's assertion and accusing him of abandoning his captain and showing no loyalty. It had been a knee-jerk decision that showed double standards, he said.

Nowhere was this view more stridently expressed than from Cricket Tasmania, whose chairman Andrew Gaggin took aim at his national counterpart in no uncertain terms.

"It is clear that the anger from the Tasmanian cricket community and general public is palpable," he seethed. "Tim Paine has been a beacon for Australian cricket over the past four years and instrumental in salvaging the reputation of the national team after the calamity of Cape Town.

"Yet at the time Cricket Australia should have supported Tim he was evidently regarded as dispensable. The treatment afforded to the Australian Test captain has been appalling, the worst since Bill Lawry (was sacked behind his back) 50 years ago."

CA was infuriated by this attack but chose not to respond.

With the players' union, the Australian Cricketers Association, also expressing unequivocal support for their senior colleague, as did all of his Test teammates, formally and informally, and several prominent past players, it seemed something resembling civil war had broken out between the various administrative elements and the playing cohort.

Relations between head office and the players' collective had long been fragile and uneasy and this had become just another example. The suspicion that Paine had been abandoned—and if it could happen to him, it could happen to anyone else—did not dissipate quickly, if at all.

At a time when the game was desperate for public support and engagement with the most important of all Test series about to begin, the whole imbroglio had deteriorated into a bit of a shambles really— and not for the first time.

Paine was the one paying the price but there was—or should have been—a limit on how heavy that was.

If I may editorialise, surrendering the captaincy—and having the words "in disgrace" attached to it forevermore—was more than enough, especially when it was set beside the emotional anguish he and his family had endured together.

That it eventually saw him fall on his sword a second time, dropping out of cricket altogether, and finding his mental health being compromised and his reputation shredded for the foreseeable future was beyond disappointing and probably unfair.

What he had done wasn't a hanging offence by any stretch of the imagination.

That is not to suggest, as many did, that it was all a storm in a tea-cup—the captaincy of the Australian Test team does not quite rival the Prime Ministership for importance as has often been romantically suggested but it does carry a prestige unequalled in any other sporting— and possibly cultural—field, so it does matter. A lot.

So was Paine right to step away from it?

Yes, in the sense that it was an honourable call, made in what he considered to be the best interests of the game and the team, an attempt to minimise distraction on the eve of a huge summer.

He was trying, remorsefully, to do the right thing by all concerned, his family no exception.

For that, he should have been respected and supported, not vilified.

Of course, his indiscretion—like the sandpaper scandal before it, and a few others before that—had damaged the reputation of Australia's most popular international sport, but the blame wasn't all his. The cover-up spread that a lot more widely.

This is not to paint him as a victim—far from it—because of course he is responsible for what he does, as are we all, and there was another party negatively involved.

However, over his roller-coaster journey Paine had done much more right than wrong and if the dust had been allowed to settle the suspicion was that most people—not everyone, admittedly—would have not only cut him some slack but wished him well in getting on with his life.

His tenure in charge began in far more demanding and unusual circumstances than had ever been the case for any new incumbent, and he mostly handled the unique challenges inside and outside the dressing room with aplomb.

The players respected him and because he never had tickets on himself the fans warmed to his "everyman" persona, while the administrators were relieved that they had pretty much hit the target with what had been originally a pretty difficult throw at the stumps, to employ an apt analogy.

He was also a better player than he was sometimes given credit for, his 36 Tests yielding 1534 runs at the very acceptable average for a No 7 of 32.6 along with 150 catches and seven stumpings, making him as good a wicket-keeper batsman as most in Australian history with the obvious exception of the incomparable Adam Gilchrist.

He was well worth his place in the team.

If perhaps he wasn't necessarily the most astute tactician and strategist ever—and he definitely wasn't—well, everyone from CA down could live with that against the backdrop of his delicate assignment.

He seemed to have the respect of the opposition, too, although that might require more forensic scrutiny.

Certainly, there was a less than angelic side, which came to the fore in an ugly clash with Indian star Ravi Ashwin in Sydney in 2021, for which he had to apologise profusely.

After an initial exchange, Paine sneered at the champion off-spinner: "At least my teammates like me, dickhead. I've got more Indian friends than you do. Even your teammates think you're a goose, don't they? Every one of them. How many IPL teams wanted you when you asked every single one of them to have ya? All I'll say is this, get your act together—it's embarrassing."

After a social media outcry, Paine called an impromptu press conference to back off. "I want to apologise for the way I went about things. I'm someone who prides themselves on the way I lead this team and yesterday was a poor reflection. I let the pressure of the game get to me. I've had a really poor game as a leader. I fell short of my expectations and my team's standards. I'm human. I want to apologise for the mistakes. I'm bitterly disappointed."

He said he spoke to Ashwin immediately after stumps and they sorted it out amicably.

However, during the same match referee David Boon fined him 15 per cent of his match fee and added a demerit point to his otherwise clean record for swearing at umpire Paul Wilson.

And in an interesting newspaper exchange with one of Australia's leading cricket writers, Robert Craddock, the London *Sun's* John Etheridge—who had been following the England team for several decades—was sceptical about Paine's universal popularity.

"The England players never believed the line about Paine being the clean-cut good guy who could restore the reputation of the Aussie team," Etheridge said. "They always thought he was a bit of a phoney."

Of course, that may or may not have been a camp-follower's contribution, on behalf of the tourists, to getting up the noses of the opposition at a sensitive time.

Everybody had an opinion on the gravity or otherwise of Paine's conduct. Prominent Sydney ethics expert Dr Simon Longstaff, who had previously conducted a review of cricket's culture, said it raised serious questions about the standards expected of leaders on the sporting fields.

"I think it is hard to say that ethical perfection is required for such a role," he said. Hear, hear!

Longstaff said it would have been better for CA to have publicly disclosed the investigation and for Paine to have expressed remorse then, in which case, "I think he would have survived it."

Part of a mature society is that it accepts people can make mistakes, can be remorseful and reform, he added.

The selection issue was left in the hands of, well, the selectors, the recently-appointed chairman George Bailey, the even fresher face Tony Dodemaide, and coach Justin Langer, which raised issues of its own.

Bailey, a former Tasmanian teammate, was a close friend and a sometime business partner, while Langer—a character well-known for his loyalty towards his friends and colleagues—was also extremely close to his captain after all they had been through together in rebuilding the team's reputation.

Bailey felt so conflicted that he said he would leave the decision to the other two, for which he was—quite rightly—castigated by former selector Mark Waugh and many others on the grounds that if you accept such an influential role you must be prepared to own all the decisions, the difficult ones no exception.

It wasn't an ideal look for Bailey, whose own qualifications for the job—he played only five Tests although he did represent Australia in 120 white ball games, some of which he captained—were on the thin side, although that is not unusual with Australian selection panels. One of the most effective chairmen, the late Lawrie Sawle, was a Sheffield Shield batsman for West Australia who never got close to playing for

Australia. And as it turned out, Bailey and his lieutenants never put a foot wrong all summer.

In the end it didn't matter.

Paine set out to prove his fitness and, hopefully, find some form by turning out in a four-day game for the Tasmanian second eleven, where he safely accepted six catches in the first innings—and didn't drop any—but failed to reach double figures with the bat in two attempts, while reporting no physical problems.

He was then selected for a domestic one-dayer in the first team a couple of days later, but suddenly withdrew the night before, saying he was taking an indefinite break from all cricket to concentrate on his mental health.

Only a week had passed since his world had come tumbling down and now, unable or unwilling to live with the fierce scrutiny applied to every move he made and every word he said, or did not say, he was gone—for how long nobody could say.

But it was clear that his international presence was over, and few expected to see him at any serious level again. If so, no matter what you thought of his conduct, it is difficult to imagine a sadder exit.

Friends and family rallied strongly, none more so than Langer, who interrupted his preparations for the looming first Test to fly to Hobart to provide support and to make certain his mate and colleague was coping.

Speaking to reporters on his return to the team camp in Brisbane, Langer struggled to control his emotions as he spoke of the "brutal" and" unforgiving" forces that had left Paine a shattered man.

"He is one of my really close friends and someone I admire enormously," he said. "He is certainly in this generation of players one of the best people I've met in the game of cricket. It was nice to go down and see him. His life's changed, obviously. We talk about looking after the boys, having each other's backs. It was a no-brainer to go and see him.

"It's a tough business. I've been in it for 30 years and you learn to grow and evolve. You're always in the spotlight. We live in a world of perfectionism, don't we?

"We're a very judgmental society. There is not one person who's asking questions, or who is listening to this, who hasn't made a mistake in their life. And our captain, one of the best, made a mistake and is paying a very heavy price for it.

"I continually see in this job, and I see in the society we live in, it can be brutal. You learn your lessons, but we live in an unforgiving society and that's a real shame."

Langer suggested the door was open for Paine to make a return to cricket at some level. "He absolutely loves cricket, he is as fit as any athlete, he's very focused, so who knows? I'm not sure we've seen the end of him but we'll wait and see."

Paine was replaced in the team for the opening Test by South Australian Alex Carey, and at the invitation of Langer and the new captain, Cummins, Adam Gilchrist was invited to perform the ritual presentation of his baggy green cap.

For the first time, this was done with TV cameras broadcasting every word uttered by Gilchrist, who was renowned in his playing days as the personification of good sportsmanship and integrity.

"There's a lot of value placed on this cap, but not for a moment is there any sense of entitlement that comes with it," he told debutant No 461. "It doesn't make you any more special than anyone else in society.

"But if you play with integrity, honesty and complete commitment to this group of people... society will ride with you in the highs. More importantly, when the lows and challenges come they will pick you up and carry you."

Given the context of the previous two or three weeks, the words were hailed around the cricket world as being perfectly chosen.

CHAPTER 4

HOW THE BOY WHO BOWLED TOO FAST BECAME THE BEST

There is nothing like it, the thrill of bowling fast, the crowd going crazy right behind you. You get a sense of teammates sensing something is happening—I love that. They say you don't have egos but we are super competitive and we all have egos.

We all want to be on the back pages of the paper, raising the bat or holding the ball up for five-for, being the matchwinner. People will pretend that's not the case but you don't get to professional sport without a bit of that in you.

It's the adrenalin, trying to make a difference. Even thinking about it I start smiling.

Quote, unquote. That was the subject of Fox Sport's excellent documentary, *The Making of Pat Cummins*, aired during the Ashes, and for anyone wanting to know more about what made the new Australian Test captain tick, it was gold.

There is an undeniable curiosity about the cricketer with the golden boy image—intelligent, humble, generous, calm, patient, responsible, polite, loyal and peaceable, with a belief that doing the right thing will usually pay off.

Too good to be true? Well, in his rant at the height of the Justin Langer resignation/sacking, former teammate Mitchell Johnson said he had been "lauded as some type of cricketing saint" before going on to savage him for his role—whatever it might have been, which wasn't clear at that stage—in that regrettable affair.

But really, unless he has been spending as much time studying stagecraft—acting, in another word—as he has in mastering the outswinger, there is no evidence to suggest that he does not personify the saying, what you see is what you get.

It's just that there is a lot to see and to get.

Test teammate Usman Khawaja, a man of great urbanity, has spoken about engaging with him in bracing debates about science, faith and evolution—about religion and life.

Cummins reads voraciously and listens carefully.

Asked to describe himself, not as a cricketer but pertaining to life in general, he said: "Pretty relaxed, pretty curious about different things. I try to have a lot of different things going on, whether it's in the business world, or meeting new people, interesting people. I find that really engaging and love it. I like to spend a lot of time with my family, try to have fun and not take anything too seriously."

I put it to him that I believe he has a lot in common with tennis champion Ashleigh Barty, both in the scale of their achievements but equally importantly, how they go about it.

Barty, who shocked the sports world by retiring aged just 25, a few weeks after the Ashes, is globally famous for her down-to-earth attitudes, humility, sportsmanship, popularity and... well, for having no tickets on herself, to employ an old Aussie expression.

Her historic win in the 2022 Australian Open—the first by an Australian woman for 44 years—came just 13 days after Cummins had completed the 4–0 demolition of England, and at that point it was difficult to think of any other candidates if you were in the business of anointing the King and Queen of Australian sport.

What they also have in common of course is that for a while Barty was also a professional cricketer, playing for the Brisbane Heat in the women's Big Bash while she took time out from her main game.

The pair are fans of each other, having been introduced by their mutual, highly-respected mind coach Ben Crowe. One of the assets they have in common is that both tend to speak about "we" not "me" when discussing their successes. To both, It's all about team. They are modest and humble.

"I've met Ash a few times and I'm absolutely a fan," says Cummins. "I think we see the world very similarly, we don't take it too seriously," Cummins says.

"We try not to let expectations weigh us down and just try to be ourselves. I think we both kind of see our day jobs as just that—they don't filter into our private lives. It's not who we are as people."

In an interview with News Corp, Barty said: "He's a brilliant guy, a legend. I love the way he goes about it. I love his attitude. He is the typical hard-working Aussie. He goes in and works hard all day long for the team."

Basically, Cummins is just like most cricketers at all levels; at heart, he loves the game for its own sake and enjoys being good at it. Yes, he gets a thrill out of bowling fast and winning a game, especially a Test match.

Yes, it has brought him fame and fortune well beyond anything he could have imagined when he first picked up a bat and ball with his two older brothers in the backyard, although that's not what he set out to achieve.

Unlike a million or more other kids down the years, he didn't go to bed dreaming of becoming the captain of Australia one day—until he suddenly found himself a professional player at the age of 17, and everything changed.

But what hasn't changed is his motivation.

In another interview specifically for this book, asked why the game turns him on so much, he said: "I love the competitiveness of cricket. The youngest of three boys, I just loved competing against older brothers.

"It's not super serious but it challenges you in so many ways. It's such a mental game. As a fast bowler it's such a physical game.

"And especially in Test cricket I just love that over the course of five days or a series it is normally the one who outlasts the other who gets the result.

"More than that, it's just fun. In the middle of a game you get to hang out with mates on the field—that was always the thing that got me out of bed each morning, training or the games, just doing it with the people you do it with."

He is talking here about under-age cricket, club cricket and every other level up to Test cricket—it has always been the enjoyment that matters.

Which doesn't mean, of course, that he was ever going to be cricket's version of Nick Kyrgios, a contemporary in the broader landscape of Australian sport, who was born with just as much talent as a tennis player and greater earning potential than most cricketers but who decided the game didn't matter enough for him to fully commit to it, and who is now widely regarded as little more than a fun-seeker who has chosen not to fully exploit gifts—of easting them, if you like—most young men would die for.

Cummins was always going to get to the top, even if it took him a while to realise that was his destiny, even if it did seem a touch unrealistic.

It was obvious to everyone else who watched him set out in junior teams as he grew up in the NSW Blue Mountains, west of Sydney, with his family, parents Peter and Maria, and brothers Matt and Tim and sisters Laura and Kara.

It was a cricket-oriented household—it was Peter's favourite sport and the brothers were all into it. "As soon as I could walk, I was chasing them," says Pat.

As Australia's most famous set of cricket brothers, Ian, Greg and Trevor Chappell, have often attested, there is always a hierarchy in these contests and the younger ones just have to find a way to keep pace.

It was no different here.

"No real sympathy was given to Pat," Matt told the documentary. "He had to deal with us from day one. He is six years younger than me and three years younger than Tim. Backyard cricket was pretty intense to say the least.

"Everything was a contest. Pat had the worst temper, didn't like losing, probably because he did lose the most early on.

"Usually how it finished was someone spitting the dummy, usually Pat, and then about seven o'clock we'd finish the game every afternoon."

Pat was only four when his future as a bowler could easily have been severely compromised, if not wrecked.

A family friend dropped him home from pre-school with five lollipops, one for each sibling. "So first thing I did was run round handing them out," he said, "but my sister Laura was in the bathroom and for some reason instead of waiting for her to come out I just opened the door a little creak and waved the lollipop through it.

"She slammed the door and off came the top of my finger, clean off, a little bit of bone sticking out. I remember screaming my head off and running for mum. I went to hospital for surgery but it was too small to sew back on.

"Mum was worried about going to kindergarten the next year, none of the girls were going to want to hold my hand walking at lunchtime. But Dad was really worried about something else. He said I've got to make sure he can still bowl.

"Because I was so young I never knew anything else so I've always bowled with a short finger."

Very perceptive of Dad, you'd have to say, to be aware at that stage of the path his boy's development would take—his special talent—and that such a problem might arise maybe 10 years down the track. Then again, it wasn't long before bowling did become an obvious factor.

Even at under-9 level in the Penrith area—he started with the Glenbrook-Blaxland Cricket Club—he was the talk of the district. By the time he graduated to the Green Shield, the under 16 level of Sydney grade cricket, he was terrorising the opposition—and their parents, who would plead for him to slow down.

He tells a story himself of playing against this one boy in junior cricket and hitting him every time they met, until his mother pleaded "please stop hurting my little boy".

Not much sympathy was forthcoming apparently.

"At 16 he had kind of grown and realised he was pretty good," says his brother Matt.

Others had come to the same obvious conclusion.

After topping the batting and bowling in the Green Shield, he was selected in a training squad for the State under 17 team, which was a big deal because it meant practice sessions at the Sydney Cricket Ground alongside NSW players and senior coaches. Test star Brett Lee came to one session and couldn't have been more impressed with what he saw.

"I remember seeing this kid, really skinny, as something special— this look in his eye," Lee recalled. "You can tell when somebody has this X-factor about him. First time I saw him, I thought this kid is something special.

"You see some bowlers who are tall and just put the ball there. Some are skinny and get the ball to go through. Pat Cummins had that steep bounce, that trajectory off the wicket, it took off like an aeroplane.

"He had that really good wrist behind the ball, that flick of the wrist, seam bolt upright. He could swing the ball both ways, something I wish I could do. I was never able to swing a brand-new ball both ways. He had that at age 17."

There was no stopping the whirlwind.

From playing for NSW under 17 and under 19 teams in 2009–10, he debuted for Penrith first grade the next year and as a fan of the Big Bash he thought he was probably capable of having a crack at that— and almost overnight, he was, playing six games for NSW, including the final, in what was when a state-based competition.

After five second eleven games for NSW, he made his Sheffield Shield debut against Tasmania, playing the final three matches of the season.

Asked now when he first thought he might be good enough to go all the way with cricket, not surprisingly he nominates that breakthrough summer.

"I started to realise then that this might actually become a full-time job," he said. "I might get paid to play cricket. How cool is this? But I still signed up for University because I couldn't imagine having a full career out of cricket and here I am 11 or 12 years later. It's been awesome."

When did it become an all-consuming ambition?

"I'm not sure it ever was. Certainly when cricket was around, I always wanted to do my best. Once I became a professional you spend a lot more hours on it and want to do really well, especially when Test cricket becomes more of a reality, playing for Australia.

"But until I became a professional it wasn't my No. 1 focus. I played on weekends and trained on weekdays and I loved it, but I was at school and doing other things. It wasn't always going to be a career path.

"It's such a small percentage of cricketers who get to have a career playing cricket and even if you get there you still have got to have so much luck go your way. It was never a career until, literally, I signed a contract."

That happened in June 2011, and the memory is vivid.

He was sitting on a train travelling to Uni when the phone rang. It was chairman of selectors Andrew Hilditch saying: "Congratulations, you've received a Cricket Australia contract."

What a moment for any young player, especially less than a month past his 18th birthday.

"I remember sitting on the train, trying not to squeal because there were people sitting around me," he says. "I'm thinking, this is wild.

"That CA contract (list) had names like Ricky Ponting, Michael Clarke—legends of the game—and I was now part of that squad of 20-odd people.

"It was my first full-time job. I remember thinking I don't have to catch the train every single day, I can go and buy myself a car. So I bought a second-hand Mazda 3 as a late birthday present."

Some thought it was a gamble on a player so young but Hilditch wasn't one of them. "We don't think it's a gamble, we think he's going to be real good," he said.

The selectors put their money where their mouths were. Cummins was in South Africa later that year with the NSW T20 team—his first overseas trip—when he was unexpectedly asked to join the national squad which was playing a series of T20s and ODIs before a two match Test series.

There, soaking up information and dressing room culture from all the big names around him—and generally having the time of his young life—he made his international debut in a T20, pinching himself because he had played only two professional games for NSW to that point "where I had taken zero wickets and gone for about eight an over."

He played all five white-ball games, leading all bowlers with 11 wickets.

He was just an intensely interested onlooker for the first Test in Cape Town, which might have been just as well because it resulted in a humiliating defeat with Australia bowled out for 47 on the way to being beaten by eight wickets.

And then, not much more than a year after playing at under 18 state level, he was told by Clarke, the captain, that he would be playing the second one in Johannesburg.

His debut became and remains etched in Australian cricket folklore as he earned man of match honours by taking 6-79 in the second innings and then hitting the winning runs with only two wickets to spare.

He also sustained an injury, the first of many that were to consign him to the wilderness for more than five years before he was able to wear the prized baggy green cap for a second time.

It wasn't only his prodigious ability that came to the fore in that unforgettable match—so did his pressure-impervious personality, which was to become an important factor in his eventual ascent to the national captaincy.

He had a lot to learn, naturally, but seemed completely unfazed by the situation.

Veteran wicketkeeper Brad Haddin recalls: "He was only a young kid at the time, very raw, very quiet. One thing I noticed, which was different from other kids, he learned very quickly. You only had to tell him once and he soaked it in.

"Patty Cummins at that time was perfect, so raw, hadn't been exposed to all the media. He was just playing cricket. Just playing with his brothers in the backyard.

"We fed off that as well. We needed something different going into that last Test after the diabolical fall of Cape Town. So he was the perfect foil for us. His performance was outstanding."

As the run chase ticked down, Haddin said, "Nathan Lyon was sitting in the corner dry-retching, as he does, and Pat was just saying, what's wrong, let's just bat, it's just a game of cricket."

True to that innocent philosophy, when he got out to the middle the young tyro had no compunction in smashing probably the best fast bowler of his era, Dayle Steyn, back over his head as he delivered 145 km/h outswingers.

"There's no way I would bat like that now—I was so naïve," Cummins said. "It's a funny thing, cricket, you're so nervous waiting to come in to bat or bowl, but once you're in the moment, you're in control so if anything bad happens at least you feel you had some sort of say in it. I guess it's one of the benefits of being 18 years old and fearless."

The five years that followed that South African experience was full of ups and downs as Cummins battled one stress injury after another, playing a fair bit of international white ball cricket but always wondering whether his body would ever again permit him to take the game on full-force again. But at least he still had it as a job—he never lost his CA contract.

And he had one other stroke of very good luck.

In October 2013, depressed at having just been told he had stress fractures again, he wandered into a Kings Cross nightclub on a quiet Sunday night—an unusual choice for him—and met a girl who knew nothing about cricket and had no idea who he was.

She was Rebecca Boston, 22, from Harrogate, England, who was on a working holiday. The conversation—he told her he was a uni student, which wasn't untrue—led to an invitation to a barbecue the next day, and very soon they were an item.

Eight years later they were engaged and became parents to a son, Albie.

"She had no idea, had never really watched cricket at all, didn't know the rules. It was great," he says.

"It felt like the first half of our relationship we have lived pretty normally and done a lot of normal things. It's been a good grounding because we do spend a lot of time apart when I'm overseas."

Family is everything, he says. As for more kids: "We'll see."

They live in comfort in a $9.5m home in Sydney's eastern suburbs and own a farm in the NSW southern highlands.

Obviously, he is financially secure for life with internet "guess-timates" claiming his net worth is about $40m. Whatever the accuracy of that, there is a huge amount of earning power to come. Soon after the Ashes, the News Corp newspapers published a list of what it said were the 100 best-paid Australian sports figures.

It was topped by basketballer Ben Simmons on an annual $45.36m, with Cummins in 11th place on $6m. The article said that $2m of that was his CA contract, which was the highest of any player.

Cummins was the highest ranked cricketer on the list, ahead of David Warner, in 20th place with $4.1m; Glenn Maxwell, 24th place, $3.5m; Jhye Richardson, 29th, $3.1m; Steve Smith 38th, $2.3m; Marcus Stoinis, 39th, $2.2m; Josh hazelwood, 48th, $1.9m; and Aaron Finch, 49th, $1.8m.

The massive amounts on offer from the Indian Premier League and other global Twenty20 tournaments account for the bulk of these riches, which was noted in the papers' assessment of where Cummins is at financially.

"That figure is likely to increase substantially as endorsements flow his way as a mega-marketable Australian captain," the article said. "Cummins has completed a $3.2m Indian Premier League deal with Kolkata Knight Riders, with the promise of another big deal on the way with the (then) imminent 2022 auction."

The $3.1m he was paid by the KKR in 2021 was a record for the IPL. In the 2022 market, however, the same franchise cut his pay packet by more than half, to $1.343m—still pretty handy for a bit over a month's work in a form of the game with a limited physical output.

There is a saying that charity begins at home, and that's true of the Cummins family—his parents have been long-time contributors to a feed-the-homeless program.

So it is no surprise that he is not unaware of his good fortune in every sense of the term and is heavily committed to charity work. He is an ambassador to UNICEF and helps fund a kindergarten for indigenous children in northern Australia.

And straight after the Ashes he launched a new organisation called Cricket for Climate aimed at persuading clubs and cricketers at every level—starting with his own club, Penrith—to step up the fight against climate change.

A who's who of the men's and women's teams—Steve Smith, David Warner, Mitchell Starc, Marnus Labuschagne, Rachael Haynes and Alyssa Healy—are also part of what they have labelled "a vanguard for a green transition".

"We've got to do out bit to make sure we try to limit temperature increases to as little as possible or else in the future cricket could be a lot harder to play," Cummins said.

Asked to expand on his community work, he says: "What motivates me is that I'm in a really lucky position so I try to help others if I can. I feel a responsibility to do some good because I'm in such a privileged position and not everyone is—I try not to lose sight of that."

UNICEF, among other organisations, can hardly believe its luck in having him come on board. Australian chief of the organisation Tony Stuart said Cummins, who first approached the UN agency during the second covid wave that swept through India while he was playing there, was no ordinary celebrity sportsman.

Young, principled and willing to offer his own time and money to support the causes he cares about, he was widely seen as representative of a new generation of leader for a sporting public fatigued with scandal, the Melbourne *Herald Sun* reported.

"In times of crisis you see what drives people, and during covid when some people were complaining about quarantines and this and that, Pat reached out to us and wanted to know what he could do to help because he knew firsthand what was happening with Covid in India with families and children," Stuart told the paper.

Cummins' authenticity and generosity—including an initial $50,000 for aid in India and further financial support for early childhood education for indigenous children in Australia—stood out, he said.

"He is so authentic, so caring, so interested in the betterment of children, globally and in Australia. And unlike some sports celebrities who delegated to their agents, Pat genuinely got involved himself."

Leadership takes many forms. The cricket captain clearly does not restrict himself to one.

CHAPTER 5

DEALING WITH FIVE YEARS IN THE WILDERNESS

They used to say it was harder getting out of the Australian Test team than getting into it, meaning that good players would usually be given every chance to prove themselves or to overcome a run of indifferent form, while ambitious wannabes had to wait their turn.

In fact, getting out of it has proved remarkably—and disappointingly—easy for a surprisingly large percentage of the 463 men who have worn the baggy green cap between the first ever Test against England in 1887 and the end of the 2021–22 Ashes series, since increased by one with Mitchell Swepson's debut in Pakistan.

Seventy-three of them played only once, which is nearly one in six.

For a long time, Pat Cummins was on that list—and feared he was doomed to be on it forever.

"I thought I was going to be that guy..." he told the Fox Sports TV documentary that was aired during what should have been his second match as captain, but which was proceeding without him because of covid complications.

That anxiety resurfaced on behalf of someone else three matches into his captaincy career when it briefly looked like new teammate Scott Boland might not get a second chance despite a dominant debut in the third Ashes Test.

When Boland was picked again for the fourth match, Cummins exclaimed: "It's huge!" He told reporters that during his long spell in the wilderness he hated it whenever anyone spoke about his own debut because he felt he had not proven anything—a needless fret given he had been a matchwinner and named man of the match.

Cummins spent far more time waiting for his second Test than he did for his first, and he was far from alone in worrying that it might never come.

That was because he had to mark time while his body caught up with his obvious talent.

Very few of those 463 debuts have been more spectacularly successful or achieved at an earlier age with so little statistical evidence that the newcomer was ready for such an assignment.

It bears repeating that only one Australian, Ian Craig in 1953, has ever been younger than Cummins was—18 and 193 days—when he was thrust into service against South African in Johannesburg on November 17, 2011.

He was selected to replace the injured Ryan Harris after Australia had been beaten by eight wickets in the first of a two-Test series, having been bowled out in humiliating fashion in the second innings for just 47, their fourth lowest Test score and the worst for 109 years.

This was hardly the platform from which anyone would want to launch a career—but for the proud and excited young tearaway, it couldn't get much worse, so he had nothing to lose.

Actually, he did—he just didn't know it. Well before the game was over, he was feeling pain in one heel. It was the first sign of a stress fracture that was to become a frustrating roadblock to his career progress for the next five and a half years.

In the first innings he had delivered 15 overs at impressive pace, claiming his maiden scalp, the accomplished Hamish Amla, and conceding just 38 runs.

But the effort of slamming his bodyweight into the rock-hard, unforgiving Wanderers pitch took a toll, and by the fourth day of the match—with the locals running up a big score with Amla and the brilliant AB de Villiers in control, each with unbeaten half-centuries—he found himself unable to match his earlier pace.

But with one pace bowler, Shane Watson, out of action with a hamstring injury and another, Mitchell Johnson, bowling off a short run, Cummins was suddenly lumped with responsibility far beyond his rookie status.

He accepted it in unforgettable fashion, taking 6-79 in the second innings—the best figures by an Australian bowler on debut for 24 years—as South Africa lost their last seven wickets for 112.

Despite a broken foot, he got through 29 overs, one fewer than Johnson and two more than workhorse Peter Siddle and almost twice as many as spinner Nathan Lyon's 16.

The following morning he coolly hit the winning runs as Australia chased down 310 to win by two wickets.

A star had undoubtedly been born—but only for the time being.

It was to be five years, three months and 27 days before Cummins would wear the baggy green for a second time.

This revived memories of probably the greatest fast bowler Australia has ever produced, Dennis Lillee, whose 11th Test—in Kingston, Jamaica, in February 1973—and his 12th—against England in Brisbane in November 1974—were separated by nearly two years as he battled stress fractures in his back which threatened to kill off his career very prematurely.

Lillee was told he would never bowl again, certainly not for Australia.

So what could be more appropriate than when the crunch came for Cummins—when he really needed help and encouragement with his own battle against his developing body—that he should turn to Lillee for help. Which, of course, he got.

But it took a while to get to that stage.

His problems had begun almost as soon as his rapid rise to stardom had, which was in the summer of 2010–11 when he played a season of first grade club cricket with Penrith and represented NSW at under 17 and under 19 level.

The following year, he played six games for NSW in the Big Bash, which was then a State-based competition rather than the franchise system that exists now, and took a competition-high 11 wickets, as did spinner Nathan Lyon, then with South Australia.

In January 2011, he made his Sheffield Shield debut against Tasmania after impressing in five second eleven matches. He played the last three matches, including the final in Hobart where he bowled 65 overs across two innings, taking 3-165.

It was far too heavy a workload for his immature body and resulted in his first stress fracture of the back.

In March, he was selected for an Australia A tour of Zimbabwe, but the injury put paid to that.

Nonetheless, such were the wraps on him—notably from national selector Greg Chappell—that he was awarded a Cricket Australia contract, which he was never to lose even through long periods of inactivity.

He had recovered well enough by September that year to join the NSW T20 team in South Africa for the Champions League playoffs but was called up to the national squad for a series of T20s and one-dayers against the Proteas.

On October 13, he made his international debut in a T20 in Cape Town, taking an impressive 3-25 off his four overs. He played five white-ball games, leading all bowlers with 11 wickets.

He could hardly believe this was happening given that it was only a year almost to the day since he was debuting in club cricket.

He was like the proverbial kid in the candy shop, waking up each morning wondering who he would sit next to at breakfast: Ricky Ponting, Michael Hussey, Shane Watson, Michael Clarke?

He had a million questions to ask them—and did.

And then—hallelujah—Clarke told him he would be playing in the second Test. Yes, a baggy green—and they'll never be able to take it away.

The advice they probably should have given him with it was "enjoy it while you can"—which he certainly did, until he could barely walk by the fourth morning.

The heel stress fracture, an injury which veteran team physiotherapist Alex Kountouris had never seen before, ruled him out of the entire home summer that followed.

By the following September (2012) he had recovered from that well enough to play in the T20 World Cup in Sri Lanka, as well as the Champions league for Sydney Thunder.

But a new stress fracture again wiped out the 2012–13 season. He was picked to go to England on an Australia A tour before the 2013 Ashes, but not to actually play any games, instead to prepare for an ensuing "A" trip to South Africa and Zimbabwe.

But again he hurt his back and was starting to wonder whether he'd ever get back fully fit.

This was about the time he started consulting Lillee, following the advice of star colleague Mitchell Johnson and paying his own way to Perth to meet the great man.

He returned to the Big Bash in January 2014 and, prioritising white ball cricket throughout that year—including a debut season in the lucrative Indian Premier League for the Kolkata Knight Riders—he featured in four matches as Australia won the 2015 World Cup in Melbourne.

In the best physical shape so far, Cummins was a late inclusion in the 2015 Ashes side when Ryan Harris announced his retirement prior to the start of the series because of a chronic knee injury.

When Josh Hazlewood was injured before the fifth Test, Cummins looked certain to get his second cap, an assignment for which he felt eminently ready, physically and mentally.

But to his dismay, the selectors opted for veteran Peter Siddle instead.

In the ODIs that followed Cummins broke down again when the stress fracture resurfaced, costing him another home summer for the fourth time in five years—and challenging his patience and morale.

He returned to the Australian one-day side against New Zealand in Sydney in December 2016 and played 11 matches between then and

February 5, returning to the Sheffield Shield on March 7 for the first time in six years, bowling 36 overs and taking eight wickets.

So, back in international cricket, back in first-class cricket. In the circumstances, these were massive milestones. Now, only Test cricket was to come.

He didn't have to wait long. He was immediately summoned to India to replace Mitchell Starc, who had a foot injury, for the third Test of a rancorous series, due to begin less than a week after the Shield game.

Not everybody, by any means, was in favour of this, the NSW medicos believing his comeback to long-form cricket should be managed slowly.

Cummins just shrugged. The point of enduring all the endless rehab and frustrating absences was to return to the Test arena, and here he was. Bring it on.

There was no longer any point of saving something in the tank.

If he was going to get injured again, he would get injured playing Test cricket.

He was walking into a minefield, with the Australians having been accused of cheating over a controversial incident involving the decision review system, the Indians claiming the batsmen in the middle—specifically, the captain Steve Smith—had been seeking advice from the dressing room before deciding whether to review.

Cummins had watched that unfold on TV at home in Sydney and knew he could expect an intense welcome.

It was just as well his back was ready for the workload because he toiled through 39 overs in India's only innings of 9-603—Australia made 451 and 6-204—picking up four good wickets, including their celebrated captain Virat Kohli for just six.

In the fourth and final match of the series, he bowled another 38 overs across two innings, for four scalps, as India cruised to an eight-wicket (and series) win.

From that point on, his Test career was interrupted only once more when he was rested from a series against Pakistan in the United Arab Emirates in 2018, as his back was "managed". He also missed the IPL tournament that year before returning to the KKR in 2020 and 2021 as the most expensive player in the tournament's history.

Perhaps it had been irresponsible for the team management to expose him to the rigours of that Test debut at such a young age, but of course no young player would have any reservations about grasping the dream opportunity when it presented itself.

"That Test match was probably the best thing I've ever done," he told cricket.com.au, the Cricket Australia website. "The opportunities it provided for me. It's one Test match. I don't think that was irresponsible at all. I wouldn't change it at all."

Cummins looks back on the many frustrations with no real regrets, now that all's well that ends well.

"Yes, it was (frustrating)," he says, "but I did play quite a bit of white-ball cricket. I would just be in for a series or two, then out for 12 months, in for a series or two and then out for 12 months.

"I just never felt I was getting the momentum that I was getting closer and closer to that second Test match. With each injury it felt like I was getting further away, not closer.

"I felt really lucky that I still had cricket as a job, but I felt like my head space was right, my form was right—it was just my body, which I couldn't control. It wasn't up for it.

"There were a couple of times I was out in the field after a spell and I'd bend to tie my shoelaces or somebody would chuck me a ball and I'd think, oh, there's a knife in my back.

"I think the most frustrating thing was that I'd been able to play World Cup, but it was only T20 cricket. I just remember thinking if my body can't get through four overs how do I expect to play Test matches?

"It was just the perpetual questions—how's your back, are you injured, are you going to play next summer, when's your next tour, when's your next game? For years I was just saying, I don't know really. You don't look injured, it's not like you're on crutches or anything. You look fine. It's a hard one to explain to people. I've got this tiny crack in my back and I'm going to miss the next nine months. There's no acute pain. You don't really feel that injured.

"I was desperate, I wouldn't have wanted not to have a career and then think, well, there were a few options I didn't try. I tried a lot of different things. It got to the stage where I just wanted to try something different. Speaking to a few people, I asked who was the best bowling coach they had ever worked with—just about everybody said DK Lillee."

The Lillee connection was crucial in more ways than one.

"I saw him when I was 21 or 22 and I thought I'm a worse bowler now than when I was 18," Cummins said. "But after a few sessions I thought, no, it's still there inside me, we've just got to unlock it again."

Not only did the legend identify flaws in his technique and show him how to fix them, while stressing the importance of fitness, strength and flexibility, he changed his mindset.

And they formed a firm friendship that continues.

On the Fox documentary, Lillee laughs when he recalls their first meeting. "I think he probably wondered what was happening when he fronted up and saw me standing here, skinny legs, pair of shorts, four days' growth, expecting me to help him solve a problem that was ruining his career," he said.

Lillee explained graphically why fast bowling could be so traumatic on the body.

"Somebody said years ago, and they were talking about baseball, that pitching was one of the most unnatural actions in sport. Somebody popped up and said what about running in for 25 or 30 metres and then jumping up and landing 11 times your bodyweight on one foot and nine or 10 times on the other one and then hurling the ball down like a baseballer. Hmmm, hadn't thought about that."

Lillee told Cummins that "most problems start early on and are caused by your run-up or something you do in your run-up. That starts a chain reaction to everything else going wrong."

Cummins was a fast learner. "Pat took to it like a duck to water, so determined," Lillee said. "Each day he'd front up and show how much he'd advanced. He was enjoying bowling with a freer action."

"DK was great, he kept things really simple," Cummins told this writer. "His key advice was always to concentrate on one thing, just the run-up, whereas with other coaches it was five things, run-up, jump, arms, legs all going in different directions. He brilliantly simplified it."

Cummins felt he wasn't being treated like just a bit of data—a science experiment—where talk of actions and techniques can quickly go into mechanics and become robotic. "That's not how I'm wired," he said. "I just wanted to compete.

"I felt like working with him not only did it relieve the stress on my back but it made me a *better* bowler. That's what excited me so much about it."

Elaborating to the Cricket Australia's website writer Louis Cameron's excellent deep-dive piece into his many injury battles, Cummins said: "I felt like I was concentrating on becoming a better bowler—not a bowler who has less stress on his body, or someone who's going to be able to bowl more overs in a week.

"I was a bowler who could actually get better—swing the ball more, pick up pace, think a batter out, the problem-solving of bowling.

"That really struck a chord with me. It really motivated me to keep working on those things. I saw the light at the end of the tunnel and found that enjoyment."

Their relationship continues. "I still reach out to DK quite a bit, just check in and pick his brain on a few things, send him some footage," Cummins says.

But it's not all about bowling.

Lillee invited his pupil home for dinner more than once and introduced him to the delights of red wine. "He loves it, and we still chat about it," Cummins says.

"He reckons I've cost him a fortune," Lillee laughs.

If so, it's been money well spent in more ways than one.

CHAPTER 6

EVEN LOSING THE TOSS PART OF A PERFECT START

When does a new Test series actually start? With the preparation over the preceding days? With team selections? With the toss of the coin? With the first delivery?

All are important and sometimes crucial factors, and Pat Cummins on his debut as Australia's captain just had to hope that at least a couple of them might work in his favour. Astonishingly, they all did.

As one of his more illustrious predecessors, the late Richie Benaud, often used to say, captaincy is 90 per cent luck and 10 per cent skill. "But don't try it without the 10 per cent," he added. It was a bit early to come to any conclusions about Cummins' skill at the caper, but as everyone was about to find out very quickly he certainly seemed to have the blessing of the game's fickle gods.

Even the fixture itself would have been a nerve-settler, the opening skirmish scheduled for the Gabba in Brisbane, where Australia had not lost for 32 years until a depleted India invaded the fortress with a remarkable win at the start of the year.

England's record there has been little short of laughable. They won at their first two appearances in 1933 and 1936, but only twice in their next 18 attempts, and one of those was in 1978 when Australia fielded virtually a second eleven because most of the best players were with the rebel World Series Cricket—as were a few of the Englishmen, to be fair.

They won again under Mike Gatting's leadership in 1986, back when Ian Botham was in his prime, and never again. Even in 2010, when they won the series 3-1, Brisbane was a high-scoring draw.

Otherwise, Australia prevailed by 10 wickets in 1990, 184 runs in 1994, settled for a draw in 1998, won by 384 in 2002, 277 in 2006, 381 in 2013 and 10 wickets in 2017. This is dominance on a grand scale, enough to meddle with the minds of any future optimists—Joe Root's outfit no exception.

The 1992 edition is endlessly famous as one of the all-time great captaincy cock-ups, when skipper Nasser Hussain won the toss on a fine summer's day perfect for batting and, to the complete astonishment of every onlooker in both countries invited Australia to bat.

His best fast bowler Steve Harmison delivered the first ball of the series straight to second slip—the widest wide ever seen at the ground—and Australia, scarcely able to believe their good fortune, cruised to 2/364 at stumps, the match already as good as won and lost.

Hussain has never lived it down. It's a recurring joke every time England turn up in town. He made the fatal decision for the wrong reasons, because he wasn't confident in his own batsmen's ability to handle the Australian attack, not as an attacking ploy. Nonetheless, I was there that day and have always believed he was a bit stiff, in that one of his best bowlers, Simon Jones, injured a knee after delivering just seven overs, in which he dismissed Justin Langer, and took no further part, while Matthew Hayden, who was 186 not out at stumps, had been dropped on the boundary relatively early. These two bits of bad luck have mostly been forgotten, but of course there is little point Hussain attempting to use them to defend himself, so he never does. He just lives with the taunting in good humour.

This time around, Brisbane was no more welcoming than ever, with the tourists' preparation severely compromised by the need to spend a fortnight in covid quarantine and then sustained heavy rain washing out most of their first attempt to play two practice matches among themselves in lieu of any first-class hit-outs against Australian opposition, as always used to be the case. Tour matches are out of fashion in both countries these days but it is still amazing that they were prepared to accept such a limited preparation.

It was just the first of what turned out to be a litany of management missteps that, collectively, proved terminal.

The Australians weren't all that much better off, although several were coming off a morale-boosting triumph in the Twenty20 World Cup and others had a limited amount of chances to tune up in the Sheffield Shield. But they had not played a Test for 10 months, whereas England had played 12 against three countries.

In both camps, selection was the subject of intense speculation.

If you count the leadership appointments of Cummins and Smith, the local panel—chairman George Bailey, coach Justin Langer and Tony Dodemaide—had no fewer than six important decisions to ponder.

The other four were to find an opening partner for David Warner, a new wicketkeeper to replace Tim Paine, to choose between Travis Head and the in-form but significantly older Usman Khawaja for the No. 5 batting slot, and whether to stick with regular new-ball bowler Mitchell Starc or go for Jhye Richardson who had been in electrifying form, especially in a Shield match at the Gabba.

They made all the calls well in advance, although not necessarily making that known, with Victoria's Marcus Harris given two weeks' free of fretting when he was informed that he would be given a chance to consolidate what had been a stop-start 10 match career at the highest level so far.

They gave the gloves to the most obvious candidate, Alex Carey, who had been a regular in the one-day side for several years, often as a top-order batsman, ahead of the younger Josh Ingles, also a highly-promising batsman—and who was born in England, moving to Australia with his family when he was 14.

And they kept the faith with the big left-armer Starc, a veteran of 61 Tests with 255 wickets to his name, an elite record by any estimation—but with a bit of a reputation for not always making the most of his express speed and ability to make the new ball swing.

These all proved to be good calls, with the possible exception of Harris, whose future—or lack of it—was never going to be determined by just one outing.

England arrived with only one selector, the all-powerful team boss Chris Silverwood, although obviously Joe Root would exert his fair share of clout.

They had plenty on their minds, too, the least of which was whether to go for Ollie Pope or Jonny Bairstow in the middle order (Pope got the nod) and the real issue, the make-up of their attack which was already without the option of their most dangerous quick, the injured and absent Jofra Archer who had intimidated the Australians up to a point at home two years earlier.

The big question—and a far from straightforward one—was whether to play both their veteran pacemen Jimmy Anderson and Chris Broad, and if not, which one?

Anderson, 39, the most successful new ball bowler in history with 632 wickets from 166 Tests, and Broad, 36, with 524 from 149, were never—at their age—going to play all five Tests but it seemed like a no-brainer that at least one would be part of the opening hostilities, especially as the likely conditions at the Gabba would suit Anderson especially, and Broad had exerted a psychological stranglehold over the prolific Warner in England two years earlier.

However, not all stats can be taken on face value. Both men had question marks against their names in Australia, where Anderson had toured four times and Broad three without making the impact they always did at home.

Anderson had played 18 Tests in Australia and averaged nearly 36 per wicket, Broad had averaged 37 from 12 matches.

Breaking it down further, Anderson against top five batsmen had 30 wickets at 47.43 and Broad 18 at 46.16, figures that do not scream "matchwinner".

This would not have been lost on England, of course.

That said, it was still to a major shock to everyone else—Cummins and the rest of the Australian camp certainly no exception—that both were left out in favour of the express Mark Wood, the emerging Ollie Robinson and the familiar Chris Woakes, with dynamic all-rounder Ben Stokes and journeyman left-arm spinner Jack Leach entrusted with the job.

Neither of the superstars were injured, they said—so this was rolling the dice, big-time.

Warner couldn't believe his luck—and duly cashed in on it.

When Cummins—resplendent in his blazer, as is the long-standing tradition—and looking more relaxed than he might have been feeling arrived for the toss with Root, they were confronted by a pitch with a tinge of green in humid, overcast weather, conditions that invited them both to defy convention and bowl first.

Plenty of wise old heads, notably two of Australia's most astute former captains, Mark Taylor and Allan Border, urged them to do so.

It was never likely to happen.

If it backfired on Cummins, it had the potential to derail his captaincy before it had begun, literally, and Root—who had declared a day earlier that this series would define his captaincy for posterity—was hardly going to risk being bracketed in infamy with Hussain.

So when he successfully called tails, Root chose to bat. As Cummings would have.

Root and his brains trust had studied all sorts of statistics in preparation for this vital call but must have missed one that mattered: the last four captains who had won the toss at the Gabba had all batted—and lost.

There was already a distinct feeling that lucky Pat had, well, got lucky again, having avoided making the wrong decision without having to say a word or do anything.

How true that proved to be—instantly.

The first delivery of the series could not have been a more powerful portent of things to come, with Starc delivering a full-pitched thunderbolt that curled slightly at the left-handed Rory Burns and crashed into his leg-stump—a golden duck for him, a disastrous beginning for his team.

And for Cummins, a scarcely believable curtain-raiser to his new gig.

Whoever was writing his scripts was on a roll already—and in no mood to stop. In his dreams, Cummins couldn't have contemplated what was about to ensue, not in its entirety, which was quite possibly the best day of his career—and there had been plenty of other good ones, all the way back to his man of the match performance in his debut Test a decade earlier.

For Starc, too, it was an intensely satisfying moment, given how many people seemed to be in favour of him making way for Richardson, and the constant criticism he was used to getting from Shane Warne wearing his commentator's hat.

Warne was on air when the wicket tumbled and seemed reluctant to admit that it had been a high-class delivery, describing it as "just a half-volley"—he should have tried telling that to the shattered Burns.

"I've been hearing it for 10 years, it's nothing new," said Starc, who celebrated extravagantly with his delighted teammates. "It must be the first of December when that starts happening (every year). You could say I carried on because I probably did. That's Ashes cricket, isn't it. It's the heightened sense of everything—there were a fair few emotions going around."

It was literally an unforgettable moment that was destined to be replayed on Ashes highlight reels forever and a day.

It wasn't a one-off either. Starc went on to become the only fast bowler on either side, Cummins included, to play all five Tests, and took 19 wickets, second only to his captain.

In quick succession, Josh hazelwood accounted for Dawid Malan and then Root—officially then the best batsman in the world—for a duck, making it 15 times either he or Cummins had dismissed him in Tests. In a sense Root was unlucky in that Hazlewood worked him over expertly for several balls before producing an absolute jaffa of a leg cutter that deviated just enough to catch the edge, proving again that he is in the very top bracket of pace bowlers anywhere.

Unfortunately this turned to be his only contribution to the series.

Cummins—who once said he regarded his dismissal of his opposite number in Brisbane four years earlier as the best wicket of his career—brought himself on to bowl at Root immediately but never got the chance, contenting himself with the wicket of England's other main weapon, Stokes, leaving the tourists in disarray at 4-29.

Like King Midas, almost everything Cummins touched turned to gold. He threw the ball to rookie all-rounder Cameron Green, whose first delivery produced his maiden Test wicket, Pope brilliantly caught by Hazelwood in the deep.

He brought himself back on after lunch and rapidly completed the annihilation, far too good for stubborn opener Haseeb Hameed and bowlers Woakes, Robinson and Wood, finishing with 5/38—his sixth five-wicket haul in his 35 Tests—as England succumbed for a totally inadequate 147.

Even the Queensland cops joined in the general pile-on that this attracted, tweeting that they were investigating "a group impersonating a Test batting order at the Gabba."

For Root, Murphy's Law seemed to be in play—anything that could go wrong so far, had done so. And would continue to do so. Australia replied with an imposing 425, thanks to a rollicking 152 off only 148 balls from the last man picked in the team, Head, a less than usually fluent 94 from Warner, an excellent 74 from Marnus Labuschagne and even a useful 35 from tailender Starc.

Root watched helplessly as several catches were dropped, Warner was bowled by Stokes off a no-ball, his star all-rounder then hurting a knee that made him virtually ineffective, and even a comical missed run-out when Warner fell over well out of his crease and dropped his bat, lying there stranded while Hameed failed to hit the stumps from a couple of metres away.

Just as dispiriting if not embarrassing was the performance of Leach, who was smashed for 102 runs—including several sixes—off just 13 overs as the Australians brilliantly executed a deliberate strategy to blast him out of the attack, forcing Root to over-use his pacemen and putting extra pressure on the underdone Stokes.

This was so successful that many commentators suggested that the left-arm tweaker—a bowling style that has never been very successful in Australia, especially at the Gabba, even for home-grown purveyors of it—could not now be selected for the rest of the series.

He was, twice, but took only six wickets in his three matches.

He seemed an unwise choice in the first place, against a team stacked with left-handers, with Broad available and Root able to bowl off-spin himself.

Root was to claim later that it was his fault, not Leach's, because the fields he had set were too aggressive—perhaps so, given that he had all his men inside the boundary when they might have had a better chance of taking a catch high in the grandstand.

Warner began the assault immediately Leach came on, hitting him over the fence twice amid a total of 17 in his second over, and Head continued it relentlessly as he roared to his ton off just 85 balls, the first one ever scored in a session at the Gabba and the equal third fastest in Ashes history behind Adam Gilchrist (57) and Gilbert Jessop (76) with Joe Darling also 85.

Having been dropped against India the previous summer, Head had plenty to prove—to himself as much as the selectors, who have always regarded him as a very good player, as his average of 39.75 from 19 previous Tests suggested, but never quite convinced that his temperament and application were all that they might be.

This was a new beginning, hopefully for the long haul—and it was destined not to stop there.

The closest any bowler came to closing him down was when the fastest one, Wood, let fly with an accidental 150km/h bean ball that Head did not pick up before it clipped his glove and smashed into the lower part of his helmet, knocking him off his feet.

Every time this happens in any cricket match now, it brings back chilling memories of former Australian batsman Philip Hughes—a close friend of Head—who was killed in similar circumstances, and so it was a massive relief when he immediately got to his feet and was able to bat on.

There were no hard feelings. "I saw it pretty much the whole way and lucky I got a bit of hand on it and that took most of the blow," Head said. "I was a bit surprised but within a couple of seconds I knew I was fine and Woody was good about it. Obviously he didn't mean to do it. So no stress."

The South Australian bears a remarkable facial resemblance to comedian Tim Gleisner, who used his own image to illustrate a series of books and newspaper columns parodying a mythical Australian middle-order batsman named Warwick Todd whose over-sized ego, cultural shortcomings and perennial struggle to hold his place in the team against a steady stream of young up and coming "losers" kept fans—and real players—entertained several years ago. Toddy was suddenly enjoying something of a revival, thanks to Head's good-humoured willingness to prolong the joke, just one reason why he is a popular character in the dressing room.

Root finally exerted a meaningful impact on the contest over the two afternoon sessions of day three when he and Malan got together after both openers were dismissed cheaply and batted through the rest of the day, reducing the deficit to just over 50, which provided hope that if this could be converted into a lead of at least 150, hopefully 200, the result could yet be turned on its head.

This was wishful thinking—in the history of Ashes cricket, 46 teams had conceded first innings leads of 278 or more and 42 had lost and four drawn. In other words, none had won.

Nonetheless, Root's return to his elegant best was a sight for sore English eyes as he reached 86 at stumps with Malan on 80. Along the way, Root passed Michael Vaughan's record of 1481 Test runs in a calendar year by an Englishmen and moved within sight of Sir Alister

Cook's benchmark for an England captain.

He looked a good thing to register his seventh century of the year and his first in Australia.

Alas, Malan was quickly out the next morning, presenting Nathan Lyon with his long-awaited 400th Test wicket, the 17th bowler to join that exclusive club and only the third Australian behind Shane Warne and Glenn McGrath.

Root added only three runs before he was caught behind off Cameron Green, giving the young all-rounder his second Test wicket—and one of the best he will ever take.

The rest was an even worse collapse than the first innings, the tourists losing eight wickets for 77 and leaving Australia just 20 to get, which they achieved for the loss of one wicket with well over a day and a half to spare. Was this a surprise to anyone—even the limited number of the Barmy Army, mostly Brisbane-based locals, who had turned out more in hope than expectation?

Well, certainly not to the bookies, who are rarely wrong—they had opened up with Australia at $1.82, odds-on, and England at $5, which turned out not to be as generous as it sounded.

This was despite pre-match suggestions by a number of commentators—not least the ever-controversial Warne—that Australia had lost its aura of invincibility at home, which were now already looking like famous last words. Of course, they weren't "last" words at all. With four Tests left, there was a lot left to be said and done. The oddsmakers were unlikely to be having any revisionist thoughts, though.

As the guillotine dropped, perhaps the most meaningful moment came when Cummins brought himself on and immediately claimed the key wicket of Stokes. He revealed later that he had intended to keep Starc bowling for at least another over until Steve Smith said "no, I think it's your turn", an intervention that suggested their unusual captain/vice-captain arrangement was already working beautifully.

Still the train-wreck wasn't complete for England.

Match referee David Boon announced that every player had been fined 100 per cent of their match fee, and the team docked eight Test Championship points, for bowling their overs far too slowly, having fallen almost 10 behind at one point.

They had averaged 71.65 balls, or less than 12 overs, an hour, which is abysmal and unforgivable. Australia went at 77.77, which isn't too flash either, but was deemed acceptable by Boon, whose only penalty for the home team was to fine Head 15 per cent of his pay for swearing at Stokes while batting.

Over rates have been a blight on the game for decades, a problem never quite solved. The players earn so much money that fines don't seem to have much effect, although in this case it might have stung.

They were reportedly being paid $27,000 each per Test, meaning the collective fine would have been about $300,000. If that was repeated in all five Tests, they would have been up for a total of $1.5m. Ouch!

Deducting points seemed like a bigger stick when a similar, if lesser penalty, against Australia in Melbourne a year earlier ended up costing it a place in the championship final, which allowed New Zealand to participate instead—and win it.

Maybe there should be a third option—deducting runs, which would have the potential to change the result of matches. All three sanctions together might have some chance of working.

Ruminating on the result, Root may or may not have been aware that no England team has won a series in Australia after losing the first Test since 1954–55.

Anyway you looked at it, this was a disastrous start. Unsurprisingly, he put the best spin on it he could, saying he didn't regret batting first, especially as Cummins would have done the same, and that he would not be changing any strategies.

As for the selection of his attack, he retorted: "It's easy in hindsight. We wanted variety. The bowling effort was good, we just put down too many chances."

As he spoke, Broad was busily composing his column for a London newspaper, in which he said he and Anderson were both expecting to play and were shocked and disappointed to be left out. "I feel I could have had a positive influence on a pitch like that," he said.

It wasn't to be the last bullets he would fire at his own team management, either during the series or when he got home.

While the fourth-day collapse was "bitterly disappointing" things could have been very different if they had showed only a fraction more resistance on day one, Root added. "And we did show we could create chances."

So what now? "We have to be brave," he said, whistling in the dark. "It's really important we don't feel sorry for ourselves. There are a lot of positives to take out.

"It would have been very easy to go out there like rabbits in the headlights and think the game was over. I think we showed good character, good fight and skill as well to get us into position where we were still in the game. It's just bitterly disappointing that we couldn't get ourselves to a total where you're in with a shout."

Root couldn't guarantee that Stokes would be fit for the second match in Adelaide less than a week later, while the Australians had their own injury problems with Josh Hazlewood nursing a side strain that would force him to miss the rest of the series and Warner a set of badly bruised ribs which were unlikely to keep him out of action.

Other than that, Cummins of course couldn't have been any more pleased with the way it had all panned out, for him personally and for his team. At no stage was he ever under significant pressure, and he didn't put a foot wrong either as a leader or as a bowler. It was almost too good to be true, really.

"I really enjoyed it," he said. "A lot went right for us, even the toss and the weather. I'm proud of everyone. It was the complete performance. Really positive."

About working with Smith, he said: "It was a bit of a different dynamic, totally manageable. I had a lot of help from Steve and a lot of the other guys who threw ideas my way, and the bowlers are all old pros. Even after the first couple of hours I found it more natural, really."

So what's not to like? Nothing at all.

Australia used to have a sporting hero who was universally known as Peter Perfect. That was the charismatic champion racing driver Peter Brock. And rugby Union captain John Eales answered to "Nobody" because nobody's perfect. Now it seemed, we might have found Patrick Perfect.

For how long—that was the question. But we were going to have to wait a little longer than expected for the answer to continue to unfold.

CHAPTER 7

THE LYON KING LIES IN WAIT

It is entirely possible that Nathan Lyon has never heard of Lady Mary Montgomerie Currie, an English poet of the late 19th century who wrote under the pseudonym Violet Fane, but her most famous few words would resonate with him after the Gabba Test. "All things come to those who wait," she wrote. Thank you, Google.

Australia's superstar off-spin bowler would have been excused if he had started to wonder about that. Of all the many story-lines attached to this game, few were more anticipated in advance than Lyon claiming his 400th wicket.

It was just a matter of when—not if—he would get it.

Or was it?

England's first innings came and went and he was still empty-handed. In their second innings, they batted through another two sessions for the loss of two wickets, neither of them to him.

Cricketers—all sportsmen for that matter—love nothing more than winding up teammates in such frustrating circumstances, and so in the dressing room that night captain Cummings cheerfully informed him he was destined to be stranded on 399 forevermore.

It was, of course, just Cummins' humorous way of easing the tension that had started to build up around the situation, a little reverse psychology.

It had indeed become a disconcertingly long vigil even if there was never the slightest doubt that all would be well in the end—well, wouldn't it?

It had been 326 days since Lyon had bowled Indian tail-ender Washington Sundar during the fourth Test at the Gabba back on January 19, at which point almost another year, or 705 days in all, had passed since he entered the "nervous 390s" by having New Zealand's BJ Watling caught—by Cummins—in Sydney on January 3, 2020.

So if the wait had become excruciating, who could blame him? It was not as if it was just another run-of-the-mill milestone—400 wickets is such a monumental performance that only two other Australians had achieved it. Shane Warne claimed 708 from his 145 Tests and Glenn McGrath 563 from 124, while it should not be forgotten that Dennis Lillee once held the Australian record with 355 but also added another 67 in World Series Cricket, which most of the players involved say was, if anything, of an even higher standard.

Lyon became the 17th to join the illustrious club, which included three other contemporary players, two of them on the spot watching as he did so—England's Jimmy Anderson and Stuart Broad—as well as India's Ravi Ashwin.

It had taken Lyon 101 Tests and just over a decade to complete the feat, which began when he made his debut in Sri Lanka on August 31, 2011, in spectacular fashion, dismissing one of the world's best players, Kumar Sangakkara, with his first delivery and going on to take 5-34 for the innings.

He was almost completely unknown to Australian cricket fans—and certainly to the surprised Sri Lankans—and could scarcely believe he was suddenly living the dream, for which he could mostly thank one of the most astute judges in the game, former Victorian captain Darren Berry who recognised his latent talent during a stint as coach of South Australia and rushed him into the State team.

Now he was as recognisable as anybody in the team, one reason being that the straggly patch of black hair he used to have had long ago given way to what might politely be referred to as the fashionable bald look, but more because he had become an immoveable fixture in the team and a regular media spokesman for it. In that role, he has not been afraid to make a few provocative calls, for instance suggesting to the Englishmen the previous time they were in Australia that he intended to end a few careers.

Within a day or two of Australia winning the first Test, he was confidently predicting a 5-0 whitewash, a line that used to be the speciality of McGrath.

His up-front personality has made him the appropriate choice for another important role—leading the dressing-room rendition of the team song after every victory.

It was bequeathed to him by a retiring Mike Hussey and Lyon says he gets nervous performing it "because the way I look at it, it is a bloody important role, not just for the players but all the staff and you might have a couple of players making their debut. I remember when Huss gave me a letter about why the song was handed over. I try to make it special and a bit funny, which is a challenge for me because I'm not that funny."

He has long answered to the soubriquet of GOAT, the acronym for greatest of all time, from the moment he became Australia's most successful off-spinner, passing Hugh Trumble's 141 wickets between 1890 and 1904 and the late Ashley Mallet and Bruce Yardley with 132 and 126 late last century.

Left-arm finger spinners have been much less prominent, the most successful being the almost totally unremembered Victorian Jack Saunders whose 78 Test wickets is the most for an Australian, and that was more than 110 years ago.

Greatest ever or not, cricket fans can be a fickle lot.

In Brisbane, a certain restlessness became evident on social media—and even the mainstream version—as Lyon laboured through 24 overs against Joe Root and Dawid Malan as they unfolded their desperate rear-guard fight in the second innings.

Amazingly, Malan revealed later that he had got an edge, or a glove, to one that popped back to Lyon for what would have been a simple caught and bowled—if there had been an appeal. But neither Lyon nor anyone else did pop the question to the umpire so the long-awaited moment passed like a ghost in the night.

His figures read 0-69, enough for one major newspaper to run with the headline "Lyon at sea, stranded on 399." A prominent journalist tweeted: "Is he still an automatic selection?"

Pre-match, even Warne had been starting to raise questions about his status, which prompted Sydney sportswriter Andrew Webster to return serve, correctly noting that the great leg-spinner had not reacted well to criticism when he was playing himself, so why was he now making a habit of bagging other Australian players, Starc the most obvious example.

Oh ye of little faith.

The new day was only minutes old when Malan advanced down the pitch to Lyon and bunted a looping, dropping delivery to Marnus Labuschagne at silly mid-on, an attacking field placing that Cummins had chosen not to employ for most of the day before, much to the frustration of former captain Ricky Ponting on TV.

Labuschagne grabbed it as gleefully as if he had just unearthed a nugget of gold—which he had, in a sense.

This was not only Lyon's moment of triumph but the breakthrough that almost certainly meant the tourists were unlikely to survive. Sure enough, Root followed a few balls later and Lyon then took total command, adding three more scalps—Pope, Robinson and Wood—to finish with figures of 34-5-91-4 as Australia charged to victory in double-quick time.

That took him to 403 wickets, two behind Curtly Ambrose, 11 behind Wasim Akram, 14 behind Harbajhan Singh and 18 behind Shaun Pollock, royal company indeed, all of which were now potentially within reach over the next month.

In fact, Lyon finished with 16 for the series—a good effort given he wasn't handed the ball at all during the fifth Test in Hobart as the pace squadron got the job done without assistance in both innings.

He went past Akram with Harbhajan just two away, a deficit certain to made up on the next assignment in Pakistan.

Excited though he undoubtedly was, Lyon took it in his stride. "It's something I'm very proud of, no doubt about that," he said. "It's been some hard toil to get it, but very rewarding.

"I'm nervous because I care. I care about everyone in the dressing room, I care about the result and I care about playing for Australia. I'm not nervous because I'm scared of failing.

"Pat was extremely calm as captain. I think when Australia play their best cricket, we're calm and playing with smiles on our faces and enjoying it. Pat really hit that home."

In the end, Lyon was a matchwinner—one among several, and by no means for the first time—which was probably rubbing salt into the open wounds of his opposite number in the other dressing room, Jack Leach, who was probably the leading candidate if the Barmy Army were trying to decide on who to blame for being a match-loser.

Like Lyon, Leach is a finger-spinner, only he uses the fingers of his left hand and therefore spins the ball in the opposite direction. That is, into left-handed batsmen, with which Australia were well-equipped with Warner, Harris, Head and Carey, plus Starc and Hazlewood.

He is not a fixture in the side and could not get a game in any of England's six home Tests earlier in the year. His history suggests he needs plenty of help from the playing surface to prosper—something few visiting spinners have ever enjoyed in Brisbane.

Leach had played only on the sub-Continent, so he was always a baffling selection, and had no answers, excuses or assistance when Warner, Labuschagne and Head expertly executed a plan to bury him as quickly and thoroughly as possible, which they did by smashing 102 off just 13 overs.

The Australians' lack of respect was summed up without mentioning his name when coach Justin Langer said: "We have an advantage because we have a world-class spin bowler."

It's not as if Leach is no good at all at what he does—in his previous 16 Tests he had 62 wickets, which is four a match give or take, the same as Lyon, at an average of 29.98, which was better than Lyon's 32.12 by a significant margin.

However, there the favourable comparisons abruptly end.

CHAPTER 8

ALL IS FORGIVEN AS SMITH TAKES CHARGE AGAIN

Redemption stories—in sport and in life generally—always go down well. There are exceptions to every rule, though. So when Steve Smith suddenly found himself once again in the exalted position of captain of the Australian Test team it was not a given that he would be universally accepted and applauded. Far from it.

However, the second Ashes Test proved to be a triumphant—if temporary—return to the highest sporting office in the land. Standing in for Pat Cummins, who had been a shock last-minute withdrawal after falling foul of covid protocols, Smith oversaw a comprehensive 275-run victory, to which he made a powerful personal contribution by scoring 93 and pouching six slips catches. And he did it without the team's two best fast bowlers, Cummins and the injured Josh Hazlewood, and with gun batsman David Warner hampered by bruised ribs suffered while batting in Brisbane.

It would have been no great surprise if he had been named man of the match.

Just as significantly, he was given a mostly—if not entirely—warm ovation when he walked out to bat in the first innings. He claimed not to have noticed, his mind being otherwise occupied, but when told about it later, he made no attempt to hide his satisfaction, and no doubt his relief. "That was nice," he said.

It was also a relief for Cricket Australia, who had agonised over the decision to appoint him as Cummins' deputy, unsure quite what the public response would be given that Smith had been stripped of the job in the first place because of his role in the ball-tampering scandal three and a half years earlier.

There were still many unwilling to forgive or forget that, and you only had to pay attention to the letters pages in the newspapers, talkback radio and social media to be in no doubt about that.

It is unlikely to ever change, which will be disappointing.

The naysayers almost certainly included a number of influential administrative figures who privately hoped it would not come to this, that it would never become necessary for him to take control again.

Naturally, no one was more sensitive to the issue than Smith himself.

Publicly, he pretty much kept his own counsel. But when the always provocative Shane Warne said he believed Smith's offence was so serious that he should not have been returned to office, and if he was it would open up Cricket Australia to ridicule and criticism, Smith confronted him by phone.

"He messaged me and said 'geez, you're a bit harsh, aren't you?'" Warne revealed. "We talked it out and that's what respect does. Just because someone doesn't like your opinion, it doesn't mean they have to get nasty and personal.

"I was happy he contacted me because I consider him a friend. Like he said to me, 'mate you've been in the game for 30-odd years, you've earned your right to have an opinion and I respect it, I just don't agree with it.'"

Former captain Greg Chappell also disagreed with the decision but for much different reasons—he thought the opportunity presented itself to blood a new potential captain, namely Marcus Labuschagne.

So when the Adelaide Test began in such bizarre circumstances—Cummins was ruled out only five hours before play began in the middle of the afternoon—Smith found himself in the spotlight more than any other player or any other issue, and there was no shortage of the latter, especially in the England camp.

For starters, Smith needed his own vice-captain. That was quickly solved with the nomination of local batsman Travis Head. Although he had been widely considered to be no good thing to be selected for the first Test, he was a pretty obvious choice because he had the gig for a while under Tim Paine and had been in red-hot form in Brisbane.

However, Head was outranked in seniority, experience and performance by Warner, who in a perfect world would have been an even more obvious choice. That was never going to happen, though. Warner had been fingered as the real mastermind of the sandpaper incident and banned from all leadership roles for life, whereas Smith had been given only two years, now long expired.

So in at least one important way Warner was still clearly considered to be on the nose in high places, and whenever it was suggested—as it was every so often—that he should also be free to hold high office even at domestic levels, the administration always dead-batted it.

It would be wrong to suggest that Warner had demonstrated insufficient remorse, but Smith raised the bar by presenting himself as an asset to the cricket community in general in every way that he could—to once again make himself "electable", as politicians say.

He wanted another crack at the job, no doubt about that, and when it became available with Paine's demise, he and Cummins were the only two realistic candidates.

CA knew that by appointing a fast bowler, especially one with a history of injuries, and who might need to be rotated from time to time to prevent overwork, there was every chance Smith would have to step in sooner or later.

They just hoped that it could be done with a minimum of blowback or controversy from fans and the media.

They got their wish, firm evidence that by and large the view was that everybody deserves a second chance in life, especially if they have done a sincere penance, and that it was now time to move on.

It would be churlish to disagree.

This was Smith's 35th match in charge and meant Australia had three different captains in as many matches, the first time that had happened since 1956, when Ray Lindwall, Ian Johnson and Ian Craig took turns.

Smith welcomed fast bowlers Jhye Richardson, who had played two Tests against Sri Lanka two years earlier, and Michael Neser, granted a long-awaited debut after having been a more or less permanent 12th man for two years.

Despite the disruptions to a winning team, Smith had a significant advantage—as is usual now, Adelaide was a day-night match, which had become an Australian specialty.

There had only ever been 16 such matches played, half of them in Australia, five of those in Adelaide, and Australia had won all of theirs, defeating New Zealand, South Africa, Pakistan, England, Sri Lanka, Pakistan, New Zealand and India.

England had played only four, losing to Australia, New Zealand and India away and drawing with the West Indies in Birmingham.

It was an enormous statistical challenge for the tourists, especially as the fifth match was also due to be played under lights, this time in Hobart.

It appeared to have muddled their thinking in advance, having left their two key strike weapons, Jimmy Anderson and Stuart Broad, out of the team in Brisbane to ensure they were fresh for Adelaide, where Anderson, especially, was seen as a threat at night because he had taken a five-for there four years earlier, albeit to no avail.

This time, they both came into the side at the expense of their only truly express bowler Mark Wood and their first-choice spinner Jack Leach, leaving them with an all fast-medium attack—with the exception of captain Joe Root's part-time off-spin—which looked decidedly unbalanced when set beside Australia's. And so it proved.

Both captains desperately wanted to bat first on the usual flawless Adelaide surface and pile up a basis for a big score before any of the five late-night sessions came into play, and when Root wrongly called tails at the toss he was already under pressure.

point, and not for the first or last time, everything that
ong for him did—painfully so.

ith, it was the opposite—he enjoyed almost the perfect
he had scored seven more runs in the first dig and held one
iance, it would have been.

igland drew first blood by dismissing out of form opener Marcus
is for three—making him the 218th worst-performed of the 225
ayers who have opened the batting in Tests at least 20 times—but
rom there it was all one-way.

Warner took 20 balls to get off the mark and an hour to move past
one but was then unstoppable until a loose cut shot off Broad left him
five short of a hundred to his obvious profound disappointment. But
he still went past David Boon's 7,426 and into 10th place on Australia's
all-time run-scoring list, and by the end of the game was just 12 behind
Mark Taylor's 7,525—from 16 fewer matches.

In his 88th match, Warner now had 24 centuries and 32 half-tons,
almost identical figures with the legendary Greg Chappell (24 and
31 from 87 outings)—a comparison that should permanently put to
bed any quibbles about his entitlement to be regarded as an all-time
great.

Labuschagne was dropped by wicketkeeper Jos Buttler on 20 and
again on 95, dropped a third time and bowled by a no-ball before
completing his sixth Test century and first against England, which took
him past 2,000 runs in just 34 innings—only Bradman (22) and Mike
Hussey got there faster.

Smith also fell marginally short of what would have been his 28th
ton as Australia rattled on 9 December for 473 but occupied the crease
for more than five hours and improved his remarkable average of 70 as
captain.

England's camp followers just shook their heads in dismay.

Sole selector Chris Silverwood and whoever else was getting a say
had got it dreadfully wrong again, going in without a specialist spinner
on a wicket where no one has ever taken more wickets than Shane

Warne and Nathan Lyon, and without their only genuinely fast attack dog, Wood.

And those who did play, including Anderson and Broad, consistently bowled the wrong length, too short. Root admitted as much at the end of the match, as if it was solely their fault, but he regularly set fields with three men deep on the leg side, which could only have been to accommodate such a strategy.

"We made the same mistake here four years ago and we haven't learned from it," he lamented lamely.

Ben Stokes attacked Labuschagne and Smith with something closely resembling the Bodyline tactics that caused such uproar 90 years earlier, but it had no effect.

Perhaps in Smith's case the strategy was a throwback to the previous Ashes series in England in 2019 when their fastest bowler, Jofra Archer, unleashed a brutal barrage of short stuff that enthralled a capacity crowd at Lord's—including the author, who was watching from the Long Room—until the chilling moment when he struck Smith, on 92, in the head.

Smith hit the deck in frightening fashion and had to leave the field, returning at the fall of the next wicket to courageously bat on, only to be quickly dismissed as he was obviously not functioning properly.

Archer, who did not come to Australia because of injury, revealed in an interview aired before the Adelaide match that he had experienced a roller-coaster of emotions when he realised his adversary could have been seriously hurt—or worse.

He warned against England again trying to undo Smith in the same way, saying the tactics at Lord's were not preconceived.

"Steve had set in for a big one, to be honest. I can't remember the exact conversation on how we ended up going the short stuff but we were just going to try everything we could so he doesn't settle," he said.

"I just ran in and let the ball go as fast as I could. The short stuff is only ever plan B."

There was certainly not much hope of intimidation this time when only 30 balls faster than 140km/h were delivered and 95 per cent of them all would have missed the stumps.

Just to accentuate the inadequacy of the make-up of the attack, fast bowler Ollie Robinson resorted to three overs of off-spin wearing sunglasses, reviving memories of former Australian player Colin Miller who cobbled together a respectable career in the 1990s by purveying equal amounts of both styles, once taking five-for with his spin against the West Indies at the Adelaide Oval—which Robinson was unlikely to have known.

The criticism was predictably ferocious, especially once the inevitable result was posted, with former Australian speedster and bowling coach Craig McDermott the most scathing.

"I just don't understand their tactics," he told *Sydney Morning Herald* cricket writer Malcolm Conn. "They bowled semi-OK in the first Test but their tactics in Adelaide were atrocious. Bowling bouncer after bouncer was a waste of time and it backfired. I don't know what their coach and bowling coach were thinking about doing. Their whole set-up and how they've gone about picking their bowlers has been very bewildering, really."

England's reply was no more encouraging initially, with both openers Burns and Hameed gone for single figures, the latter gifting Neser a maiden wicket with an inept half-drive to mid-on.

As in Brisbane, Root, 62, and Malan, 80, turned the tide with a patient partnership of 138, the captain succumbing for the second time to impressive young all-rounder Cameron Green, sparking a collapse of 8-86.

That meant that in two partnerships, Root and Malan had contributed 2-300, while at that point every other partnership so far had amounted to 24/313.

The ensuing collapse left them 237 behind and at the mercy of the follow-on.

But to the puzzlement of many, Australia almost never sends the opposition straight back in again these days, usually preferring to give the bowlers more rest—but perhaps, some think, because of a lingering unease dating back 20 years when Steve Waugh famously did so In India and lost an unlosable match.

So Smith opted for another 61 overs of glorified batting practice before again declaring nine down, this time with an extravagant lead of 467—and 135 overs in which to complete the coup de grace. It looked like a formality.

Could things get any worse for Root? You bet they could.

Before play on day four he was facing throw-downs in the nets without wearing a box and was hit in the goolies—or "the abdomen," as the ensuing news release coyly preferred to say—and was taken to hospital for scans and missed an hour or so of play.

Much later in the day, while mounting another rear-guard action at the crease, he was hit in exactly the same delicate area, this time not by a gentle throw-down but a 140km/h thunderbolt from Mitchell Starc.

At least he was wearing the usual protection this time but that didn't make it any less painful as he collapsed onto the pitch and rolled around in agony, waving away the aerial "Flying Fox" camera as he unzipped his pants to check out the damage.

The Australians tried their best, not altogether successfully, not to smirk, not because they wished him any injury of course, but for some reason these incidents always seem to be amusing—except for the poor unfortunate on the receiving end.

Root was fully entitled to retire hurt but, perhaps because of a sense of duty given the need for his team to display a bit of fortitude for once, he eventually batted on, only for Starc to put him out of his misery by having him caught behind off what was the last ball of the day.

That left England at 4-82 with so little apparent prospect of surviving long into the final day that Cricket Australia waived admission fees in favour of a gold coin for charity.

When Ben Stokes and Ollie Pope quickly departed on resumption, it was as good as over—and almost certainly would have been if wicketkeeper Alex Carey had not made his first mistake of his new tenure, inexplicably watching an edge from Buttler, who was on a pair, fly waist-high between himself and Warner at first slip.

It didn't seem to matter. Buttler was better-known as a white ball blaster—he had thrashed a century in a T20 World Cup match against Australia only a few weeks earlier—rather than a grafter likely to pull down the shutters in a long siege.

But that's exactly what he did, sharing in a stubborn partnership of more than three hours with all-rounder Woakes which had onlookers beginning to query the wisdom of the follow-on decision, while also a reminder that Australia had twice failed to bowl out India on fifth days the previous summer.

It didn't change the result but it did restore some much-needed respect and morale for the tourists.

Buttler was the second last man out, having faced 196 balls for his 25 before pretty much sabotaging himself by stepping on his stumps while playing back to Richardson.

Has anyone ever had a weirder match? He held three stunning diving catches behind the stumps but dropped a couple of sitters, made a duck in the first innings and then proved almost impossible to get out in the second one, before falling to one of rarest of all forms of dismissal. It was a cruel denouement to an impressive display of character and determination, of which there had been precious little

The fightback—which took the match into the last session of the last day and within 20 overs of a different outcome—was some consolation to the visitors but did not disguise the reality that they had been out-thought and out-played in every facet of the game.

All the most effective players were wearing a baggy green cap; Labuschagne, whose second innings half-century ensured he won the man of the match award, Warner and Smith contributed the three highest scores. Smith was by far the best fieldsman, and Starc, with six wickets and Richardson, with a five-for in the second innings, were streets ahead of any of the opposition bowlers.

At the presentations, Smith made a point of offering a special shout-out to Starc, who had come into the match under extra pressure with the absence of Cummins and Hazelwood but responded superbly—as he always does in day-night games. His four in the first innings made him the first bowler from anywhere to claim 50 with the pink ball.

Smith said he had never seen the big left-armer bowl better. It took him to 264 career wickets, leap-frogging Jason Gillespie into eighth spot on the Australian list, sixth among fast bowlers. The 300-club beckoned.

The thrashing took England past 4,000 days since they had last won a Test in Australia and left them on the brink of a series defeat, trailing 0-2.

Only once in the history of the Ashes had a side ever come back from two down to win. That was in 1936–37 when Australia did so, but that team was led by Don Bradman, who made three huge scores in the remaining matches, which perhaps illustrated the immensity of the challenge that now lay ahead for Root.

He was, naturally, asked whether he was confident the situation could be retrieved... well, you would hardly expect him to say no. So he whistled in the dark—again.

"Absolutely," he said. "We have to. We have what it takes to win here, but we have to be better and not make the same mistakes. We are capable of it and we have shown it in small pockets. We feel we have been competitive in patches in both matches. The attitude today was brilliant, we just have to have more of it. We expect to have the same mentality for the rest of the series."

Needless to say, that confidence was not widely shared among the notoriously hard-marking Fleet Street press corps.

Smith, naturally, was delighted. "It was fun. I enjoyed myself," he said.

Certainly the gods seemed to be smiling on him.

In his second innings, he edged his first ball from Broad straight to Buttler, who grassed it, preventing a rare golden duck. Second ball, he looked so plumb lbw that Broad didn't even bother interrupting his celebration with the formality of an appeal—only for the umpire to give it not out and a subsequent review also unsuccessful even though it showed the ball would have hit off stump.

"Never seen a luckier start to an innings," said TV commentator Ricky Ponting.

And midway through England's second innings, he suggested to Starc that he switch from around the wicket to over the wicket against Pope—and the next ball was edged straight to the slips, where it was caught by a grinning Smith.

More to the point, perhaps, Australian cricket in general enjoyed having him back at the helm, not that anyone would now want him there permanently in place of Cummins. The transition to the new leadership set-up might have been only two matches old, but there was already everything to like about it—and nothing to worry about.

The public backlash against Smith that some people in high places expected never eventuated, at least not in any significant form.

Perhaps it all happened so quickly that there was no time for dissenters to get their act together, and in any case the Adelaide cricket public love the game so much that they were never likely to make life uncomfortable for a player well on his way to becoming a legend of the game.

Smith captained the team calmly and well, was never under pressure, led by example with the bat and in the field, and delivered a victory that would only make Cummins' re-entry all the smoother.

His redemption was as complete as it was ever likely to be—and even Warne was no longer querying it.

CHAPTER 9

ONE OUT OF THE BOX FOR KING MIDAS

After taking an unwanted break in Adelaide from his new job, Pat Cummins returned to work in Melbourne and slotted straight back on to the throne as if he was, indeed, King Midas, turning everything he touched to gold.

Even the mighty MCG seemed to have fallen under his spell—perhaps deliberately.

The great stadium has never really had a reputation as a fast bowler's playground—although the great Dennis Lillee used to enjoy it, as did the West Indies terror squads of the eighties on occasions—but this time it became obvious before play even began that something profoundly different might be about to take place.

As a fast bowler—the best in the world, officially—Cummins couldn't have scripted it better himself, although he might have struggled to come up with the incredible nature of the eventual denouement involving a player most fans had never seen in action.

The first clue that something had changed dramatically came when the captains came together for the toss beside a pitch that was greener than any in recent memory at the ground—certainly many shades removed from the one Joe Root's team had encountered on their last visit four years earlier.

In that match, England's Alistair Cook batted for two days for 244 not out—a ground record for a visiting batsman—while only 24 wickets fell across the five days in one of the most boring stalemates imaginable.

The pitch was reported as sub-standard to the ICC, which warned a repeat could see the MCG lose its Test status—an unthinkable contingency, which resulted in a total overhaul of the methods used to prepare and install the drop-in strips.

This time curator Matt Page cut the grass to a height of 11mm, a generous cover by any standards. To say the least, it proved to be bowler friendly and difficult to bat on, but that's never been against the Laws of Cricket and it produced absorbing cricket—if not for very long.

When the game finished in less than seven sessions, Australia winning by an innings and 14, even the Melbourne Cricket Club was wondering whether there might have been a slight over-correction and a few old batsmen in the commentary boxes were making it clear they were glad they didn't have to cope with it.

On social media, one unimpressed observer, calling himself "the voice of experience", labelled it the worst he had seen at the ground, adding: "They must have top-dressed the old one with Viagra!"

But none of that disguised the fact that the quality of the fast bowling on offer was outstanding, and not just from Cummins and his colleagues. England's ageless Jimmy Anderson turned back the clock with a masterclass too, as futile as it turned out to be.

Nobody was quicker to take advantage than Cummins.

Despite still being without key bowler Josh Hazlewood and the five-wicket star from Adelaide, Jhye Richardson, and with little-known Victorian Scott Boland making his debut, Cummins had no hesitation in bowling first when he won the toss for the first time.

It was a good toss to win because Root was desperate to do the same.

In his first over with the new ball, Cummins immediately took a wicket—his 100th on Australian soil—when he had the barely competent Haseed Hameed caught behind, following up quickly with the scalp of the other opener Zac Crawley, caught in the gully.

England were 2-13, thanks entirely to the rampaging Australian skipper, and already looking likely to crash to their third heavy defeat in as many matches, formally ending their forlorn hopes of retrieving the Ashes.

Even so, the full measure of the tourists' descent into cricket Hell was still to reveal itself—but only for a couple of days.

As they had awoken on the morning of the match, news came through that former English captain Ray Illingworth had died from cancer at 89.

There were no shortage of respectful obituaries pointing out that while the old Yorkshireman was not necessarily a great player, he was a tough, shrewd and courageous leader of men, whose finest achievement was to captain England to a 2-0 victory in Australia in 1970–71.

Perhaps his memory might become a sad source of inspiration for the current squad. Or perhaps not. Maybe he would soon be rolling in his grave.

If they were ever to scramble their way back into the series, Melbourne was probably their best chance of doing it.

Of their six previous Tests there dating back to just before the turn of the 21st century, England had won two and drawn one, a respectable recent history.

Like all touring teams, the English enjoy playing there simply because it is such an iconic venue, the birthplace of Test cricket in 1887, always huge crowds in attendance, creating an atmosphere unlike any other ground in Australia or the world.

To play in a Boxing Day Test is an experience like no other, no matter where you're from.

But if you're out of form and under pressure when you get there—either as an individual or as a team—it's a tough place to recover.

On day one, England never looked like doing it, bowled out for 187—the 13th time for the year they had failed to reach 200. Hameed's duck was their 50th for the year, the record being 54 in 1998—and which was destined to last only for another 48 hours.

As usual, only Root offered any meaningful resistance, getting to exactly 50—for the ninth time in Australia—before nicking off, this time to Starc, for the fifth consecutive innings.

At least he batted to his average. In fact, Melbourne's prolific social media statistician @sirswampthing wryly pointed out that his average had slumped from 50.015873016 to 50.15789474. This, he said, was a change of 0.0000083542, the lowest ever change in anyone's average from one innings to another.

Where would we all be without such priceless information?

Cummins took the first three wickets, making him the first to reach 10 for the series even though he had participated in only three of five innings. Of 20 bowlers to have taken 100 wickets in Australia, he had the best average and strike-rate.

Australia's reply—interrupted by a 30-minute delay on day two after six non-playing members of the England camp returned positive covid tests—was held together by Victorian opener Marcus Harris, who was probably on his last chance after failing to make any impact in the first two Tests.

Harris's 69 was no thing of beauty—he injured a finger along the way, it took four and a half hours, he played and missed regularly, he was given out lbw to Ben Stokes on 36 only to be reprieved by the third umpire, he should have been stumped off Jack Leach on 63—but the value of it could be measured in that he succeeded where Warner (to a lesser extent), Smith, Labuschagne, Head and Green did not.

When you look at it that way, it was priceless both for the team and personally, hauling his stuttering career back from the brink of oblivion and resisting England's most positive attempt to exert some control in the series so far.

Australia had lost six wickets before they took a first innings lead, bringing the match alive and restoring a pulse to England's forlorn hopes of getting back into the fight for the urn if they could only improve their second innings and set a challenging run chase.

For that, they could thank the 39-year-old Anderson, who exploited the conditions with every skerrick of his vast experience, taking four for 33 off 23 overs—England's first bag of more than three wickets, and in some opinions his best performance in five visits to Australia even though he had a five-for under lights four years earlier.

He dismissed Harris, Warner, Smith and Cummins and had every other batsman struggling to survive or even score.

It was immaculate. There were no wides or no-balls and his economy rate was 1.43. In one six-over spell, the only run he conceded was a half-chance to the diving wicketkeeper and he claimed the prize wicket of Smith, bowled.

He said he felt it was the best he had bowled in Australia since the series win in 2010–11.

His expert use of the helpful pitch made you wonder why his long-time partner Stuart Broad wasn't playing, for the second time in three matches.

England's use of their squadron of right-arm pace bowlers had been hard to fathom from the moment they left both Anderson and Broad—owners of more than 1100 Test wickets between them—out of the opener at the Gabba.

Neither was impressed by their treatment and didn't forget to say so in newspaper columns.

As he toiled away at the MCG, Anderson never smiled, not even when he took a wicket.

These days, as the excellent British writer Jonathan Liew pointed out in *The Guardian*, he doesn't seem to enjoy it—the wickets are met with a snarl, the plays-and-misses with a grimace. Watching him can be a draining experience, Liew wrote.

"He has the knack of making professional sport look like hard labour, especially as he has become reduced to defending lost causes, bailing out failing batsmen. But when conditions are good and the ball is doing a bit, there are still few bowlers you would rather watch."

Hear, hear. Only four months earlier I had been hitting the keyboard myself about being transfixed by Anderson's absolute masterclass in new-ball bowling against the cream of the Indian batting.

"Swinging the Duke orb both ways with precise placement at brisk pace, defying some of the world's best batsmen to pick what exactly was coming next, he had KL Rahul, Cheswar Pujara and the great man himself, Virat Kohli, all caught behind at the cost of six runs off eight overs. Has he ever bowled better?" I asked.

He didn't get a chance to improve on those superb figures because the world's second ranked Test team were bowled out for a humiliating 78 before he could have a second spell.

As impossible as it seemed in a craft that is largely physical, it did seem that the older he was getting the better he was bowling.

Having made a certainty of one more Ashes trip, he had a point to prove. In 18 Tests across those four tours he had taken 60 wickets at 35.43 with just one bag of five. In England, where his 95 Tests had yielded 402 wickets, his average was 24.20.

So it was always going to be a matter of waiting to see what we got from him when he got here—and if the answer was mixed, then this one performance in Melbourne went a long way to balancing perceptions.

Sadly for him and his many admirers, it didn't change anything in the big picture.

Within an hour of him coming off the field late on day two, it had all been for nothing, the contest was as good as over—England had been blown away again.

Cummins and Starc had unleashed one of the best double-edged new ball onslaughts anybody could remember witnessing at the MCG, not necessarily lightning fast or physically frightening a la Lillee and Thommo or the old Windies back in the day—but intensely challenging, virtually every ball.

Fast bowling doesn't get much better.

For those of us who were present back then, it revived memories of the time in 1981—also in the late afternoon—when Lillee ripped through the West Indies with four wickets, bowling Viv Richards with the last ball of the day.

It has always been high on the list of the MCG's great moments in sport, and some have it as No. 1.

The Cummins and Starc show, in similar circumstances, won't be quickly forgotten either, especially by those at the other end

Starc removed Crawley and Malan and then Boland got Hameed and nightwatchman Leach to leave England tottering at 4-22, dead in the water. For a long minute or two no replacement batsman arrived on the field, leaving everyone to wonder if they had surrendered—until finally Stokes emerged to join his captain.

This probably wasn't the sort of experience that Root would have requested from who whoever was writing his scripts, but on the other hand, as Mike Atherton pointed out, the adrenalin would have been pumping so hard that he would certainly have known he was alive.

Crawley agreed. "I loved walking out to bat on Boxing Day—it was one of the best moments of my career. That second evening with the crowd there—it didn't go my way, but I'll look back on that with quite a few fond memories," he said on Twitter.

They could all perhaps console themselves that it will never get any harder than this, Atherton said.

Allan Border, agreed. An old-school hard-head when he captained Australia, he said: "I rarely feel sorry for England—but for one individual, yes. Hameed as a young opener, he had absolutely no chance of scoring runs. The crowd baying for blood, the fast bowlers—they were throwing hand grenades, every ball was doing something and you expected a wicket just about every ball. He's fought like anything to get through and hasn't quite made it. He must think Test cricket is the hardest game in the world."

The only question was whether Root and Stokes could eke out some sort of lead at least, but that was emphatically answered when Starc produced the delivery of the match to take out Stokes' middle stump.

What followed was barely believable, as the debutant Boland took the next four wickets in 19 balls to finish with the spectacular figures of six for seven off four overs and claim the man of the match award.

Out for 68, the shell-shocked rabble hadn't even made it to lunch, let alone the mid-point of the series—which would have been the drinks break in the second session—and the Ashes had been surrendered in record time.

They had lost 20 wickets for 273—four years after Cook had scored 0-244 himself at the same ground.

This was cricket as blood sport, one English newspaper said as the predictable recriminations began to pour down on Root, Silverwood and anyone else in a position to be held responsible, particularly the England Cricket Board itself.

Inevitably, Root's head was placed on the chopping block by some, most notably the ever-trenchant Geoff Boycott, who said he wasn't trying to be hurtful to "a man we all love"—a fellow Yorkshireman—or controversial for the sake of it.

"Nobody would want to give up the captaincy but it's not about Root, it is about getting guys to perform better," he said. "At the end of this series, the question should be asked would England benefit from a change of captain?"

Stoically, Root was not about to take the easy way out by abdicating, at least not yet. "The series isn't over yet," he said. "We've got two very big games and, more than anything, it'd be wrong to look past that. I'm in the middle of a very important series. My energy has to be all about trying to win the next game. I can't be selfish and start thinking about myself. I'm sure we can come back hard in the last two Tests."

Silverwood also dug in amid even more intense speculation that he was a dead man walking, especially with his boss—English team director Ashley Giles—arriving for the Sydney Test armed with plenty of hard questions needing answers.

Asked if the players would still back him, Silverwood said: "I think they are. We had a good, honest chat. We just have to put performances together and start pushing back."

As it was about to turn out, Silverwood was to play no part in the following Test, told to isolate in Melbourne because of a positive covid case in his family.

Needless to say, the mood in the two camps—personified by the captains—could not have been any more starkly different.

Now the only fast bowler ever to claim the Ashes as captain, Cummins was living the dream.

"I grew up playing in the backyard and watching Steve Waugh, Ricky Ponting, those guys, in Ashes series," he said. "It felt a million miles away from me playing cricket in the backyard. Yet here I am a decade later in that position. It's madness. The MCG is a good reminder each year when you play on Boxing Day. You turn up and do the national anthems, you've got a packed house and millions of people watching from home. It's a great reminder each year that you're part of Australian cricket history. It always takes me back to my childhood. It's nowhere near what I imagined my life could become as a young kid. To be in that similar position to those guys (Waugh and Ponting) is just awesome. Those guys were the captains I grew up watching and idolising. When I think about what it means, I think more about what it means for our group of players. All round, everyone has performed, everyone has contributed. It's all gone to plan so far. Even when England played really well on day two, we managed to wrestle it back late in the day. It's just worked out fantastically. Winning early on day three at the MCG just doesn't happen, so it's a fantastic result. To go 3-0 up, it's the first Ashes victory for a lot of the guys in the team. It's what dreams are made of, the way we played."

Cummins singled out Starc for special praise. The big left-armer, who had struggled through the previous summer because his father was dying, had to repel a challenge from Richardson for his place in the first Test, with his regular critic Shane Warne leading the charge for him to be dropped.

He then took a wicket with the first ball of the series and continued to lead from the front in the absence of his regular partner Hazlewood, taking key wickets at all the right times. Not only that, he was scoring such useful runs from No 8—35, 39, 19 and 24 not out—that he found himself elevated to No. 5 on the ICC rankings for all-rounders, one ahead of Stokes.

"I have never seen him bowl better," Cummins said.

His form did not go unnoticed. Not long afterwards he won the Allan Border medal for player of the year for the first time.

CHAPTER 10

SIX OF THE BEST FOR STARTERS

Australia's long cricket history is replete with many outstanding Test debuts, Pat Cummins' high on the list. But few will be remembered for quite as many reasons as Scott Boland's scarcely credible performance when his opportunity finally arrived after a lifetime—in cricket terms—of patiently waiting.

Selected out of the blue for the iconic Boxing Day Test at the MCG, Boland immediately became a matchwinner, taking seven wickets for the match, including six for seven in the second innings—the sort of figures you might only ever see in scorebooks devoted to young kids in the park—and was instantly hailed as the newest hero of Australian sport.

It wasn't just because of his performance—as monumental as that was—but every bit as importantly, he had just become only the second indigenous male, and the fourth of either gender, to play Test cricket for Australia.

Given that the game has been played at that level for 144 years, it is a dispiriting statistic so this was being hailed as exactly the sort of inspirational breakthrough that cricket desperately needed. Some even, a tad extravagantly, compared it with Cathy Freeman's immortal gold medal win on the track at the Sydney Olympics 21 years earlier.

The game has long been left for dead in this respect by the football codes, especially the AFL, while 2021 had also celebrated hugely impactful achievements by indigenous stars, tennis player Ash Barty winning Wimbledon and basketballer Patty Mills collecting the Sport Australia Hall of Fame's prestigious The Don award as the nation's most inspirational athlete for his efforts at the Olympics and in the American NBA.

This was suddenly illustrious company for Boland—literally so because Barty was at the MCG to watch his first appearance - but nobody was about to dispute his right to stand in it.

There had been quite a few heroes—some familiar, some introducing themselves—in a busy year at the Olympics and elsewhere and the applause for this one was the equal of any, especially if you were among the 42,000 people who were there to see it unfold—an "I was there" moment destined to take its place in the mighty stadium's long list of unforgettable feats.

For most onlookers—and probably the shell-shocked English batsmen who were left humiliated—it came completely out of the blue, like the most captivating sports stories so often do.

Very few saw it coming in any shape or form, with the obvious exception of the in-form selection panel of George Bailey, Tony Dodemaide and coach Justin Langer, who had identified him as a possible bolter by inviting him into the travelling squad without actually making it known publicly.

They were well aware of his superior record long-term at the MCG, where he had taken eight wickets in a man-of-the-match performance in the Sheffield Shield for Victoria just a few weeks earlier.

The main reason it was so surprising was that the Victorian fast-medium bowler was 32 when selector Dodemaide informed him on Christmas Eve that he would be a part of what is always the biggest date on the cricket calendar and bigger still when it's against England, with the Ashes at stake.

He went weak at the knees.

Chances like this rarely if ever arrive for fast bowlers of such advanced vintage—no one older had done so since a lanky South Australian named Geffrey Noblet played against South Africa in Port

Elizabeth in 1950, aged 33. (And no, we haven't mis-spelled his Christian name—that was the work of whoever had been entrusted to register his birth, and he never bothered correcting the mistake.)

It was hard to get a game in those days with Ray Lindwall, Keith Miller and Bill Johnston—all matchwinners—shutting out all other would-be new ball exponents.

But, hey, Boland could relate to that—as the Ashes campaign approached he knew that the new captain, Cummins, veteran stars Josh Hazlewood and Mitchell Starc, young all-rounder Cameron Green and two fringe candidates in Jhye Richardson and Michael Neser were all much more likely to play before him. And did. So when he finally emerged, blinking, into the limelight it was as Australia's seventh choice pace man.

Seventh! Touring parties that go on the road for months on end never have that many fast bowlers. England arrived with only six, and that was only after star all-rounder Ben Stokes announced his availability after the original party had been chosen.

Boland's age and his remote place in the pecking order were, however, both eclipsed as talking points by the fact that he was about to join another very good fast bowler, Jason Gillespie, as the only male indigenous Test players, along with two women, Aunty Faith Thomas and Ash Gardner.

But even that had an age connotation.

Gillespie went to enjoy a hugely successful career—his 259 wickets put him in eighth place on the Australian all-time list until Starc overtook him during this series—before it petered out in spectacular fashion when he made a double-century while batting as a nightwatchman in Bangladesh.

That was Gillespie's 71st Test and he celebrated his 31st birthday during his mammoth innings—so in other words he was done and dusted at a younger age than Boland was able to get started.

When Gillespie arrived on the scene against the West Indies in 1996, nobody from Cricket Australia or the media even realised he was

Aboriginal, his father belonging to the Kamilaroi people of north and central NSW.

He didn't see the need to tell anyone of his First Nations heritage, it just sort of leaked out as he went along. Which is definitely not to suggest that he was in any way not proud of it, he just shyly didn't shout it from the rooftops.

"I always found it weird that it took so long to come out because I always knew I was of Indigenous descent and all my mates knew it," he said later. "I was never asked initially. It was a strange one. Then when it got out I could not believe how much publicity it got. I had naively assumed there were a lot of people in Australia with Indigenous blood and then when you research it you realise we are quite unique. I was incredibly proud."

Boland was in his mid-twenties before he discovered that he was connected through his maternal grandmother to the Wurundjeri people of Victoria's Western District. Without making a fuss about it, he embraced this new status enthusiastically.

Western Victoria was the home of the 13 Aboriginal cricketers who toured England in 1868, a decade before white Australian teams did the same, and in 2018—150 years later—Boland, his brother Nick and two other first-class players, Dan Christian and D'Arcy Short, took part in an all-indigenous tribute tour which also featured a women's team.

One of the original team's better players was an all-rounder named Johnny Mullagh, real name Unaarrimia, who was also to become a significant part of the Scott Boland story.

Some Test cricketers—such as Boland's new captain, Cummins—are obviously destined to go all the way from childhood, dominating from the word go and rarely having to wait for recognition. That was never really Scott Boland, who was obviously talented but had a lot of work to do to make it to the top.

As he progressed through the suburban ranks in Melbourne—slowly—he was a knockabout, known by the unflattering nickname of Barrell, who ballooned to nearly 120kg and was told he wouldn't get a game at senior level at Frankston Peninsula Cricket Club unless he got a lot fitter.

As he shed weight he started bowling faster and faster, the work paid off and he eventually made it into the Victorian Shield team where he had to struggle to find a place in a strong attack, including Test players Peter Siddle and James Pattinson.

However, by the time he made it to Boxing Day his credentials were a bit more substantial than his low profile might have suggested to most people—but not to Bailey and Co, obviously.

He had played 17 white-ball internationals—14 ODIs and three T20s—with modest success on tours of the West Indies, Sri Lanka and South Africa, had been called up on standby for the Hobart Test against the Windies in 2014–15, had won the Sheffield Shield player of the year award when Victoria won it in 2018–19, and had taken 275 wickets in 80 first class matches.

He had also acquired reputation for being particularly hard to handle on the sometimes-unpredictable MCG track, while his unflappable nature and willing work ethic were also seen as assets.

Even so, most considered him a rank outsider to usurp either Richardson or Neser, and if he did, it would be on a temporary basis and he would most likely end up in the One Test Wonders club, which has more than 70 members.

Presented with cap No 463 by Hazlewood, he told anyone who asked that he just hoped he could make some sort of impact.

So did Dodemaide, who was the last Victorian pace bowler to make his debut on his home ground on Boxing Day, which was against New Zealand back in 1987—when he took six wickets in the first innings and seven in all, which now sems like an eerie coincidence.

The excited newcomer was happy to be bailed up by a photographer at training, but when the snapper took one shot and declared himself done, Boland replied: "Are you sure? You only took one. It's my debut and I wouldn't mind it being a decent photo."

Photographer, curtly: "You do your job and I'll do mine, mate."

Boland wasn't to know, of course, that he was soon to become the subject of hundreds of photos, some of which were destined for the front pages of every daily newspaper in the land, and for lift-out hero posters.

He cracked it for a mention in the official "welcome to country" by senior Wurundjeri elder Aunty Joy Wandin Murphy

When play began after a half-hour rain delay, Boland had to wait his turn behind Starc and Cummins of course, and worked hard for his first wicket, which came when he trapped Mark Wood in front, with umpire Paul Reiffel—himself a former Test pace bowler from Victoria—taking his time make the decision, which then had to be confirmed by the third umpire.

The reaction from both the crowd and his teammates stunned him.

"Obviously I was really excited when the finger went up—all my teammates really got around me, which made it really special, and when I went down to the boundary the crowd was going nuts," he told reporters.

England were bowled out for a mediocre 185 with Boland taking an unremarkable 1-48 off 13 overs, as well as holding two challenging catches in the outfield.

Twenty-four hours later, he was back in action as England batsmen began their second dig with an hour to play on day two. After Cummins and Starc terrorised them with one of best double-edged new-ball spells most onlookers could remember, Boland then chimed in by dismissing opener Haseeb Hameed and nightwatchman Jack Leach in quick succession, leaving England floundering at 4-22.

Next morning, he again had to wait until Starc had disposed of Stokes but then took matters entirely into his own hands by accounting for Bairstow, Root, Wood and Robinson within 11 deliveries.

In total, his bag of five had come off just 19 balls, equalling the record for the fastest to reach this milestone, set by Australian seamer Ernie Toshack in 1947–48 and matched by Stuart Broad at Trent Bridge, Nottingham, in 2015 when Michael Clarke's Australian side was infamously routed for 60.

The old enemy had been humiliated for 68 and the Ashes had been defended two hours before the series even reached the halfway point.

At this point, Boland's Dad Mick, a busy health-care worker, had just completed a rushed trip to the MCG after knocking off work, hoping to see his son put in an afternoon shift himself—and missed every ball of it.

Boland's wife Daphne, a police officer, and their daughters Charli and Andi also missed part of the Test because family members of the team were told to stay away after positive covid cases materialised in the England camp.

It turned out it wasn't the start of the family connection with Australia's most important sports venue—Boland's grandfather Brian played there regularly during his 56 VFL games for Richmond and Hawthorn in the fifties, four of which were with teammate Ron Rieffel, Paul's father.

Dad might have missed the wickets but he arrived in time to see his son standing in the middle of the ground, surrounded by teammates, with the crowd of 42,000 chanting his name.

He had the match ball in his hand, still shining it as if he wanted to keep bowling. Most bowlers, when they have taken a five-for, hold the ball high to show it off—he seemed reluctant to raise it above head high, scarcely able to believe what had just occurred.

Another huge moment—prouder still perhaps—arrived quickly when it was announced that he had won the man of the match award, which for the MCG Test is now always named the Johnny Mullagh medal in honour of the original Aboriginal cricketer.

The trophy, made from the buckle of a belt worn by Mullagh, was to be presented by Belinda Duarte, a direct descendant of another member of that long-ago team, Dick-a-dick, a member of the MCG Trust, and who has held a number of senior positions of influence in the development of Indigenous people.

She had been waiting outside the MCC committee room to discover who the recipient would be and, when told, she burst into tears.

She said later she could feel the ancient life force of her people sweeping across the ground.

"Some would say the old people had something to do with this," she said. "We carry our old people everywhere. There were so many indicators they were by his side. Oh my God, I just felt extraordinarily emotional. I had so many mob contacting me by text saying 'Oh my God, I think you're going to present it to Boland.' I'm a big believer in the work of our people and the spirit of our people and our ancestors."

She said Boland—who had told her he couldn't breathe during his first innings because he was so nervous—encapsulated the spirit of his forebears from 1868.

"It would be such a personal experience reconnecting back to the origins of those men—their courage and commitment at a time when they were treated as lesser people," she said. "Scott's journey—what I love is he is very similar to those people from the Western District. They speak with actions and those actions are often extraordinarily powerful. What a beautiful way to celebrate his ancestry, his connection to the Western District and our people will be celebrating up that way because it's part of the fabric of who we are. It's the story of our people."

In a match-eve interview with the Melbourne *Sunday Age*, Duarte had said she had trouble getting her head around what the 1868 cricketers must have felt about their experience.

"I think about how brave as a group they must have been, or about their curiosity in exploring to take on this trip. Today, to go away for a year we might feel like 'that's an eternity' but back then there was no confirmation or guarantee that they were going to get back or that they would survive. To think they had only been learning to play cricket for four years. This team in its own right, and Uncle Johnny Mullagh with his symbolic representation, captures that team and the history of this country. Sport is so much the identity of Australia. The good, the bad, the ugly and the beautiful."

Boland's own reflections were largely focused on his link with

Gillespie and what it might mean for younger Indigenous sportsmen.

"It means a lot to join a pretty small club," he said. "Hopefully it's just the start of something bigger for the indigenous community in cricket. I hope I can be a role model for kids who want to play cricket The indigenous community in AFL and rugby are so big, hopefully one day Aboriginal cricket can be just as big."

Boland has been assisted in his journey by Cricket Australia's Indigenous Advisory committee, which had been exploring ways to promote greater involvement.

They included a designated round of the Big bash T20 tournament, and—not without some opposition—had officially stopped referring to January 26 matches being played on Australia Day, which some sections of the community refer to as Invasion Day.

The committee's co-chair Justin Mohamed said the decision was still being robustly discussed. "What we learned is that we have to communicate and that communication is a lot stronger now," he said.

It was mostly about education, he said, and now acknowledging that the 26th has "different meanings and represents different things, especially for First Nations people."

It takes time, he said.

"We've seen that with other sports—people forget many years ago that Richmond was the only team in the AFL that had an Indigenous jumper. The Dreamtime at the MCG game was a concept made up between two clubs (Essendon and Richmond) but then it turns into the indigenous round and that flows. So it takes time and we've broken the ice on it. CA has worked a lot on getting that communication and having those conversations. It's a journey we have to walk together as a nation, and CA's doing that at the moment with its footprint on what happens on that particular day."

For all his heroics, there was still no guarantee that Boland would play the next Test match in Sydney—or, indeed, ever again. That's how stiff the competition had become for bowling assignments in the Australian team.

Seldom, if ever, have any set of Australian selectors been presented with quite such a dilemma, a dream and a nightmare at one and the same time.

However, with Hazlewood and Richardson still not fully recovered Boland not only kept his place but he resumed precisely where he had left off, taking another seven wickets—including Joe Root for a duck—which guaranteed him a third crack in Hobart.

There, he got four more, for a series total of 18 from three matches, at the almost unheard-of average of 9.55—almost exactly half the cost of Cummins' 21 scalps at 18.04 and little more than a third of Starc's 19 at 25.36.

Asked if he had been surprised by his new man's spectacular arrival, Cummins said: "Well, I knew he was capable—but this was just incredible."

He certainly got no argument about that.

CHAPTER 11

FIGHTING FOR PRIDE TO THE LAST BALL

When all is lost, the least you can hope for it that your supporters have not deserted you.

England were grateful for that small mercy as they prepared to try to salvage some pride in the fourth Test in Sydney.

The Barmy Army, their travelling fan club which has accompanied the team around the world since first appearing in Australia several years ago, are more famous for their beer-fuelled, witty singalongs—usually taunting the opposition—than for any serious, official dialogue about the fortunes of their heroes.

But they are nothing if not passionate and loyal—as they decided to make abundantly clear as the team's mood and morale threatened to hit rock bottom.

On arrival in Sydney they posted a statement which said they were "gutted and distraught" that the Ashes had been lost so soon, but "no matter what we remain unconditionally supportive of the team—we will never waver."

They would be making their voice heard with the England Cricket Board, they said, having noted "it was clear there are fundamental and structural issues with the county game and its level of prioritisation is not working for the Test team."

That must have been a positive note for Joe Root and his shell-shocked rabble to take fresh block—but did they have the character and courage to fight back?

And what did Australian sports fans actually want to see? More of the same, or a more captivating contest, if not necessarily a different result?

The hope, surely, was that the Sydney encounter—always an iconic event no matter what the state of play, and the second biggest crowd-puller of any series—would provide a more sustained and genuine battle than the previous match, which was all over in very little more than two days.

Maybe the cricket Gods felt they owed it to all concerned—or maybe the tourists did—to deliver something special, something memorable, something to underscore what all true cricket aficionados have always known, that Test cricket's capacity for producing great theatre far outranks any other form of the game and is right up there with any other sport.

The match went right to the last available minute of play, and then some, and to the final delivery, with two vastly different outcomes—another large Australian victory or an honourable (for England) draw—still possible.

Even though they had been thoroughly outplayed—Australia would surely have won by well over 100 runs if more time had been on offer, or not lost to wet weather on each of the five days—it is not patronising to suggest that England were entitled to be proud of their great escape.

That's because it was achieved with, yes, character and courage.

It was something better for the Army to sing about.

Four men in particular led the way—Jonny Bairstow and Ben Stokes made important runs while dealing with significant injury, Jos Buttler did his best to carry on despite being so damaged that he had to return home immediately after the match, and Stuart Broad took England's first five-wicket haul of the series— while others found something extra to hold firm under pressure in the pulsating final session.

Impressed and grateful, Root said: "There was clearly a lot of pain relief required. It's not just a physical element but the psychological, knowing you're going into a pressure situation not 100 per cent, to be able to perform at the level that some of the guys did was phenomenal and shows a huge amount or character."

Bairstow would have won the man of the match award if not for a sublime performance by Australian batsman Usman Khawaja, who scored hundreds in each innings, 137 and 101 not out.

It was an interesting match-up given that neither of them was considered to be in their team's best eleven when the series kicked off a month earlier.

Indeed, Khawaja might not have got an opportunity, in this series or any other, to revive a Test career that was in danger of withering on the vine if it had not been for the great X-factor in everybody's lives over the preceding two years—the ubiquitous covid virus.

Proving that there is always a silver lining to every cloud, he was recalled after Travis Head—who had narrowly beaten him to the last uncertain batting spot in the first place—was ruled out of this match because of a brush with the virus.

Khawaja's credentials for that spot, or to open the batting instead of the unstable Marcus Harris, were if a little short of impeccable than at least very substantial—44 Tests for 2,887 runs at 40.66 with eight centuries, plus several very productive seasons of Sheffield Shield cricket since his last appearance.

Those figures—taken without any context—make you wonder why he was ever dropped, which he was not once but several times.

By this stage it was pretty much impossible to argue that he wasn't a superior player than Harris, and certainly much more experienced, and to many observers, better than Head too. So his exile was puzzling.

But he was 35, five years older than Head and four older than Harris and selectors are always likely to look to the future when such line-ball calls have to be made.

However, this after all was the Ashes—Australian cricket's Grand Final, where the immediate challenge is what counts, not what might be around the next corner.

The selectors were having a blinder in every other respect—they opted for Head in Brisbane and he made a hundred, they called up Jhye Richardson to replace the injured Josh Hazlewood in Adelaide and he claimed a match-winning five wickets in the second innings, and they pulled a smokey with Scott Boland in Melbourne and he dominated like few rookies before him.

And now Khawaja for Head and back-to-back centuries are the result.

It was enough to make you wonder whether England would have been any more successful if they had been up against Australia A.

If chairman George Bailey, Tony Dodemaide and coach Justin Langer were to be given anything less than a 10 out of 10 for their work, the decision to overlook Khawaja in the first place was the only possible quibble.

But not even Khawaja was entering into that debate—not even after his triumphant comeback was consummated by becoming only the third Australian behind Doug Walters and Ricky Ponting to lodge back-to-back hundreds at the SCG.

He said he understood the selectors' thought processes—their preference for continuity—had no issues with them and did not expect to be an automatic inclusion for the fifth Test no matter how well he had played in this one.

Where once he would have fretted over each and every call the selectors made about him, the politics and the pecking orders, now he had learned whatever will be will be—so there was no point stressing about it.

Khawaja, Pakistan-born and the first Muslim to play cricket for Australia, is an inspirational and valuable figure in a country that continues to struggle with issues of culture and identity.

It took him a long time to understand where his life could take him, having been constantly told as a young player that he would struggle to succeed in what was essentially a white man's game.

He once told an TV interviewer that there were times he wished he had a white skin. As a non-drinker—a rarity in most sporting environments, cricket certainly no exception—he often felt the odd man out, cricket writer Robert Craddock observed: "It weighed heavily on him and is why he is a staunch campaigner for more multiculturism in cricket."

Khawaja's philosophies on life—not just cricket—had been shaped by an uncommon range of experiences, achievements, frustrations and patience. In a word, maturity—and with that, confidence to be who and what he is, comfortable in his own skin as a citizen and a sportsman.

It shone through with rare clarity after each of his comeback innings, which drew multiple standing ovations from the Sydney crowd, who still considered him one of their own—he grew up only a few streets away from the SCG and played junior cricket alongside his future Test teammate David Warner—even though he had opted to continue his career in Queensland.

"I've gone through a lot of hard times, broken down a lot of barriers to get to where I am right now and I think at some level people can relate to that and they can see it and I love them for it," he said. "My parents still live in Parramatta. I still have a lot of connections to Sydney in a lot of respects. I'm a Queenslander now but I don't forget where I came from, I never have. The SCG. Honestly, it was the most touching, humbling, amazing feeling out there, getting that 100 and the roar that went up, the chanting 'Uzzie'... It's stuff you dream of. I never expected that to happen. It was unbelievable. They talk about the American Dream. I call it the Australian Dream. I joke about it but I'm quite serious. I'm living the Australian dream. My parents came here from Pakistan to give me and my family a better life. They've come all the way here and I'm representing Australia at the national sport. I've put a lot of hard work in. A lot of time behind the scenes that people don't see. I have a lot of support from my family, my parents and in particular my wife Rachel. You never take anything for granted. I was never really sure if I was going to represent Australia again, let alone score a hundred for Australia."

Khawaja's first knock was little short of a masterpiece. He arrived at the crease at 3-117, with Warner, Harris and Labuschagne failing to capitalise on starts, and hardly put foot a foot wrong against some much improved bowling from the recalled Broad as well as Jimmy Anderson and Mark Wood.

Never regarded in his previous incarnation as particularly comfortable against spin, he also dealt fluently with Jack Leach, except for one very difficult chance that eluded both the wicketkeeper and the slip.

On a strip with more grass than usual at the SCG, batting wasn't easy but his languid style was both easy on the eye and immensely effective as he and Steve Smith put on 117 to ensure that the captain's decision to bat first was not going to come into question despite the uncertain start.

Khawaja's eventual 137 came off 260 balls with 13 fours and enabled Cummins to declare at 8-416, virtually a position of safety from defeat already.

An hour later, England were 4-36 and yet another embarrassing capitulation was looming.

Root had his second duck of the series, courtesy of Scott Boland, who was continuing his MCG rampage with two more wickets without conceding a run, which meant he had now taken 8-7 across two innings.

He bowled five consecutive maidens before conceding a single off the second last ball of his sixth over, with the CricViz data system declaring his combined handiwork in Melbourne and Sydney was the most accurate period of bowling seen since their records began in 2006.

Enter Bairstow.

You kind of know when he comes on the scene there's a fair chance you're going to get a fight. Maybe it's his flame-red hair and bulky build—or that his reputation precedes him.

Hmmm, that might be a bit unfair but the Australians—and most fans—wouldn't have forgotten his colourful contribution to the early stages of the previous tour four years earlier when he was accused of head-butting young Australian batsmen Cameron Bancroft when they met for the first time in a Perth bar.

They quickly claimed a psychological victory when they sledged him about it when he came out to bat in the first Test of that series, which might have been why he got out to a very poor shot at a crucial stage of the second innings.

This time round, though, the 32-year-old Yorkshireman was a more accomplished performer—on arrival, a veteran of 78 Tests with 4381 runs at 33.70 with six centuries and a highly respectable record as a wicketkeeper when required to double up on that job—and no stranger to tough times. A hard nut to crack.

He has had more challenges in life than most young sportsmen, the full extent of which became public only during that previous tour when he published an autobiography titled *A Clear Blue Sky*, which was widely acclaimed as the best sports book published in England that year.

It was a compelling, emotional story full of both tragedy and resilience on his own part and that of his mother Janet and younger sister Becky.

It revolves around how he arrived home from football training— he was a talented enough junior soccer player to be invited to trial for Leeds United—at the age of eight to find, together with Becky, that his dad David had hanged himself, apparently in a fit of depression over financial problems and his wife Janet's battle with cancer.

David Bairstow, who was 46, had also played cricket for England as a wicketkeeper batsman, although not quite as successfully as his son—four tests and 21 ODIs, with moderate results.

He was a gregarious, upbeat personality—I can confirm that, having enjoyed a convivial hour or two with him in a bar in South Africa many years ago—who was a popular legend in cricket-mad Yorkshire.

He left no clues about his state of mind when he made his terrible decision more than two decades ago, although apparently he had come to terms with the end of his cricket career only reluctantly and had struggled with the transition to business.

The tragedy happened the day before Janet's birthday and he had even booked a restaurant to celebrate and organised a babysitter for Jonny and Becky.

Janet, his second wife and a cricket administrator at the Yorkshire County club herself, then had to bring up two children as well as coping with two separate battles with cancer. She succeeded on both fronts but not without plenty of stress—and plenty of pent-up anger, she said.

Jonny helped her through the first battle and went on to achieve his dream of following in his father's footsteps. But then she was stricken again, this time while he was on tour with England in India.

The news hit him like a thunderbolt. "I didn't know anything about it," he said at the time. "Mum kept it from me and Becky looked after her because I was away and she didn't want it to affect my cricket. To find out after I had just warmed up for a game was hellishly tough and the journey back was horrendous. You hear the word cancer and you don't know how bad it is."

Happily, she recovered and in 2020 was elected the first female vice-president of the crustiest old club in the country, an honour she regarded as a reward for acting as a mother figure to hundreds of players across several generations.

Although not greatly gifted, the elder Bairstow had enjoyed a well-earned reputation for trying his guts out in pursuit of team glory—and when the time comes to assess his son's career, the events of Sydney, 2021, will ensure he is credited with inheriting that invaluable quality.

As he and his fellow redhead Stokes—batting with a strained thigh suffered while trying to pepper the Australian batsmen with short bowling—set about addressing the all-too-familiar situation, Bairstow was cracked on an unprotected part of his thumb by a high-velocity missile from Cummins.

As he writhed in agony in the hands of medical staff while the game stopped for several long minutes, it seemed certain he would have to retire hurt.

But he opted to soldier on, completing what he described as by far the hardest hundred of his career. "Just with the circumstances, it takes quite a bit to get one off the park," he said. "It was one of those where it was a decision I made to stay out there."

Sadly, the respect for this courageous performance wasn't quite universal. As he and Stokes walked off for the tea break, they stopped to confront a spectator who was attempting to give both batsmen grief about their weight.

"Stokes, you're fat," one said.

"Take your jumper off, Bairstow, lose some weight Bairstow."

Stokes' only response was a glare—perhaps because, as one columnist archly suggested, he is one cricketer who knows that young men on the drink sometimes do and say things they later regret, a reference to the street brawl that cost the all-rounder the previous Ashes tour.

But the combative Bairstow returned fire. "Pal, that's right, just turn around and walk away. Weak as piss," he fumed.

In the corresponding Test a year earlier, Indian bowler Mohammed Siraj alleged he had been racially abused by spectators seated behind where he was fielding.

Recalling that, a well-travelled—in terms of watching his favourite sport—observer wrote a column in the Melbourne *Age* suggesting Sydney was home to the worst-behaved cricket fans in the world.

The pair added 128, before Stokes departed for an aggressive 69, which was a few more than he should have got after a bizarre escape when he played no shot to a ball from young pace bowler Cameron Green which then clipped his off-stump at 142km/h without dislodging the bails.

It was such a strange occurrence that umpire Paul Reiffel gave him out lbw even though the ball wasn't within a foot of his pads, which a grinning Stokes quickly had overturned on review, of course.

The partnership allowed England to avoid being asked to follow-on, an unusual strategy these days but a distinct possibility in this case given the highly uncertain weather forecast.

Australia's second innings was, basically, Act Two of the Khawaja show, co-starring all-rounder Green, whose 74 was only the second significant contribution with the bat of his brief career—and a reward for the work he had been putting in on his technique, which had been coming under intense scrutiny from people who know about such things.

Cummins waited until Khawaja had completed his second century late on day four, and then a little longer, before declaring 387 in front with enough time to bowl seven overs, which Hameed and Crawley nervously survived.

And so decision-day dawned with England needing to survive for 109 overs to salvage a face-saving draw—victory was not quite impossible, but beyond improbable—while Australia needed to take 10 wickets. The Ashes script so far suggested they should do that comfortably, but recent history was not so sure as they had twice failed to bowl out India on day five the previous summer.

When seven more overs were lost to yet more rain immediately after lunch—making a total of more than 60 across the five days—the equation evened out again.

An engrossing battle unfolded. Australia pressed hard with the early wickets of Hameed and Malan, Root unable to hold out much longer. Crawley resisted with a classy 77 and Stokes, a second half-century, and Bairstow, still unable to hold the bat comfortably as he gritted his way to 41, took the fight deep into the final session.

Bairstow was still in occupation when the second new ball arrived and Cummins, applying his Midas touch one more time, ripped out Buttler and Wood with vicious, unplayable in-swingers, both of which were painstakingly reviewed, adding to the mounting drama.

It left just the tailenders Leach, Broad and Anderson in support of Bairstow.

Then Scott Boland's fairytale introduction to Test cricket continued when he had Bairstow caught at bat-pad, his seventh wicket for the match, giving him the astonishing career analysis of 14 at an average of under nine.

It left the nine, ten, jack to survive for almost 11 overs, a long-odds proposition with Cummins, Starc and Boland all armed with a still newish ball.

With six overs remaining, Nathan Lyon returned with all nine fielders crowded around the bat in search of the final two wickets, most urgently Leach, who had frustrated them in the famous match in Headingley two and a half years earlier when he hung out while Stokes completed a miracle victory.

Lyon couldn't break through, and with three overs still to play out, the umpires told Cummins he couldn't use himself or Boland because it was too dark for fast bowling.

So, who? Cummins was to laugh later that both Labuschagne and Smith, both part-time leg-spinners, considered themselves the best at that task, so it was a toss-up.

He threw the ball to Smith, who had not taken a Test wicket for five years—but who then promptly had Leach edging to Warner at slip.

Two overs to go, numbers 10 and 11 at the crease, one wicket left—this was high theatre indeed.

Broad, who actually has a Test century and 13 fifties to his name, dealt with Lyon, and Anderson—who had been not out more than 100 times in Tests, a record—did the same with Smith's second over.

The 5-0 whitewash had been averted. A measure of English pride had been restored.

The irony was lost on nobody that it had come down to a duel between England's two best bowlers and Australia's pre-eminent batsman—but with roles reversed.

For the first time in his brief captaincy career, Cummins came in for criticism with a strong school of thought insisting that he had delayed the declaration too long, piling up runs that were never going to be needed given that England had been bowled out for fewer than 300 every other time.

He shrugged it off, saying he thought well over 100 overs was enough to work with, given that the extra runs allowed him to attack creatively on a wicket that was still not playing many tricks. In fact, he thought England's remaining victory target of just over 350 was achievable.

"It gave them a little bit of a cherry if a couple of batters got in," he said.

Like everyone else, he enjoyed the climatic tug-of-war immensely and had no regrets. "I feel I was able to make quite a few calls, some came off and some didn't, but it was a lot of fun," he said. "When you are that far ahead in a game, of course you want to win it. We got close but just not close enough."

Root said averting the whitewash was "hugely important—especially on the back of the previous Test, which was a really dark day for English Test cricket. It would have been easy to roll over and feel sorry for ourselves. The guys were trying to put some pride back into the badge and show how much they care about playing for England.

"We didn't win the Test match and were a very long way behind the game but to still find a way to get the draw shows the character, the pride and the desire the guys have when they put on an England shirt.

"Relief is the overwhelming emotion and I'm quite proud too. We had a lot thrown at us and guys have really stood up and showed a lot of character and pride. I feel a big sense of pride."

Given all that had gone before, Root was entitled to his declaration of pride—and yes, some of his troops did display some desperately needed fortitude at long last—but the stark reality was that they were still as little as one ball away from yet another heavy defeat. And that was with no little assistance from their opponents, who dropped six catches, missed a run-out and handed one wicket back because of a no-ball.

These uncharacteristic errors aside, they were far and away the better team—again.

As the teams gathered in Hobart for the final showdown, the Australians were acutely aware of that—and in no mood for mercy.

CHAPTER 12

HOP TO IT—A BROADSIDE FOR FRIENDS AND FOES

Stuart Broad signed off on his Ashes campaign the way he should have clocked on—by dismissing David Warner for a duck.

This was Australia's second innings of the fifth Test in Hobart, and therefore the end of the fascinating duel between these two superstars, at least for the time being and very possibly forever.

At 35 years old, both men were deep into the twilight of wonderful careers and no certainty to be participating in the next Ashes series in England more than a year later.

Certainly, it was extremely difficult to envisage Broad making a fourth tour of Australia in four years' time, even though he would then be 39, the same age as his long-time new-ball partner Jimmy Anderson was when he arrived for his own fifth tour.

That suspicion was all but confirmed when he and Anderson were both dropped from the team to tour the West Indies, the next assignment after the Ashes, even though the ECB insisted it was not necessarily the end for either.

Australia will miss Broad—but possibly not as much as he will miss Australia.

It has been a long love-hate relationship—well, hate is too strong a word and maybe love is too—based on more than his brilliance with the ball in his hand, a commodity statistically saluted when he dismissed Warner for the 14th time, and the ninth time since the start of the 2019 series in England.

It was his 129th Ashes wicket, passing the record holder Lord Ian Botham, and five ahead of the late Bob Willis and 17 more than Anderson. Botham, however, played in a handful of Tests in which the Ashes were not at stake, and finished with 148 all up, the most of any bowler against Australia, ahead of the West Indies' Courtney Walsh 135 and NZ's Richard Hadlee 130. Broad finished the series with 13 wickets and a total of 130 against the old enemy.

But like Botham before him, Broad exuded a personal appeal for Australian fans, even if the relationship was decidedly ambiguous for a while.

On this tour, he came across as the most interesting personality in a touring party that was scarcely over-stocked with entertaining characters, a white headband securing his ample blond hair making him instantly recognisable on the field, happy to make himself seen and heard—even amusing the Hobart crowd by pausing in his run-in to shout out to a robotic camera circling the perimeter of the ground and intruding on his eye-line. Next day, Fox Sports equipped the camera with its own white headband as a peace gesture.

There is no doubt—certainly in his own mind—that more use should have been made of him, more quickly, by the England team management. And he did not neglect to let them know how he felt about that.

Of all the many mistakes England perpetrated from the moment they landed in Australia, perhaps the most egregious was their use—or non-use—of Broad. No, they didn't get it quite right with his long-time partner in crime, Jimmy Anderson, either, who played only three games, or Mark Wood, who was left out in Adelaide when his searing pace was sorely missed.

And that just makes it worse. But as soon as the old urn was lost, with Broad having been given a minimal chance to exert any influence, he demonstrated what might have been by taking five wickets in the first innings of the fourth Test in Sydney.

It was the only such bag of the tour until Wood followed suit with the pink ball in Hobart, his career-best haul of 6-37 providing his team with by far their best chance of winning a match, which they promptly squandered in embarrassing fashion.

Broad's Sydney scalps came at a personal cost of more than 100 runs and could not prevent the Australians declaring with more than 400 on the board and two wickets short of being bowled out—but at least England narrowly avoided losing the match.

However, it was a clear pointer to what might have been if he and Anderson had not been mysteriously omitted from the team for the series opener at the Gabba, where the conditions on the first morning would have suited them both nicely—if they had been playing, and if the captain Joe Root had the gumption to send Australia in when he won the toss. Instead, England were bowled out for 147, never recovered and lost by eight wickets. To most experienced observers, the Ashes were already won and lost.

Broad did not take the snub kindly and without becoming in any way obnoxious about it, he never let sole selector Chris Silverwood and Root and whoever else might have had a hand in it forget it. His pride wouldn't allow that. The same went for Anderson to a lesser extent, but it was Broad who led the charge, culminating in him dropping a few truth bombs at his media conference the night of his five-for—not so much a tirade as a passionate dissection of the flawed strategic thinking that had produced such a disastrous outcome.

It was so impressive that the team media manager congratulated him on it before he had even left the room, to the surprise of most of the journalists present, few if any of whom had ever heard such an accolade for a dissertation critical of his own senior heavy-hitters, all the way up to the England Cricket Board.

Some thought it an impertinence that he as lucky to get away with.

But at 35 and with 150 Test matches behind him, coming from a family background with strong roots in the game—his father Chris played 26 Tests as an opening batsman and later became a match referee—and with a deep-seated love for it, Broad was perfectly equipped, entitled and willing to make his views known. Which is why one of London's major newspapers, the *Daily Mail*, paid him handsomely to write a weekly column, which was one of the most entertaining, informative and trenchant of its genre.

As described earlier in these pages, he had used that platform to express surprise and dismay that he wasn't given an opportunity in Brisbane or in Adelaide, the two venues where he felt he could have been of most use.

So he played only one of three Tests where the Ashes were still alive.

Australian cricket fans were just as puzzled by this as he was. They have long enjoyed a feisty and ambiguous relationship with him, especially in Brisbane where the daily newspaper, the *Courier Mail*, once branded him a fraud and a cheat and refused to publish his name.

That unprecedented attack—partly in jest, perhaps, but partly not, maybe—didn't faze Broad, who had learned to appreciate the Australian penchant for a bit of mongrel on the cricket field during a season with the obscure Hoppers Crossing club just outside Melbourne when he was 18.

"I went over as a young kid, public school cricket, all nicey-nicey, flat wickets, knock it around... and then I stepped out there and it was like being in a fight," he once told the British media.

"They were coming at you all the time. That taught me toughness and that was good for me because it hardened me up."

He described one match where he batted for 60 overs, for 70 runs, just to defy a much older opposition bowler who had tried to bully him.

"That was the moment when I stopped being a polite schoolboy cricketer who liked to hit nice cover drives for fun and decided this was going to be my life and that I loved the edgy, competitive element even more," he said.

His father agreed. "In the hostile atmosphere of Australian league matches the boy became a man and the man discovered he liked something other than cricket: he liked cricket with needle," he said, clearly well pleased by such a development.

This "no need to be nice" attitude famously surfaced during the first Test of the 2013 Ashes series at Trent Bridge, Nottingham, when batsman Broad edged spin bowler Ashton Agar via wicketkeeper Brad Haddin's gloves to first slip, where he was caught.

But he refused to walk and was given not out to the astonishment of the Australian players—and anyone else who witnessed it—with Broad, who was on 37 at the time, adding another 28 runs and England going on to win by just 14.

Australia's coach Darren Lehmann later labelled him "a blatant cheat" and called on the Australian public to "make him cry" when the battle resumed in Brisbane a few months later—a comment that almost certainly did not escape the editorial heavy-hitters at the *Courier Mail.*

The paper was already feuding with another visiting star, Kevin Pietersen, who had made an art form of sledging the Queensland capital in general, but that "was just a dress rehearsal to test the mood of the tourists for our assault on the real villain," the Editor, Christopher Dore, later wrote in a column.

"We had thought about going after Joe Root, but he seemed unworthy," Dore continued. "And Ian Bell. But truthfully, despite his impressive figures in recent years, most of us can't take him seriously. He will always be Shane Warne's bunny.

"A week out from the Test, Allan Border told us that going after Broad would be a bad idea—he thrives on the attention. That changed our thinking. What if we were to do the opposite and ignore him instead? Give him the silent treatment.

"Of course, we were never going to convince a good-natured Australian crowd to be mute. But we could brush him entirely in print, as a symbolic protest. And so the Broad ban was born."

The paper decided to refer to him only as the "27-year-old English medium pace bowler" in all reports. "We felt this was an even graver insult than turning him into an asterisk and refusing to publish his image. What fast bowler wouldn't be furious about being relegated to mediocrity?"

Broad's counter-attack was swift and deadly—if ultimately futile.

He was the star of day one, taking five of the eight wickets that fell, making it 6-81 the next day when Australia was out for 295, putting England on top.

The crowd of some 42,000, fired up by what they had read, baited him all day with chants of "Broad's a wanker."

Did that upset him? Not one bit.

Grinning broadly, he walked into his media conference after play carrying a copy of the Courier Mail under his arm. When his editorial tormentors saw this back in the newspaper office, they cheered. "He got the joke," wrote Dore. "In the vernacular from the stands, maybe he's not such a smug pommy dickhead after all. After such a commanding performance we couldn't possibly go through with the promise to wipe Broad from the paper the next day. But we couldn't back down now. We had to go harder."

The upshot was a front-page headline *The Phantom Menace* with the hero cut out of the main picture and referred to in the scorecard and match reports as 27YEMP.

"By midway through the next day's play we were contemplating surrender," said the red-faced editor. "For the next day would we run a white flag and an open letter of apology to Broad or publish an Australian citizenship form on the front and invite him to sign up, given that he seemed to have seen the error of his ways. He hadn't cheated in the first two days and appeared to share several characteristics for which Australians were renowned—bravery, good humour, exceptional talent, fighting spirit and a mop of blond hair surely only the Pacific Ocean and the searing antipodean sun could have had a hand in creating."

Broad good-humouredly told them they had picked on the wrong victim.

"Our psychologist did tests to see what sort of personalities we all are," he said at the presser. "There are three guys in this side who thrive properly on getting abused: Kevin Pietersen, myself and Matty Prior, so they picked the good men to go at. There's a little more niggle playing against the Aussies, it means that much that I feel it does bring out the best in me. I didn't give it the time of day, particularly. You don't need any more inspiration than playing for your country in Australia's backyard in the first Test of a series. I'm pleased my mum wasn't in the stadium. But I was singing along at one stage. It gets in our head and you find yourself whistling it at the end of your mark. I'd braced myself and actually it was good fun."

The fun dried up quickly enough, however. With big left-arm quick Mitchell Johnson embarking on one of the most terrifying series-long onslaughts in memory, taking 4-61 and 5-42, Australia bowled England out for 136 and 179 to win by the massive margin of 382 runs with a day to spare. They went on to complete a 5-0 whitewash, regaining the Ashes for the first time since 2006–07.

Broad was England's most successful bowler with 21 wickets, six more than Ben Stokes and seven more than Jimmy Anderson—and a thirst for revenge.

He obtained it more than once.

In 2015, he took advantage of a green-top track at Nottingham to register his career-best figures of 8-15, as Australia were bowled out for 60 and defeated by an innings and plenty.

Then in 2019, when he was again England's best bowler with 23 wickets in a series drawn 2-2, one notable feature being Broad's complete stranglehold over star opener David Warner, who he dismissed seven times in the space of 104 balls.

That statistic alone suggested he would be a must-play in Australia this time—but in the end he played only three of the five matches, taking 13 wickets, which was still second only to Wood's 17.

In his Sydney outburst he claimed the squad had become too obsessed with long-term planning during the covid pandemic and had lost sight of the importance of winning each battle as it came.

"There's loads of reasons—not excuses—why (2021) had not been a successful year at home or in Australia," he said.

"Covid has played quite a big part in it, but there's a mindset within this group now that, instead of looking ahead at what's coming in the next year, the next Ashes series, actually we need to get back to the real basics of what's ahead of us right now. How are we going to win the next Test match?

"Sometimes when your brain gets too far away from what's in front of you, you're not focused on delivering what you need to deliver in that Test match. We don't know what the world's going to look like or what cricket is going to look like in June and in next November, but can we win tomorrow? Can we win the next opportunity that's in front of us? I think that should be a real focus for the England cricket team going forward, because it's all well and good planning for the next away Ashes and the World Test Championship, but actually if you don't win the battle in front of you it's all irrelevant."

Noting that England had failed to reach 300 in any innings while the Ashes were still alive—which remained the case for the rest of the series—Broad turned the blowtorch on his team's batsmen.

"You can dissect loads from this tour but actually first innings runs is where you live in Test cricket and we've failed to deliver," he said. "Honestly, it doesn't matter what bowlers you play if you are getting bowled out for 140. That might be a bit brutal but that's the truth in Test cricket."

So, 17 years after his Hoppers Crossing initiation, will this be the last Australia sees of him?

Not necessarily, he says, pointing to Anderson's amazing longevity and insisting he still has what it takes himself to remain a world-class competitor.

"Jimmy's been an inspiration to me," he said. "I see how much drive he's still got at 39, how much energy he puts in, not just to the match days, but the training and the skill development," the Cricinfo website's Andrew Miller reported him saying.

"He is truly the most professional I've seen him in the past two years, so why can't I replicate it? I'm not as skilful as Jimmy and I haven't got as much armoury in my locker, but I've got the motivation and the drive similar to him, and I'm as disciplined as he is. And I feel like I can contribute as much as Jimmy has since that age. He's a driving force behind my mindset and hopefully I get to play more Test cricket with him. A few years ago I was umming and aahing and I spent a lot of time talking to my dad about it. He has a great belief that you should play the sport you love for as long as you can. While the fire still burns you should play because nothing replicates it in life. Nothing can bring you the satisfaction, the pain, the highs and the lows. They are quite addictive."

If he doesn't quite make it back as a Test player, no doubt the boys at Hoppers Crossing would welcome him back with open arms—and even the *Courier Mail* would have no objections.

CHAPTER 13

CONVICTED OF THROWING IN THE TOWEL IN DISGRACE

The English cricket team's grasp of Australian history probably wouldn't have extended to the fact that the handsome Tasmanian capital city now known as Hobart was originally established in 1804 as a penal colony, where 70,000 convicts were transported for their various sins.

Losing the Ashes wasn't against the law back then of course—cricket's cherished concept was still nearly 80 years from its birth—and still isn't, as much as certain elements of the English media consider it to be a hanging offence.

So when Joe Root and his troops disembarked from their flight from Sydney to prepare for the fifth and final Test, there was no need for any sense of trepidation that they might be locked up and fed bread and water—things were grim, but they weren't quite that bad.

Indeed, there was more likely a certain optimism that here, at last, was an authentic chance to salvage something tangible from their tour from Hell.

And they were right—this was the opportunity they were waiting for. All they had to do was grasp it. Not once but twice. But in the end, and a very quick end it was too, they—like their ancient forbears—were sent on their way in disgrace, shame and embarrassment.

Worse, they surrendered their pride and dignity.

The Tasmanian cricket family were left with mixed feelings about what was a massive and historic occasion for them—like Australian cricket fans everywhere, they were pleased to see their team win of course, but disappointed that the tourists proved incapable of stretching the contest into a fourth or fifth day—and night.

In some ways it was a limp end to what the State Government had declared to be the biggest sporting event the island had ever hosted.

It wasn't even on anyone's agenda when the Ashes began in December, not long after Cricket Australia had cancelled, for political reasons, what would have been the first ever Test against Afghanistan, which was to have been Tasmania's moment in the sun for the season. A welcome one, but a far cry from the big-time of the oldest and most prestigious series on the international calendar.

Tasmania's 13 previous Tests had been against Sri Lanka (3), New Zealand (3), Pakistan (2), West Indies (2) and South Africa (1), for nine wins, two defeats and two draws, all in low-profile time frames.

That changed when West Australian Premier Mark McGowan's obsession with keeping his state free of the covid virus made it impossible for Perth to host the fifth Test—and possibly the decider for all anyone knew then—in its flash new(ish) Optus Stadium, as scheduled.

It prompted a fierce bidding war between Sydney and Melbourne, with Canberra throwing a few hopeful shots, with the Victorian capital the early favourite because of the mighty MCG's capacity to generate far more box-office money than tiny Tasmania.

But the Tasmanians are becoming used to fighting on these sorts of fronts, having been locked into a long battle with the AFL for their own footy team, which they seemed on the verge of winning. They had also lured the thriving National Basketball League back, creating a new team called the JackJumpers.

Their tactic with Cricket Australia was to point out that they were a full member of the organisation and had never had the privilege of hosting an Ashes match. It was a matter of fairness, of doing the right thing rather than counting the contents of the cash register.

To the surprise of many, sentiment triumphed over financial pragmatism.

It was also agreed that the match would be played as a day-nighter with a pink ball, also a Test first for Bellerive Oval—and an extra challenge for the tourists, given Australia's unbeaten record under lights.

As veteran writer Scyld Berry, a former Editor of Wisden who has seen more Test cricket than anyone alive, pointed out, this would be the 76th ground on which England had played—and the only one in Australia that might make them feel at home, given the coolish weather and the likely state of the pitch.

The only negative in the build-up was when news broke that Hobart's favourite cricketer, the immediate past Test captain Tim Paine, would be making himself scarce interstate for the duration of the match, rejecting all invitations to be one of Cricket Tasmania's—and Cricket Australia's—guests of honour.

This was entirely understandable—he would have become the subject of intense media interest, intrusion even, which was the last thing he or his family needed after all they had been through while the texting scandal that cost him his career was at its height.

Former teammates and the players' union, the Australian Cricketers Association, had kept in touch with him, media reports suggesting the players were still upset at what they perceived to be a lack of support from head office in times of trouble.

"We've been talking regularly, a couple of times a week. He's going okay, is how I'd describe Tim," ACA chief Todd Greenberg told SEN radio. "He's incredibly disappointed he's not playing cricket and I'm disappointed he's not playing cricket. But we're keeping in close contact and we'll help him through it. We made it very clear to Cricket Australia we thought there was a different way that could have been handled, but we're not always going to agree. The players felt it could have been handled differently, and they felt like the governing body didn't have their back at that particular time. We're creating trust between the players and the governing body and that's a big part of that. We took some steps backwards in that scenario, that's just being brutally honest."

The outcome of that affair had never sat well with the Tasmanian officials either and they, too, had not been backward in making their views known to their CA counterparts. But Paine wasn't there and there was no point in allowing his absence to become a party-pooper— although the last had not been heard of it.

The Australian selectors were left with no choice but to stick with Usman Khawaja after his twin centuries in the previous match and with regular No. 5 Travis Head an automatic returnee after a brush with covid, the only way to do that was to axe the struggling opener Marcus Harris.

That brought Warner and Khawaja back together at the top of the order, prompting some warm reminiscing about how they had first played as teammates at the age of seven and had come up through the ranks together—friends and former coaches describing them as completely different personalities bonded by a key common trait: honesty.

It was even turned into a ballad by legendary singer and songwriter Paul Kelly, the first verse of which went like this:

Khawaja loves the game of cricket since he was a boy,
With his good friend Davey it was their pride and joy.
He took the train down to the SCG, he said
One day we'll play there you and me
He loved his bat and ball and gloves
he loved his batting pads.
He played a million weekend games
In front of mums and dads.

The England brains trust were far busier, making five changes. They sacked the hapless opener Haseeb Hameed, who had averaged 10, and replaced him with Rory Burns, who had already missed two matches after a string of failures.

Jonny Bairstow, scorer of the only century of the tour in Sydney, couldn't continue because of a broken thumb and was replaced by the previously discarded Ollie Pope, while underwhelming spinner Jack Leach made away—again—for struggling all-rounder Chris Woakes to have another crack.

And they even had to raid the Big Bash to summon Sydney Thunder's Sam Billings to keep wickets in place of the also injured—and desperately out of form—Jos Buttler, who was already on the way home.

Billings received a warm welcome from Pat Cummins, with whom he had played for Penrith in Sydney club cricket a few years earlier. Cummins sent him a copy of the scorecard from the day he himself had made 110 not out—and Billings a duck. It was as close as the Australian captain ever gets to a sledge and Billings got the intended laugh out of it.

Despite this upheaval, and with morale boosted by the draw in Sydney, the mood in the England camp was relatively upbeat—and improved markedly when Root won the toss and chose to bowl first on the greenest wicket of the series, which Cummins was also bent on doing if he got the chance.

Well inside an hour of the first ball being bowled after a short rain delay, Root was on cloud nine with Australia in deep trouble at 3/12 with Warner and Smith gone for ducks and Khawaja for six, while Labuschagne had also been dropped.

Broad and Robinson bowled superbly on a wicket offering plenty of assistance, and you did have to wonder what might have happened if Cummins had won the toss and unleashed his own superior pace attack on England's brittle batting—the tourists might have struggled to survive the first session.

Enter Travis Head. The South Australian played the best innings of the summer as he and Labuschagne decided that in the circumstances attack was the best means of defence and went after the bowling, which itself quickly lost its menace.

Rattling along at virtually a run a ball, they added 71 before Labuschagne, on 44, was dismissed almost comically when he stepped across to the off-side, lost control of his feet and toppled to the pitch, allowing Broad's delivery to pass behind him and knock out his middle stump. Even Labuschagne's teammates in the viewing room couldn't help laughing at it, the captain included.

Head then added another 121 with Cameron Green, whose confident 74—his second half-century of the series—removed all remaining doubt, not that there was much, that he was coming of age as the real-deal all-rounder Australia had been seeking for many decades.

Green wasn't finished yet—far from it.

Head brought up his second century of the series in 112 balls and then got out off the next one, but the job was done. No one else on either side batted with so much positive intent, with the exception of tail-ender Nathan Lyon who whacked three sixes in an entertaining 31 that took Australia past 300.

Head's efforts earned him the player of the match award and the player of the series.

It was a pleasing total given that England were yet to make that many in any innings of any Test.

And when Burns was run out for a duck, lazily declining to dive for his crease as Labuschagne threw down the stumps from the infield, nobody was betting on them doing so this time either.

Sure enough, they collapsed again with Cummins ripping through their top order—Crawley, Malan and Root—on the way to 4-45 while Starc, 3-53, completed yet another demolition, England out for 188.

But England still weren't out of contention, especially when Broad again pulled off his favourite trick, dismissing Warner for his second duck of the match off the third ball of the innings.

Cummins had noted before the game that while it didn't matter that Australia were now playing with two 35-year-old opening batsmen, that couldn't go on forever—the day would come when newer, younger blood would have to found.

So here was the veteran—the team's oldest player—contemplating a pair, simple slips catch dropped, and after falling just short of centuries in the first two Tests, now with a total of 71 runs from his last five innings.

Could that be the sound of a distant bell beginning to toll—as it eventually tolls for everyone?

Wickets continued to tumble regularly with only Alex Carey's fortunate 49—he was reprieved twice when bowled by a no-ball on 19 and later given out lbw only for the review system to rule that the delivery had pitched fractionally outside leg—allowing Australia to scramble to 155.

This was almost entirely down to Mark Wood's career-best 6-37, only his team's second bag of five or more, and a total of nine for the match.

Wood had been ineffective in the first innings, going wicketless and for seven an over. But this time, generating fierce pace consistently around the 150km/h mark, he returned fire every bit as hostilely as the Australian quicks had to him and his teammates.

What took him so long?

He ended up easily his team's most successful bowler with 17 wickets at 26.64—four more than Broad at an almost identical average—but only five of them came while the Ashes were still alive, and only 46 of his 121 overs were delivered when it mattered most.

It's just one more puzzling piece in the generally unfathomable bowling strategy that was employed from start to—almost—finish.

Wood's wrecking ball left England with a run chase of 271, with time no object—ostensibly an eminently achievable assignment, when you considered that in holding out for the draw in Sydney they had scored 9-270 in the fourth innings.

There had been 50 previous Tests in Australia, according to the king of cricket stats Ric Finlay, where England had chased 271 or more in the last innings, for 39 defeats, eight draws and three wins.

So while it was far from impossible, no one was backing them to do it, probably not even themselves.

However, when Burns and Crawley strung together the best opening partnership so far—by far—to be 0-68 on the stroke of the tea break, the target now just over 200 with all 10 wickets in hand, the TV graphic WINVIZ that assesses outcome probabilities at any given juncture had England favourites for the first time in any match.

On the last ball before the break, Burns—who had decided to do away with his usual man-bun and allow his long hair to cascade down around his shoulders, presumably for luck or maybe some sort of Samson complex—chopped on to Green and was out for 26.

In the Australian dressing room during the brief pause, all was calm—in accordance with Captain Pat's standard mantra. No need to panic. We've got this.

What followed was nothing short of a bloodbath.

Cummins stuck with Green, who smashed a thunderbolt into David Malan's helmet and then promptly had him playing on too. One run later, he had Crawley caught behind and at 3-83 the vultures smelt blood.

Green's three successive wickets took him to 13 for the series, a huge contribution from the No 4 pace option, especially as they cost only 15.76 each and were mostly top-order batsmen, including the superstar Root twice.

He was now a legitimate front-line attacking weapon—as distinct from a relief soldier employed to plug gaps—and had also improved markedly as a batsman, justifying his occupation of one of the top six slots.

When Stokes, 5, and Root, 11, quickly followed, the jig was up at 5-101. It took only another seven overs to complete the rout, England losing 10-56 to be bowled out for 125, gone from a position of strength to yet another thrashing, this time by 146 runs.

Fittingly and symbolically, Captain Pat administered the coup-de-grace himself, smashing down the stumps of Wood and Robinson, an emphatic exclamation mark on what had been a total personal triumph from start to finish.

The tail-enders had made no attempt to defy him or Boland, who also had the good fortune to be bowling at the end—amazingly, the 400-wicket spinner Lyon was not required to bowl a single ball for the entire match.

Robinson's dismissal was especially spineless, making no real attempt—other than a wild swing from somewhere near the square-leg umpire—to defend his wicket.

One former captain Michael Vaughan angrily described it on one TV channel as "throwing in the towel" and another, Ian Botham, said on the other network that he was embarrassed on the players' behalf. Similar vitriol rained down from every quarter of the travelling media contingent—and rightly so.

From any vantage point, it was a pathetic capitulation unworthy of professional players in any sport.

There wasn't much poor Root could say, except express yet more frustration and concede the obvious—that they had been well and truly outplayed by a much better team. "Full credit to Australia," he said.

Cummins told the MC of the presentation ceremony, Adam Gilchrist, that it was a childhood dream come true for him, and that he was pumped for the other 14 players who had taken part, some of whom had missed matches on tough selection calls.

In typical fashion, he commiserated with the opposition, without patronising them, saying he knew the circumstances of the trip—a reference to the many covid bubble restrictions—had made it difficult for them. "Thanks for coming, I know it wasn't easy," he said.

Certainly, this was a far cry from the same presentation ceremony after the fifth Test in Sydney four years earlier, when some marketing lamebrain arranged for a large, inflated hand with its four fingers upraised to be the backdrop.

It created social media uproar—insulting triumphalism, tasteless and gross, unsporting—and took a lot of living down.

Needless to say, there was no such confronting symbolism on display this time.

Perhaps the only uncomfortable note came from a social media protest from Tim Paine's brother Nick, who posted: "Pretty hard to watch this knowing full well that one of the key people in resurrecting the reputation of Cricket Australia was shafted by that very organisation because of a personal mistake he made nearly four years ago.

"He deserved this send-off on his home ground in front of his family and friends and long-time supporters. It's just a real shame that one mistake in life (that the person was cleared and exonerated by an inquiry) can end a kid's dream but then for others who make them, they come back and it's all OK and, in a way, forgotten. Double standards from an organisation that clearly doesn't have the back of its people. A local boy on a local ground in front of his people. Gut-wrenching stuff."

It was accompanied by a broken-heart emoji.

While the family's on-going angst was understandable, the timing of this outburst was tone-deaf, ignoring that this was a moment to celebrate the achievements of the new captain and his team—as it now was, not Tim's team. And that team was precisely where Cricket Australia needed it to be, looking forward with confidence, not backwards to darker days.

The one remaining ritual to be observed was, naturally, for the players from both sides to have a drink with each other, which was always likely to stretch well into the wee hours given that it was well past midnight before some had cleared a multitude of media commitments, packed up and made it back to the city hotel where both lots were staying. Some, including Root, never even bothered changing out of their playing strips.

The party was still going at 6am when the police arrived to shut it down after a complaint about loud music, and Root, Anderson and three of the Australians, Lyon, Head and Carey, were told it was probably time they went to bed—which they did without demur.

These proceedings were filmed and made their way into the Australian media which the England Cricket Board found so unwelcome that it ordered an inquiry, not into the drinking—who could reasonably find anything wrong with that? —but into how and why it became so public.

It quickly emerged that their assistant coach, former Test batsman Graham Thorpe, had been responsible, for reasons he thought were in the players' best interests—that is, to provide evidence that their behaviour had in no way been outrageous.

He was reported to be in trouble with his bosses, and sure enough he was promptly sacked when he got home—although that was probably always going to happen given that he was the batting coach of a team that could never make 300.

Cricket Australia couldn't have cared less about the incident—and rightly so. If the day ever comes when having a drink with your opposition after the battles are won and lost is discouraged cricket will have lost its heart and soul.

CHAPTER 14

FULL SPEED A-HEAD ON THE WAY TO A MEDAL

Nothing about the Ashes is more appropriate than the award for the player of the series. It is the Compton-Miller Medal, named after the dashing England batsman Denis Compton and the cavalier Australian all-rounder Keith Miller.

They were more than wonderful cricketers, they played the game as if it was sport and not war, a distinction not lost on either because their careers both straddled the second great conflict—Miller famously participating as a fighter pilot.

Their almost identical outlooks on life made them firm friends on and off the field of play, which is why Miller named the oldest of his three sons Denis.

I got to know Miller well in his later years when he was frequenting press boxes and journalists' watering holes and always found him to be hugely helpful, never more so when I needed to prepare Don Bradman's obituary well in advance. "Nugget" wasn't The Don's most ardent fan but that didn't mean his mostly off-the-record insights and recollections weren't respectful, informative and honest.

I only met Compton once—but what a meeting, if you'll pardon the indulgence of saying so.

At a loose end in London one afternoon, I found myself passing the Cricketers Club and decided to see if I could sign myself in for a look around—and yes, maybe a drink. As legendary songwriter Kris Kristofferson sings in To Beat The Devil, I could see that there was just one old man sittin' at the bar.

It wasn't hard to recognise him as the one and only D. C. S. Compton, who introduced himself and sked if he could buy me a drink. When he learned that I was Australian and worked in the media, he wanted to know if I knew his old mate Miller.

When I truthfully said I did, a bottle of white wine was uncorked and for the next four hours or so—as more bottles came and went—he regaled me with endless anecdotes about what he and the great man had got up to around London and elsewhere in their halcyon days. Some of them were even about cricket. I doubt I have ever had a more entertaining day, even if, for some strange reason, I don't seem to recall some of the finer details.

Both men were also first-class footballers, Compton playing First Division soccer for Arsenal and Miller playing VFL for St Kilda and Victoria.

Sadly, both are long gone. Compton died at 80 in 1997 and Miller at 84 in Melbourne in 2005, where he was given a State funeral that packed out the city's biggest church, St Paul's Cathedral.

The medal in their joint honour was struck in 2005, the first winner being England's Andrew Flintoff with an illustrious cohort following—Ricky Ponting, Andrew Strauss, Alistair Cook, Ian Bell, Mitchell Johnson and Steve Smith twice.

Travis Head has now been added to the list.

No voting details were made available, but it is likely that he narrowly beat three other prime candidates, Pat Cummins, Scott Boland and Cameron Green.

It was the right call on numbers alone—from his four Tests Head contributed a series-high 357 runs at 59.50 with two match-winning centuries and another half-century.

But it wasn't just the weight of runs, it was the way the aggressive South Australian went about it, scoring at about a run a ball in his two biggest knocks and completely changing the momentum after the English bowlers had briefly taken control in Hobart.

Compton and Miller would both have thoroughly approved of

Head's entertaining outlook and methods.

Given that he had played 19 previous Tests and even risen to vice-captain without quite nailing a permanent spot—he had been dropped against India the previous summer—it was a career changing tour de force.

He also won the Test player of the year and the domestic player of the year in the Cricket Australia awards.

He offered credit for the transformation to Cummins, yet another accolade for Captain Pat's leadership style.

He was told there would be no repercussions if he sometimes got out playing ambitious shots as had often been the case at all levels, leading to some unattractive dismissals when big scores were at his mercy.

He was encouraged to be himself even if it sometimes looked bad.

"Travis goes about it a little bit differently to most other batters, which is his biggest strength," Cummins told reporters. "As a captain I don't care if he gets out in non-traditional ways. I just want him to go out, be free and play his game. We can be the type of team that are brave enough to take that positivity overseas if we need to. That puts us in a great place."

Head said the conversations he had with Cummins linked well with work he had done in Adelaide with Tim Neilsen, a former national team coach.

"I went through a period of time where I understood dismissals might not look the best and I might get caught at third man or flap at a ball—and obviously I don't want to do that—but in saying that, no dismissal ever looks pretty. Any outs are a bad out," he said.

"Pat's given me the confidence to and go out and play and he's sort of alluded to that (by saying) 'Look, if you're taking the game on and get done at third man a couple of times and you're playing the right way it's no skin off my nose,' and he backs me 100 per cent. That gave me the confidence going into this series to be myself and play the situation as I see it."

It worked so well that Head found himself elevated seven places in the ICC batting rankings to equal fifth alongside India's Rohit Sharma, and below teammate Marnus Labuschagne, Root, New Zealand captain Kane Williamson and Steve Smith, and one above former Indian captain Virat Kohli.

Cummins retained his spot at the top of the bowling rankings, ahead of prolific Indian spinner Ravi Ashwin, which was no surprise given that he topped the Ashes wickets list despite missing the second match.

He had now done that in each of the three Ashes series he had played.

His 21 wickets at 18.04 were well ahead of Mitchell Starc's 19 (from five matches) at 25.36 and Scott Boland's 18 at an amazing 9.55 from just three matches. All three topped England's best, Mark Wood with 17 and 26.64 from four outings.

It took Cummins into 20th place on the all-time Australian wickets list with 185 from 38 matches, going past Geoff Lawson, 180, and the aforementioned Keith Miller and Terry Alderman, both 170. Lawson played eight more matches than Cummins, Miller 15 more and Alderman three more.

It left Cummins one behind the late, great Alan Davidson—who died during the season—from 44 matches, and 15 shy of the next one up, Jeff Thomson, who needed 51 matches for his 200. Barring accidents, Cummins' rate of progress was going to leave those luminaries well in the shade in the not-too-distant future, too.

Miller's place in this table of greatness is relevant in that, at the risk of repeating observations made at the beginning of this book, Cummins has long been regarded—by the author, anyway—as a bit of a Miller clone, both in performance and appearance and even attitude.

That comparison has now become obsolete for a number of reasons.

For one, Cummins—little more than halfway through his career—has the numbers on the board to suggest that he is indisputably a superior bowler, even if Miller might have been up against far better

English batting line-ups and the equal of anybody when he decided to really let rip at maximum power.

Secondly, Cummins' batting has not progressed—as it once promised to—to the point where he can be regarded as a genuine all-rounder, certainly not in Miller's class. Miller averaged 36.97 and hit seven centuries—the numbers of a genuine batsman—while Cummins averaged 14 in this Ashes, just below his overall 16 with two fifties and a highest score of 63.

Thirdly—and far more importantly—in the long search for the new Keith Miller, which has preoccupied Australian cricket since the great man finished playing in the 1950s, more than 70 years ago, a more authentic claimant to the title has now emerged—a genuine one, in the unanimous opinion of all the good judges.

Take a bow, Cameron Green.

The 22-year-old West Australian, who made his Test debut the previous season against India after two or three years of irresistible performances in the Sheffield Shield, took a few matches to find his feet (literally, in terms of his batting technique) at the ultimate level.

But he did so emphatically during the Ashes, collecting 228 runs with two impressive half-centuries at an average of 32.57 and took 13 wickets at the miserly average of 15.76.

That compares more than favourably with Miller's output on the fabled 1948 Invincibles tour of England, where he also claimed 13 wickets—more expensively, at 23.55—and made 184 runs at 26.28.

(Incidentally, it is not always remembered that while that tour—Bradman's triumphant farewell to England—saw Australia go through unbeaten in Tests and all other matches, hence the soubriquet The Invincibles, for once the world's greatest cricketer was not his team's most successful batsmen. He averaged 72.57, well below his fabled career mark of 96.94, while Arthur Morris and Sid Barnes went at 87 and 82 respectively.)

In his last Ashes series in Australia, in 1954–55, Miller scored 167 at 23.85 with no half-centuries and took 10 wickets at 24.30.

Such selective comparisons may be slightly odious, but the point is hard to argue with—at this stage of his embryonic career, and notwithstanding the questionable quality of the opposition in this, his breakthrough campaign, Green has nothing to fear from any old-timers who insist that there will never be another Miller.

Well, there won't be, not when you consider the many other assets that made him a national hero—but in purely cricket terms, he might have met his match now. Time will tell, of course.

Certainly, Green does not want for a certain excitement factor—he is as fast as Cummins and the rest of the more senior pace attack, with the possible exception of Starc, regularly clocking in at above 140km/h on the speed gun; and being as tall as an AFL ruckman the bounce he was able to generate from helpful pitches bordered on frightening.

And he bats in the top six, which is absolute gold for any selection panel. Former captain—and selector—Greg Chappell, one of the more erudite commentators these days, spelt it out in his summary of the series in The Age newspaper.

"(A) huge positive was the continued growth of Cameron Green into the all-rounder every selector and team pines for. Finding a player who commands a place as a genuine batting or bowling option is akin to winning Lotto. It's why Mitch Marsh was previously afforded so many opportunities. No matter what conditions are prevalent, a genuine all-rounder allows selectors to pick a balanced team. The overs Green can bowl takes the pressure off Cummins so he doesn't have to over-bowl to keep applying pressure. When your fourth seamer can bowl in excess of 140km/h, extract steepling bounce and can bat in the top six, you have the flexibility, nay luxury, to pick an extra spinner if needed."

Green is a fast learner too, not afraid to take advice. After a number of disappointing dismissals—he started the series with a golden duck in Brisbane and had other scores of 2, 17 and 5 in his first five innings, which had some commentators starting to fret; even experienced club players and coaches were picking faults in his footwork.

And when Rocky Ponting did the same on TV, then passed on his observations to the team coaching staff, Green immediately set about rectifying the problem, with immediate results—impressive knocks of 74 in each of the last two Tests. He publicly thanked Ponting.

Averages are never the be-all and end-all in cricket, but they don't tell many lies either.

The Ashes tables clearly demonstrate the yawning gulf between the teams.

Australia had seven batsmen—including bowler Starc—averaging better than 30, with the only one who suffered the indignity of being dropped at any stage, opener Marcus Harris, a tick behind on 29.83.

Only two Englishmen matched that, with Root barely getting there with 32.20 and Jonny Bairstow going at 48.50 from his two opportunities.

Australians scored five of the six centuries.

They also had five bowlers—Cummins, Starc, Boland, Lyon and Green—who had between 13 and 21 wickets, while the tourists had only Wood, 17, and Broad, 13, at that level, with Robinson on 11.

If you were selecting a combined side it is difficult to see where any England player, even Root, would get a guernsey. Who would any of them displace?

The margins were all comprehensive—nine wickets in Brisbane, 275 runs in Adelaide, and innings and 14 in Melbourne and 146 runs in Hobart, and if the Sydney draw had lasted a few minutes longer for a result to be completed, it would have been about 140 runs there too. One match finished before lunch on the third day, another in three days and a third in four days.

This overwhelming result meant Australia got a turbo-charged start to the second edition of the World Test Championship, which Cummins has declared to be high on his wish-list after narrowly missing out on the final the previous year, and watching New Zealand pull it off.

It left Australia a single point behind India, who also had four wins but also two draws from three series, not one. Sri Lanka, with two from two against the West Indies, was the only other unbeaten team.

England were stone motherless last, with one win from 10 matches, and having also forfeited 10 points for bowling their overs too slowly.

In the separate ICC Test rankings, Australia were No. 1 ahead of New Zealand.

Not the least remarkable aspect of Australia's performance was what and who they did without.

They lost their incumbent captain and first choice wicketkeeper before the action started, lost probably their second-best bowler Josh Hazlewood after just one match, lost new captain and No. 1 bowler Cummins and batsman of the series, Head, for a match each and played three debutants.

They resurrected the career of a middle-aged batsman, Khawaja, who couldn't get a game initially, and watched the modern-day Bradman, Smith, average barely 30—less than half his career benchmark—while David Warner also failed to reach three figures and averaged 34.12, failing in three matches and finishing with a pair of ducks.

If England had known all that was about to happen when they first arrived, they would have considered themselves to be in with a very big shout—and so would have the bookmakers.

They would have all been wrong, which is as good a measure as any of the quality of Australia's performance.

Nothing about the Ashes is more appropriate than the award for the player of the series. It is the Compton-Miller Medal, named after the dashing England batsman Denis Compton and the cavalier Australian all-rounder Keith Miller.

They were more than wonderful cricketers, they played the game as if it was sport and not war, a distinction not lost on either because their careers both straddled the second great conflict—Miller famously participating as a fighter pilot.

Their almost identical outlooks on life made them firm friends on and off the field of play, which is why Miller named the oldest of his three sons Denis.

I got to know Miller well in his later years when he was frequenting press boxes and journalists' watering holes and always found him to be hugely helpful, never more so when I needed to prepare Don Bradman's obituary well in advance. "Nugget" wasn't The Don's most ardent fan but that didn't mean his mostly off-the-record insights and recollections weren't respectful, informative and honest.

I only met Compton once—but what a meeting, if you'll pardon the indulgence of saying so.

At a loose end in London one afternoon, I found myself passing the Cricketers Club and decided to see if I could sign myself in for a look around—and yes, maybe a drink. As legendary songwriter Kris Kristofferson sings in *To Beat The Devil*, I could see that there was just one old man sittin' at the bar.

It wasn't hard to recognise him as the one and only D. C. S. Compton, who introduced himself and sked if he could buy me a drink. When he learned that I was Australian and worked in the media, he wanted to know if I knew his old mate Miller.

When I truthfully said I did, a bottle of white wine was uncorked and for the next four hours or so—as more bottles came and went—he regaled me with endless anecdotes about what he and the great man had got up to around London and elsewhere in their halcyon days. Some of them were even about cricket. I doubt I have ever had a more entertaining day, even if, for some strange reason, I don't seem to recall some of the finer details.

Both men were also first-class footballers, Compton playing First Division soccer for Arsenal and Miller playing VFL for St Kilda and Victoria.

Sadly, both are long gone. Compton died at 80 in 1997 and Miller at 84 in Melbourne in 2005, where he was given a State funeral that packed out the city's biggest church, St Paul's Cathedral.

The medal in their joint honour was struck in 2005, the first winner being England's Andrew Flintoff with an illustrious cohort following—Ricky Ponting, Andrew Strauss, Alistair Cook, Ian Bell,

Mitchell Johnson and Steve Smith twice.

Travis Head has now been added to the list.

No voting details were made available, but it is likely that he narrowly beat three other prime candidates, Pat Cummins, Scott Boland and Cameron Green.

It was the right call on numbers alone—from his four Tests Head contributed a series-high 357 runs at 59.50 with two match-winning centuries and another half-century.

But it wasn't just the weight of runs, it was the way the aggressive South Australian went about it, scoring at about a run a ball in his two biggest knocks and completely changing the momentum after the English bowlers had briefly taken control in Hobart.

Compton and Miller would both have thoroughly approved of Head's entertaining outlook and methods.

Given that he had played 19 previous Tests and even risen to vice-captain without quite nailing a permanent spot—he had been dropped against India the previous summer—it was a career changing *tour de force*.

He also won the Test player of the year and the domestic player of the year in the Cricket Australia awards.

He offered credit for the transformation to Cummins, yet another accolade for Captain Pat's leadership style.

He was told there would be no repercussions if he sometimes got out playing ambitious shots as had often been the case at all levels, leading to some unattractive dismissals when big scores were at his mercy.

He was encouraged to be himself even if it sometimes looked bad.

"Travis goes about it a little bit differently to most other batters, which is his biggest strength," Cummins told reporters. "As a captain I don't care if he gets out in non-traditional ways. I just want him to go out, be free and play his game. We can be the type of team that are brave enough to take that positivity overseas if we need to. That puts us in a great place."

Head said the conversations he had with Cummins linked well with work he had done in Adelaide with Tim Neilsen, a former national team coach.

"I went through a period of time where I understood dismissals might not look the best and I might get caught at third man or flap at a ball—and obviously I don't want to do that—but in saying that, no dismissal ever looks pretty. Any outs are a bad out," he said.

"Pat's given me the confidence to and go out and play and he's sort of alluded to that (by saying) 'Look, if you're taking the game on and get done at third man a couple of times and you're playing the right way it's no skin off my nose,' and he backs me 100 per cent. That gave me the confidence going into this series to be myself and play the situation as I see it."

It worked so well that Head found himself elevated seven places in the ICC batting rankings to equal fifth alongside India's Rohit Sharma, and below teammate Marnus Labuschagne, Root, New Zealand captain Kane Williamson and Steve Smith, and one above former Indian captain Virat Kohli.

Cummins retained his spot at the top of the bowling rankings, ahead of prolific Indian spinner Ravi Ashwin, which was no surprise given that he topped the Ashes wickets list despite missing the second match.

He had now done that in each of the three Ashes series he had played.

His 21 wickets at 18.04 were well ahead of Mitchell Starc's 19 (from five matches) at 25.36 and Scott Boland's 18 at an amazing 9.55 from just three matches. All three topped England's best, Mark Wood with 17 and 26.64 from four outings.

It took Cummins into 20th place on the all-time Australian wickets list with 185 from 38 matches, going past Geoff Lawson, 180, and the aforementioned Keith Miller and Terry Alderman, both 170. Lawson played eight more matches than Cummins, Miller 15 more and Alderman three more.

It left Cummins one behind the late, great Alan Davidson—who died during the season—from 44 matches, and 15 shy of the next one up, Jeff Thomson, who needed 51 matches for his 200. Barring accidents, Cummins' rate of progress was going to leave those luminaries well in the shade in the not-too-distant future, too.

Miller's place in this table of greatness is relevant in that, at the risk of repeating observations made at the beginning of this book, Cummins has long been regarded—by the author, anyway—as a bit of a Miller clone, both in performance and appearance and even attitude.

That comparison has now become obsolete for a number of reasons.

For one, Cummins—little more than halfway through his career—has the numbers on the board to suggest that he is indisputably a superior bowler, even if Miller might have been up against far better English batting line-ups and the equal of anybody when he decided to really let rip at maximum power.

Secondly, Cummins' batting has not progressed—as it once promised to—to the point where he can be regarded as a genuine all-rounder, certainly not in Miller's class. Miller averaged 36.97 and hit seven centuries—the numbers of a genuine batsman—while Cummins averaged 14 in this Ashes, just below his overall 16 with two fifties and a highest score of 63.

Thirdly—and far more importantly—in the long search for the new Keith Miller, which has preoccupied Australian cricket since the great man finished playing in the 1950s, more than 70 years ago, a more authentic claimant to the title has now emerged—a genuine one, in the unanimous opinion of all the good judges.

Take a bow, Cameron Green.

The 22-year-old West Australian, who made his Test debut the previous season against India after two or three years of irresistible performances in the Sheffield Shield, took a few matches to find his feet (literally, in terms of his batting technique) at the ultimate level.

But he did so emphatically during the Ashes, collecting 228 runs with two impressive half-centuries at an average of 32.57 and took 13 wickets at the miserly average of 15.76.

That compares more than favourably with Miller's output on the fabled 1948 Invincibles tour of England, where he also claimed 13 wickets—more expensively, at 23.55—and made 184 runs at 26.28.

(Incidentally, it is not always remembered that while that tour—Bradman's triumphant farewell to England—saw Australia go through unbeaten in Tests and all other matches, hence the soubriquet The Invincibles, for once the world's greatest cricketer was not his team's most successful batsmen. He averaged 72.57, well below his fabled career mark of 96.94, while Arthur Morris and Sid Barnes went at 87 and 82 respectively.)

In his last Ashes series in Australia, in 1954–55, Miller scored 167 at 23.85 with no half-centuries and took 10 wickets at 24.30.

Such selective comparisons may be slightly odious, but the point is hard to argue with—at this stage of his embryonic career, and notwithstanding the questionable quality of the opposition in this, his breakthrough campaign, Green has nothing to fear from any old-timers who insist that there will never be another Miller.

Well, there won't be, not when you consider the many other assets that made him a national hero—but in purely cricket terms, he might have met his match now. Time will tell, of course.

Certainly, Green does not want for a certain excitement factor—he is as fast as Cummins and the rest of the more senior pace attack, with the possible exception of Starc, regularly clocking in at above 140km/h on the speed gun; and being as tall as an AFL ruckman the bounce he was able to generate from helpful pitches bordered on frightening.

And he bats in the top six, which is absolute gold for any selection panel. Former captain—and selector—Greg Chappell, one of the more erudite commentators these days, spelt it out in his summary of the series in *The Age* newspaper.

"(A) huge positive was the continued growth of Cameron Green into the all-rounder every selector and team pines for. Finding a player who commands a place as a genuine batting or bowling option is akin to winning Lotto. It's why Mitch Marsh was previously afforded so many opportunities. No matter what conditions are prevalent, a genuine all-rounder allows selectors to pick a balanced team. The overs Green can bowl takes the pressure off Cummins so he doesn't have to over-bowl to keep applying pressure. When your fourth seamer can bowl in excess of 140km/h, extract steepling bounce and can bat in the top six, you have the flexibility, nay luxury, to pick an extra spinner if needed."

Green is a fast learner too, not afraid to take advice. After a number of disappointing dismissals—he started the series with a golden duck in Brisbane and had other scores of 2, 17 and 5 in his first five innings, which had some commentators starting to fret; even experienced club players and coaches were picking faults in his footwork.

And when Rocky Ponting did the same on TV, then passed on his observations to the team coaching staff, Green immediately set about rectifying the problem, with immediate results—impressive knocks of 74 in each of the last two Tests. He publicly thanked Ponting.

Averages are never the be-all and end-all in cricket, but they don't tell many lies either.

The Ashes tables clearly demonstrate the yawning gulf between the teams.

Australia had seven batsmen—including bowler Starc—averaging better than 30, with the only one who suffered the indignity of being dropped at any stage, opener Marcus Harris, a tick behind on 29.83.

Only two Englishmen matched that, with Root barely getting there with 32.20 and Jonny Bairstow going at 48.50 from his two opportunities.

Australians scored five of the six centuries.

They also had five bowlers—Cummins, Starc, Boland, Lyon and Green—who had between 13 and 21 wickets, while the tourists had only Wood, 17, and Broad, 13, at that level, with Robinson on 11.

If you were selecting a combined side it is difficult to see where any

England player, even Root, would get a guernsey. Who would any of them displace?

The margins were all comprehensive—nine wickets in Brisbane, 275 runs in Adelaide, and innings and 14 in Melbourne and 146 runs in Hobart, and if the Sydney draw had lasted a few minutes longer for a result to be completed, it would have been about 140 runs there too. One match finished before lunch on the third day, another in three days and a third in four days.

This overwhelming result meant Australia got a turbo-charged start to the second edition of the World Test Championship, which Cummins has declared to be high on his wish-list after narrowly missing out on the final the previous year, and watching New Zealand pull it off.

It left Australia a single point behind India, who also had four wins but also two draws from three series, not one. Sri Lanka, with two from two against the West Indies, was the only other unbeaten team.

England were stone motherless last, with one win from 10 matches, and having also forfeited 10 points for bowling their overs too slowly.

In the separate ICC Test rankings, Australia were No. 1 ahead of New Zealand.

Not the least remarkable aspect of Australia's performance was what and who they did without.

They lost their incumbent captain and first choice wicketkeeper before the action started, lost probably their second-best bowler Josh Hazlewood after just one match, lost new captain and No. 1 bowler Cummins and batsman of the series, Head, for a match each and played three debutants.

They resurrected the career of a middle-aged batsman, Khawaja, who couldn't get a game initially, and watched the modern-day Bradman, Smith, average barely 30—less than half his career benchmark—while David Warner also failed to reach three figures and averaged 34.12, failing in three matches and finishing with a pair of ducks.

If England had known all that was about to happen when they first arrived, they would have considered themselves to be in with a very big shout—and so would have the bookmakers.

They would have all been wrong, which is as good a measure as any of the quality of Australia's performance.

CHAPTER 15

GET OUT OF JAIL CARD FOR JINXED JOE

The longer his ill-fated tour went, the deeper into despair it descended, the more certain it seemed that Joe Root's long tenure as England captain was in mortal danger. Much of the unforgiving home media was gunning for him, while nobody—not even Root himself—was seriously disputing that he had made his share of mistakes in most if not all five matches, even if the responsibility for some of them had to be shared with coach and nominal sole selector Chris Silverwood.

His batting fell well short of his usual high standards, too, suggesting the pressure might have got to him.

Still, the question always was: If not him, who?

The surprising answer? Nobody.

Three weeks after the last ball was bowled in Hobart, the team was announced for England's next red-ball assignment, a tour of the West Indies—and there he was, Joe Root captain. Against all the odds he had survived, probably because of a lack of realistic alternatives.

Otherwise, though, the backlash was predictably savage.

First to go was Director of Cricket Ashley Giles, whose three-year tenure included the appointment of Silverwood, with an extraordinary amount of influence and power.

Silverwood, 46, a genial character who was well-liked by the players but found out as a strategist and communicator, quickly followed his boss out the door, along with batting coach Graham Thorpe.

Former captain Andrew Strauss took over as interim cricket boss and oversaw the selection of the team to tour the Caribbean, axing the bulk of the ill-fated Ashes outfit—veteran bowlers Jimmy Anderson and Stuart Broad, as well as batsmen Dawid Malan, Rory Burns and Haseeb Hameed, wicketkeepers Jos Buttler and Sam Billings and unused spinner Dom Bess. Former all-rounder Paul Collingwood was appointed interim coach.

Anderson and Broad were bitterly unhappy even though they were told by Strauss that they were not being axed permanently—an assurance that they were hardly likely to accept without scepticism given their ages, 35 and 40.

So much carnage did nothing to scotch suggestions that there may never have been a worse team to tour Australia.

There have certainly been a few who have failed to win a match, six of them including three of the previous four—but has there ever been one that has covered itself in so little glory, enjoyed itself less or been quite so comprehensively put to the sword?

Well, the stand-out candidate would be Alistair Cook's 2013-14 outfit, who were terrorised into submission—if not abject surrender—by fast bowler Mitchell Johnson, losing by 381 runs, 218 runs, 150 runs, eight wickets and 281 runs in what was only their third 5-0 whitewash in history.

Johnson's literally frightening pace reaped 37 wickets at just 13.97 in what might have been the greatest display of sustained fast bowling the Ashes had ever seen, with batsmen clearly—and willing to say so—alarmed for their safety. One, Jonathan Trott, found the experience so traumatic that after struggling to make 19 in the first Test he flew home, stressed out.

In his autobiography Trott later said that facing fast, short bowling was the cause of his problems. "I felt I was being questioned as a man—I felt my dignity was being stripped away with every short ball I ducked or parried. It was degrading."

And in 2006–07, another whitewash, captain Andrew Flintoff became so frustrated with the outcomes and his own struggle with the responsibilities of leadership that his already well-developed fondness for a cool drink on a hot day took over, turning the tour into—his words— "a booze cruise".

No, Test cricket, like life itself, was never meant to be easy—but the Johnson onslaught must have been about as difficult as it has ever got for anyone.

And no, it wasn't like that for Root's team this time around—but what the scorebooks had to say wasn't much different in the final analysis.

In various ways, it was still the tour from hell—another one.

No one had a harder time than Root, who even ended up with the indignity of having the Hobart cops tell him it was well past his bedtime as he and Anderson—still in their playing kit—were kicking on with a few of the opposition at 6.30am after the fifth Test ended in a defeat that was nothing short of embarrassing and humiliating.

Australian sports fans do not—ever—feel sorry for English cricketers when they come to this country, but Root is universally recognised, by off-field friend and on-field foe, to be a pleasant, intelligent, humble and immensely talented personality, and so while his every dismissal and tactical faux-pas were cause for celebration there was, mostly, a backdrop of goodwill.

It sometimes seemed he was jinxed, that whatever could go wrong usually did.

Root had arrived on the back of a superb year—personally if not quite so much from a team perspective—in which he had scored 1,455 runs, putting him sight of Pakistani Mohammed Yousef's record of 1,788 in 2006. His 253 in the first three Tests on tour left him 80 short of that and just two short of Windies superstar Viv Richards' 1,710 in 1976.

He was officially ranked as the best batsman in the world, and on the verge of overtaking Cook as England's longest-serving captain, which he duly did.

He readily agreed that while his record in charge was well up to scratch—his 27 wins from 56 matches were the most of any of his 79 predecessors, including Cook's 24 from 59—his reputation and legacy would be defined by what was about to take place. "The Ashes is how all England captains are judged," was the unanimous refrain from ex-players and the hard-marking English media.

"Of course, it will define my captaincy, I'm not naïve enough to think it won't," Root said. "You look at how hard it has been for English teams over the years (in Australia). It's been something that doesn't happen very often."

As famous last words go, they were pretty much 24-carat not so much a definition as an epitaph. Root was doomed to complete the tour as the only English captain to have lost two such campaigns in a row, failing to win a single match on either.

He was also part of the disastrous 2013–14 trip which was a whitewash, and which saw him dropped from the team for the final Test.

From a results perspective it has been one long nightmare.

His own performances haven't exactly been a cause for much celebration either.

His two previous tours produced six 50s and no centuries from nine Tests and an average of 38, acceptable for most but not befitting his status as one of the Big Four batsmen of the international game.

This time, it was worse, three 50s, still no centuries, and an even more mediocre average of 32.20. It didn't take long for that to cost him his spot at the top of the ICC batting rankings, overtaken by Marnus Labuschagne.

Australian teams—and most others for that matter—always go hard at the opposition captain, believing that if you cut off the head the body dies.

They gang-tackle them, aided and abetted by vocal crowds, flat decks, harsh outfields and hot sun, all of which can combine to grind the best and worst of them into dust.

Even such experienced, resilient characters as Wasim Akram,

Richie Richardson, Alec Stewart, Graham Gooch, Flintoff and Sachin Tendulkar have succumbed in the not-too-distant past.

This time it was Root's turn and he was no more successful at combating it.

The bowlers worked on his penchant for deflecting the ball away on the off-side, a productive method at home but less controllable on the bouncier Australian pitches, resulting in regular nicks into the cordon.

Although probably not deliberately, they made it physically excruciating too, Root being struck where it most hurts—the, ahem, abdomen, as their media man opted to describe it—multiple times.

In fact, getting hit became an occupational hazard for all batsmen on both sides, which was no great surprise given the spicey nature of all five pitches on which they had to cope with relentless fast bowling.

It was the only area in which there was no gulf between the teams.

According to the CricViz database, there were 151 blows to the hands, the body and the helmet, split equally between the two teams. This compared with 134 four years previously.

Mark Wood, consistently the fastest bowler on either side, was the most dangerous, striking batsmen 29 times, but two of his teammates, Hameed and Bairstow were hit the most often—Hameed nine times or once every 31.7 balls and Bairstow 10 times, once every 35.6 balls.

Predictably, Pat Cummins and Mitchell Starc, with 28 and 20 hits, inflicted the most pain on the Englishmen.

Root, of course, could not be blamed for everything that went wrong. For instance, it was scarcely his fault that the team had to be quarantined in a bubble on arrival and then spent the rest of the tour unable to mix socially with local people as would be the case on any normal tour or overseas holiday.

And nor could he do anything about the preparation for the first Test being highly compromised with only two practice matches arranged and wild Queensland weather then sabotaging both.

Nor was it his fault that a racism row exploded around his county club Yorkshire just as the tour began, but it did create one more early source of attention that he didn't need, even if it blew over quickly.

But once the action started, he was under the hammer from the word go, big-time.

His first act was to win the toss in Brisbane and then decline to take the aggressive if risky option of bowling first on a pitch that was clearly inviting him to do so, and which many old hands in the commentary box insisted would have been the right call.

Instead, he watched his team get bowled out for just 147—failing to trouble the scorers himself—and lose by almost an innings. The rot had set in already.

It wasn't just the result that drew heavy flak, but the team selection, with the team's two most experienced bowlers, Anderson and Broad, left out even though both were fit and raring to go.

One selection controversy followed another virtually to the very end of the campaign, and although Silverwood was technically the sole selector obviously these big calls would not be made without the captain's input.

And so Root's captaincy credentials and skills began to be questioned at almost every turn, a situation not helped when Broad began making his dissatisfaction public in his newspaper columns.

As defeat followed defeat and the fate of the Ashes was decided in double quick time, critics—the ones well-credentialled themselves, and the self-proclaimed experts on social media—were queueing up to get stuck into him.

Ian Chappell led the charge even before a single mistake had been made, saying Root "had an imagination problem" which would be important in Australia, and that he should bat at No 3, not his regular No 4—a suggestion that he appears likely to belatedly take up in the West Indies and thereafter.

He would have to make 500 for England to have any chance, Chappell said—Root got nowhere near that, restricted to 322 at 32.20.

When Root admitted his bowlers had been getting it wrong with the lengths they were bowling, Ricky Ponting gave him a burst for not being in control enough to make sure that wasn't happening.

At home, the ever-trenchant Geoff Boycott weighed in after the third and deciding Test that Root, good bloke though he was, should step down because he lacked the necessary authority and skills.

The travelling English media were no less savage in their day-to-day assessments, but of course Root—and anyone else who has ever represented England at sport—wouldn't have been expecting anything else from the world's most unforgiving sports-writing cohort.

Despite his good previous success rate, there had been multiple occasions where his apparent reluctance to take any risks in search of victory had provoked criticism, most recently when he refused to chase down a victory target of 273 from 75 overs after a generous declaration by New Zealand earlier in the year.

His reserved, undemonstrative personality—bordering on bland— was widely regarded in Australia as being unsuited to hard-edged combat.

And of course, everything his opposite number Pat Cummins—a captain with virtually no leadership experience or qualifications at all—did was turning to gold, making Root look even more inadequate.

Eventually it became so uncomfortable that damage-control leaks began emerging from the dressing rooms that Root still had the confidence and the support of the players, which must have been true enough given that there were no whispers of dissent. Or might it have been some players worried about their own futures, and believing that the devil they know might be preferable to one they don't?

Ben Stokes, the most obvious replacement if there was to be one, then or in the future, was one of the more powerful voices to register support, saying that he had no ambitions for the job anyway. Chris Woakes also made a point of joining in.

Root himself showed no signs of cracking, no inclination to fall on his sword.

And neither did Silverwood, whose tenure was generally—and

correctly, as it turned out—perceived to be on far more tenuous ground than the captain's.

Both insisted they were still the best men for the job.

After the wreckage of Hobart, Root told reporters: "I'd love the opportunity to take this team forward and to turn things around. We're going through a real tough stage as a group of players. The performances haven't been good enough but I'd love the opportunity to turn things round and for us to start putting in performances you'd expect from an English Test team."

Asked whether he was merely hoping for an opportunity to quit the captaincy on a high after a more successful series, Root was adamant.

"I believe I am the right man to take this team forward, in my own eyes, and if that decision is taken out of my hands, so be it."

Having been publicly outspoken about the deficiencies of both his batsmen and bowler over the series, he said the squad had to accept they were clearly second best.

"We've let ourselves down because we've not given a fair account of what we're capable of. But at the same time, it's quite evident that Australia are, at this moment in time, a better team than we are, in all areas.

"It hurts me to say that but it's the reality of things and we've got to accept that and find a way of doing better—very quickly."

Finding a way of doing better—quickly—is of course, not simply the role of the captain or the coach, or any other one man. The widely-acknowledged lesson from this debacle—and it wasn't a new one—was that the governors of the game in the country that invented it, the English Cricket Board, had allowed the domestic system to become far too attached to the white ball formats which was sabotaging the production of players capable of adapting to the more intense demands of five-day red-ball cricket.

This had delivered the most recent one-day World Cup but had made Test wins as scarce as elephants on the streets of London.

England has always been a land in love with tradition, especially in sport, and cricket's governors have seldom seen the need to interfere with the time-honoured county competition, which comprises 18 clubs all of which share first-class status—but some of which, these days, often fall well short of that.

Most experts agree they have too many mediocre players, diluting the quality of the competition. "Any player coming into our Test team is doing so in spite of, not because of, the county system," Root has said.

Australia, by contrast, has only six first class teams and the standard and competitiveness is clearly superior—and manages to keep its head well above water in every format, not to mention dominating women's cricket. The England women's team also failed to win a match in five attempts in three formats after the men had gone home.

There is little doubt that if England had to start again from scratch, with up-to-date thinking, they would not replicate what they have got now. They would, and should reduce it to eight or 10 teams, and if that means 10 counties get their noses seriously out of joint and fade from mainstream view then the end will almost certainly justify the means.

It will take some tough talking to achieve but the ECB has access to plenty of smart thinkers who know what is required—such as former captains Mike Atherton, Nasser Hussain, Michael Vaughan and Sir Alistair Cook—and who would not worry about stepping on toes. They should be utilised before it's too late.

Few, if any, speak on all these matters with more authority or a louder voice than Atherton, cricket correspondent for *The Times* of London and a ubiquitous commentator on radio and TV in Australia during the summer.

In a double-page deep dive into England's many problems—also published in the News Corp papers in Australia—he described the Ashes series, which at that point still had two matches to play out, as "gruesome, the worst I have covered as a journalist."

He said English fans had a right to be angry because they care, and that the administration had taken its eye off the red ball first class game.

He recommended Silverwood be sacked and that Root had to take responsibility for the many mistakes and should step down and be replaced by Stokes.

He said players should not be paid (overly-generous) central contract retainers when they are otherwise occupied elsewhere, such as the Indian Premier League, and that a way must be found to improve the quality of county cricket, perhaps by promotion and relegation if there is no political will to reduce the number of teams.

And finally, while the aim should be to produce a good Test in all conditions with the World Test Championship a focus, specific attention must be given to winning in Australia.

As he added, there were a lot of problems to work through and it was easy to pick holes in anything anyone suggested—but something more coherent and sensible was essential. Doing nothing was not an option.

Australia was in the rear-view mirror—exactly where the touring party were pleased to have it—before it emerged, as these things often do, that the campaign had been even more shambolic than it had appeared to the naked eye.

In a scathing report in London's *The Telegraph*, cricket writer Nick Hoult said a worrying drinking culture involving both players and staff had developed from the outset, a result of life in the quarantine bubble, and which had people struggling to focus on the task at hand.

The cosiness of the set-up had been a major talking point within the group, he said.

One player refused a skinfold test—a gauge of body fat—and accused management of fat-shaming him. The test was never carried out. Fitness levels generally dipped as the tour went on, fast bowler Ollie Robinson a constant case in point.

Senior players were left out of tactical discussions, Hoult wrote, and one was angered to learn he had been dropped by reading about it in the press.

Batsmen and bowlers argued with each other at team meetings and some players did not take enough individual responsibility.

Hoult's expose did not appear to attract any denials, at least none that filtered back to Australia.

No wonder, then, that Root didn't seem to have a smile on his face very often.

If it bordered on tragic for English fans, then Greg Chappell wrote that it could have been billed as a reprisal of Shakespeare's comedy *Much Ado About Nothing*. But it transformed into *A Comedy of Errors*, he wrote, adding sadly: "I have never looked forward to a contest so much and enjoyed it so little."

If he was looking for a seconder to that melancholy sentiment, Joe Root was probably his man.

CHAPTER 16

A LOT AT STAKE AS COVID CHAOS AND CONFUSION REIGN

Pat Cummins' Test record will forever be missing a match, not because he lost form and was dropped, not because he was ill or injured, not because of any family drama and not because the selectors had decided to "rotate" their fast bowlers—but because he decided to go out for a steak dinner with an old mate.

That casual social engagement was on the eve of the second Test in Adelaide, from which he was a shock scratching the next morning because he had come into contact in the restaurant with a fellow diner who then almost immediately learned he had tested positive to the covid virus.

That made Cummins a close contact and under the South Australian Government's ultra-strict policies for combating the pandemic he was obliged to isolate for a week, ruling him out of what would have been only his second match as Australian captain.

It was at that stage the most obvious example of the pandemic's potential to disrupt the entire tour perhaps to the point where it might not be possible to finish it. For administrators, it was their worst nightmare threatening to come true.

There were plenty more such dramas to come and they were by no means confined to the Ashes—the rest of the cricket season, including the popular Big Bash T20 tournament and the Sheffield Shield, was thrown into chaos, as was virtually every other major sport, notably soccer, basketball and women's AFL.

And of course by far the biggest news event of the summer—the Ashes included—was the covid-related deportation of the world's best tennis player, Novak Djokovic, after the Serbian superstar flew into the country without being vaccinated in the optimistic hope he would be allowed to contest the Australian Open.

The Government and the courts sent him home—and rightly so.

Cricket never did quite get to the other end unscathed—a short series of one-day games scheduled for two weeks after the fifth Test were abandoned—or at least postponed— after New Zealand players declined to jump through all the biosecurity hoops that would have been involved, saying it just wasn't worth it. A planned return visit a few weeks later was also scrapped.

Five T20s against Sri Lanka went ahead as scheduled but the Kiwi void came at a hefty cost in lost TV rights, not to mention gate takings.

And the Sheffield Shield struggled across the line with states playing an uneven number of matches necessitating a pro-rata points distribution.

It could all have been so much worse—including the Cummins incident.

The skipper dined at the Little Hunter Steakhouse—a popular establishment where a ribeye will set you back more than $50—with Harry Conway, a NSW and Big Bash cricketer, and they were approached at their table by another Sydney club player who just wanted to say hello—but who then, within minutes, was notified by text message that he had tested positive.

Cummins' teammates Nathan Lyon and Mitchell Starc were seated at the same eatery—but were at a table outside on the footpath. If they had also been inside, they, too, would have been deemed close contacts and would not have been able to play.

Starc revealed later that he and Lyon had sat outside only because they were jokingly "brushing" Cummins after he had earlier failed to reply to a text message about their dinner plans.

If they had gone inside Australia would have been without their entire attack from the first Test, given that Josh Hazlewood was unavailable with injury.

That's how precarious the situation had become. The series would be played out on a knife's edge.

Early in the match a BBC journalist had also returned a positive result after taking the compulsory test six days after arrival in the state, so he and several others in the British broadcaster's Test Match Special crew were sent into isolation.

The journalist had interviewed English batsman Dawid Malan after play on the Saturday night but was wearing a mask and so there was no issue in Malan's participation in the rest of the match.

Cricket Australia still made the call to suspend all on-field interviews for the last two days.

But in chaotic scenes on the Sunday morning, ABC commentators—who had been working alongside their visiting counterparts—were told not to go to the ground, with Jim Maxwell, Ian Chappell and Andrew Moore flying straight home to Sydney.

The national broadcaster called the day's play out of remote studios while at the ground all media, written and broadcast, were under strict instructions to wear masks while working and to take regular tests.

After returning a second negative test Cummins was given permission to fly back to his young family in Sydney, but by chartered plane—a costly exercise—several days before his isolation expired, while Cricket Australia and the SA Government entered into a "blame game" debate about whether he had been prematurely ruled out of the Test.

The local health officials, meanwhile, changed the rules so that visitors would no longer have to do a test on arrival, which meant the asymptomatic cricketer who briefly chatted with Cummins and Conway would not have had one and therefore not been told he was positive—and Cummins would not have had a problem. He could have played and the broadcast teams could have worked through.

The South Australian Premier Steven Marshall claimed it was not his health officials who had ruled Cummins out—"we hadn't even interviewed him"—but CA, "because (they) probably formed the opinion that they didn't want to have a chance for the entire two teams to be deemed close contacts and ruin the entire Test series."

But CEO Nick Hockley insisted there had been an emergency meeting with SA Health "that left us with no option."

Whatever the finer points of that argy-bargy were, nobody was taking any chances from this point on, with already strict protocols about movement and socialising upgraded.

Full lockdowns with players restricted to their hotel rooms were ruled out because there was every possibility they might have prompted a mutiny anyway.

Hockley didn't need reminding that several leading players—Cummins, Steve Smith, Warner, Glenn Maxwell, Jhye Richardson and Daniel Sams—had all declined to tour the West Indies and Bangladesh for white-ball games during the winter, with bubble fatigue among the reasons they provided.

All national players had been coping with quarantine bubbles for the two years that the pandemic had been impacting on elite sport and there was a limit to how much more of it they were prepared to take. They wanted—demanded?—some freedom.

While professional cricket tours are working environments and not holiday jaunts, their appeal to those who undertake them—or aspire to—is that they do also offer a certain socially relaxed and convivial lifestyle after hours, and it is no surprise that when this becomes unavailable it has a negative effect on the mood and mental health of the participants.

After two years of working around it, players—and administrators—in all countries have learned to deal with it, but that doesn't mean it isn't still a significant problem.

"We're very conscious of taking a precautionary approach—we're very conscious of their mental well-being," Hockley said.

Players were told to always dine outdoors and in groups of no more than three and to avoid bars and any other crowded places.

"We have to check in with each other to see what restaurants everyone is going to, it's just being smart," said batsman David Warner.

Any shopping had to be done online while getting haircuts or working out in public gyms were banned.

The English players were living under similar safeguards.

Their travelling media had also been doing it the hard way, most journalists unable to get into Brisbane for the first Test and forced to work off the TV from hotel rooms in Sydney.

To add to the vast expense, CA was flying the Test players and the Big Bash teams around the country either in chartered jets or on commercial flights with a row of extra seats booked to separate them from all other passengers.

As draining on the coffers as this was, it was a drop in the bucket compared to the tens of millions of dollars in lost broadcast rights and other expenses if the series had to be abandoned.

But it was like a game of whack-a-mole—hit one problem on the head and another would crop up immediately. No one was exempt.

A second Australian player, Travis Head, copped a dose of the bug in Melbourne and missed the Sydney Test, as did match referee David Boon, England coach Chris Silverwood and even Hockley.

On day two of the short-lived Melbourne Test, play started half an hour late because the English team were delayed at their hotel while they waited for rapid antigen test results to come back after four members of their touring party—family members and support staff—developed symptoms after celebrating Christmas at a restaurant in St Kilda.

Channel 7 had to replace its commentary team for the first session but the match continued—not that it had long to go, Australia winning inside seven sessions—without further incident.

The broadcasters, 7 and Fox Sport, were walking a similar tightrope as the administrators were, flying 100 or so staff—and huge amounts of equipment—around the country, and setting up studio hubs for worst-case scenarios with commentators.

For instance, Ricky Ponting worked from his home in Melbourne during the Sydney Test.

But by far the biggest headache surrounded the fifth Test, which was scheduled to be played in Perth in mid-January.

The West Australian Premier Mark McGowan, whose massive Parliamentary majority meant he was almost a law unto himself, had spent the entire two years of the pandemic virtually seceding from the rest of Australia as he made it almost impossible for people from interstate to cross his borders without submitting to extensive biosecurity protocols.

Naturally, when it became clear that one of the jewels in the national sporting crown, the AFL Grand Final, could not be played in Melbourne because of the virus's heavy presence there, McGowan found a way to host it for the first time ever—and did so with enormous success.

But with a week's bye before the big game, it was relatively easy for the teams and anyone else who needed to be there to get to Perth in time to fulfil their quarantine obligations.

It wasn't that convenient for the cricket.

With McGowan insisting on 14 days isolation for all travellers from Sydney, where the fourth Test was due to end on January 9, for everyone involved—players, broadcasters, staff, travelling supporters—the time frame for a January 14 start in Perth just wasn't feasible.

Even if it was possible to tweak it somehow, it wasn't going to wash with the England team, who were not remotely interested in doing any more hard quarantine at all.

They had reluctantly agreed to an initial fortnight on arrival in Brisbane—albeit in a luxury resort—after weeks of scuttlebutt suggesting the tour might not take place at all if the protocols were going to be too restrictive.

Perth was certainly a bridge too far.

From McGowan, there was no wriggle room available. "It's up to them whether they want to adhere to these rules or not," he said.

Nobody did want to.

It was a desperately disappointing decision for the Western Australian Cricket Association, who were now seeing the city's showpiece venue, Optus Stadium, bereft of top cricket for the second year in a row, the previous year's scheduled Test against Afghanistan, a historic occasion, also cancelled because of COVID-19.

McGowan's Sports Minister Tony Buti made an audacious Hail Mary bid to salvage the situation by suggesting that they could take over Adelaide's second Test—the teams would have been coming in from Brisbane, to which the same protocols did not apply—and the South Australians could have the final one.

Yeah, right. Buti was laughed out of court, and the match was put for tender, attracting bids from Melbourne, Sydney, Hobart and Canberra.

English commentator Michael Vaughan campaigned for the final three Tests to all be played in Melbourne, arguing it would mitigate the risks inherent in keeping the travelling circus on the road—and probably be more profitable.

Sydney and Hobart were having none of that, of course.

Insisting that they were owed the privilege of an Ashes match, the Tasmanians got the nod and grabbed it with both hands, the day-night encounter going off without an organisational hitch and Australia marching to victory No. 4 with two days to spare while the WA fans watched it on TV and cried into their beers.

Meanwhile, the Big Bash also descended into disarray, with so many players and associates testing positive that several clubs were forced to recruit top-up players from club cricket, with CA going so far as to establish a pool of replacements who could play for any franchise that asked them—or even more than one, in some cases.

Some players simply opted out, such as former Test fast bowler James Pattison who flimsily claimed he needed to concentrate on preparing for a winter stint in English county cricket, but also admitted he had had enough of bubble life. He was just sick of it, if not in quite the same way as others were.

There were so many cases that reports emerged that most players had simply assumed that all of them would become infected at some point—"all in the same boat" syndrome.

No team were more seriously disadvantaged than the Melbourne Stars with as many as 15 cases in their camp at one stage. That made it practically impossible for them to win for two or three matches in a row, calling into question the integrity of the competition.

As the finals approached, several games were relocated to Victoria, where the MCG, Marvel Stadium, Junction Oval and the Geelong football ground between them were able to absorb the extra traffic.

After playing only their first match at home, the Scorchers were permanently on the road, unable to return to Perth and chose to play their finals at Marvel Stadium. There, they duly took down the Sydney Sixers to win their fourth title, a record for the competition.

It was a minor miracle that the tournament made it all the way to the finish line.

Much the same could be said for the Ashes, which is why Hockley issued a media release after the fifth Test which bordered on understatement.

Thanking all concerned—the England board and their team, coaches and officials, partners, host venues, governments, state associations and the public—for their participation, he described the season as "extraordinary."

It had been, he said, "a true testament to the resilience and unwavering spirit of the international cricket family who have been supportive through periods of uncertainty and change as we navigated the unique challenges posed by the COVID-19 pandemic."

Amen to that.

CHAPTER 17

FAST BOWLING CAPTAIN PUTS PLENTY OF RUNS ON THE BOARD

Pat Cummins' report card from his first term in charge of the Test team is a pretty simple, straightforward document. He gets at least an A, probably an A-plus.

He led the team in four of the five Ashes matches and won three of them by big margins. He fell just one wicket short of doing the same in the other one and despite missing one match through no fault of his own he took more wickets than any other bowler on either side.

He also handled himself with impressive aplomb—earning wide applause—when he faced the media to explain his and his teammates' role and attitudes in the messy departure of their coach Justin Langer three weeks after the last ball was bowled.

The only quibble—and it's a pretty flimsy one—was that in the Sydney Test, the one he didn't win, he might have delayed his second innings declaration a fraction too long, which in the end meant he ran out of time, just, to complete the victory late on the last day.

In the greater scheme of things, that blip became more or less meaningless, with Australia having already retained the Ashes in less than 12 days of combat and going on to record a 4-0 overall scoreline with their demoralised opponents admitting they had been thrashed by a much better side.

Cummins had come into the contest with almost no captaincy experience whatsoever, other than a handful of one-day games for NSW, and was pitted against Joe Root, who was about to become the most experienced England Test captain in history. Cummins won that one-on-one duel by a knockout.

For a cricketer who often talks about the enjoyment he gets out of just playing the game he has loved since he was a kid, that must have been fun?

It sure was, he says.

Asked to rate the experience on a scale of 1 to 10, he told me: "I think 10 because we just had an absolute ball. The players got on so well. There was never a bad day. We just absolutely loved it."

There were only 21 playing days out of a scheduled 25, one of those lasting less than a session, and there was a blink-and-you'll-miss-it quality.

"It just felt like it went really quickly. Normally Ashes series are a bit longer, the previous couple I played in had a lot of five-day matches, but this one just felt like a blur and suddenly Hobart was done," he said.

"It was totally smooth. There weren't any hiccups other than small ones with covid restrictions and injuries and we just dealt with those really well."

If there were any tensions involving the increasingly insecure Langer, the captain was keeping them well and truly to himself, not just while the campaign was ticking along but for the two or three weeks afterwards that it took for that to come to a head.

Only then, under pressure from the media and past players, did he address that issue publicly.

The magnitude of the win—even if it was against one of the weakest and most poorly-led English outfits to tour Australia for a long time—was a towering personal triumph and point of great pride for the baggy green cap's new leader. But no one was about to hear him say that.

Asked if he saw it that way, he said: "I absolutely see it as a team thing. As captain, I had some role to play in the environment but every one of the boys were fantastic in the roles they had. It really, really feels like the beginning of a long stretch for this team."

If anyone genuinely feared that appointing a fast bowler captain for the first time in history—other than a one-match fill-in by Ray Lindwall way back in 1956—might prove unworkable because of the dual workload, they were quickly able to relax.

Cummins' figures—and his ability to enforce important breakthroughs at crucial junctures—were ample proof of that.

He had no problems mixing and matching his attack, he said. "I just leaned on other people." And veteran spinner Nathan Lyon said: "It's been really interesting having the No. 1 bowler's mindset as captain. Pat is very approachable and it has helped me, and Mitch (Starc) is getting the rewards he deserves."

Cummins was more than willing to seek advice, especially from his deputy Steve Smith.

"In my time I've had Michael Clarke, Steve Smith and Tim Paine as Test captains and Aaron Finch in white-ball as well as a lot of others in in domestic and T20 competitions, and I think you pick the best bits and pieces from each different one. I've picked up tit-bits from a lot of captains. I'd say the role that naturally fits me is trying to manage relationships."

Asked if he sought or accepted advice from old hands who were no longer directly involved—and there's always plenty of that available any time you turn on the TV commentary—he said: "Yeah, I think you have to pick a couple. If you listen to too many it tends to cancel each other out and becomes really cluttered. I've got a couple whose decision-making I really trust and that's part of our support staff. There are a lot of different voices there and I want to hear those different opinions."

Not the least impressive aspect of Cummins' leadership was the spirit in which the series was played, for which he was given most of the credit—although the tourists certainly reciprocated. The captains did not discuss it beforehand, Cummins said, but it was a deliberate initiative on Australia's part and presumably from the other side as well.

There were several obvious instances.

In Sydney, England players warmly applauded Usman Khawaja's century, and when Jonny Bairstow got his, Khawaja and David Warner offered fist bumps. Lyon was seen giving Root tips on off-spin bowling, while Starc was laughing and joking with Root the day after hitting him with a low blow where it hursts most the previous day.

When breaks in play arrived, opponents shared friendly exchanges as they left the field.

There was plenty of banter but little or no objectionable taunting or insults.

This was very different from previous tours, most notably in 2013–14 when Michael Clarke told tailender Jimmy Anderson to "get reading for a fucking broken arm" and Warner spoke about the "scared eyes" of Jonathan Trott as he suffered a mental breakdown in the middle of the Gabba.

There have been many other examples, against all teams. Even the previous summer, then captain Tim Paine found himself apologising for a crude take-down of Indian bowler Ravi Ashwin.

"Yes, it was a hot topic and I think everyone really loved the spirit in which it was played," said Cummins, who has never fitted the mould of the wild-eyed, loose-tongued fast bowler who gave the batsman both barrels at every opportunity. Merv Hughes, he has never been.

If intimidation is required, he is well-equipped to provide it in different ways.

He has always said he regards sledging as a waste of time and energy.

Under him, that quickly became more or less official team policy.

"We all spoke about it beforehand and we all bought into it, it wasn't just me," he said. "I kind of laid out what I like and the environment I wanted to set and tried to shape that. We sat down and nutted it out."

It wasn't new.

"In recent years we have been really good. There are moments when it gets heated, and the media take that and make it what (they) need it to be, we just try to keep it friendly and happy, and the media love that too. It's something we have to continue. I don't like wasting time on sledging and those type of things, I just try to be myself out there."

Elaborating on this in a different interview with a British newspaper, he said: "You have to be aware of it. From a couple of years ago it was obvious the world wanted all cricket teams, particularly the Aussie cricket team, to tone it down a little bit. I keep encouraging all our players to be themselves. They do not have to try to impress anyone or sledge just because it might have been done like that in the past. Just be themselves. It is something to keep an eye on. But I've been really proud of how the lads have conducted themselves. If I need to pull someone up, I will, but everyone is an adult here. They have heard it loud and clear from the outside what is expected of us from cricket fans in Australia."

If there is one word that has seemed to come to define Cummins' management style, it is "calm". He uses it frequently himself. Is it a reflection of his personality?

"I hope so," he says. "It's something I really try to maintain. I think that's when a lot of us really play our best."

Prominent cricket journalist Ben Horne compared him to one of the most famous of all Australian captains, Richie Benaud, who was originally from the same Sydney district of Penrith, a working-class area where pretentiousness is not a common feature of life.

Horne wrote that Cummins believed that the best way to combat the stresses of international cricket was not to be washed away by them.

Veteran commentator and former captain Bill Lawry, who started his very successful Test career under Benaud's captaincy, said that was exactly how he remembered the doyen.

"As a leader Richie had no airs. He was a man of few words. There was no opening speech, there was no drama," Lawry said at a function to name the Sydney Cricket Ground's new media centre after Benaud.

In one of the most astute assessments of the new skipper, Horne wrote in the News Corp papers: "Like Benaud, Cummins is not one for Churchillian addresses, he leads by example. For more than a decade now—and not the fault of any one person—there has been a franticness about the Australian team. Eleventh-hour selection decisions, mixed messages, erratic and unbecoming on-field behaviour and a lack of clarity about what the team actually stands for. But Cummins has calmed the waters. Genuine and sensitive and a clear communicator, he might be the antithesis of macho captains of the past but, in his own way, Cummins is a strong and decisive personality who instils confidence in those around him. Players know he's a natural-born winner—relentless—and they feed off it."

While popularity is not necessarily a prerequisite of the post, it does seem to be an asset that comes naturally to Cummins. Is it important to him?

"You like to say it's not but, yes, being popular, everyone is always conscious of that," he says.

But to him, it's more about cultivating good relationships. "That makes a lot of other things easier, so when I talk about getting the best out of players, knowing what makes them tick, those things, it's through good relationships, not necessarily being super popular."

That goes for another important aspect of the job, dealing with the media, which is easy when things are going well, not so much when the flak starts flying.

Fortunately, there was no flak while the Ashes was playing out—but when the Langer drama hit the fan a couple of weeks later, he got his first taste of what the heat could feel like with accusations that he had not demonstrated enough transparency as it became increasingly apparent that he was not in the besieged coach's corner.

While the process played out in head office—messily—he was in a delicate situation no matter what he did or did not say, until finally Langer had left the building and he was free to address it publicly.

Otherwise, former fast bowler Geoff Lawson, also an astute newspaper columnist for the *Sydney Morning Herald* and *The Age* made the accurate observation that Cummins "handles press conferences with a refreshing air of no nonsense, common sense and that ring-of-confidence smile that is quickly becoming a trademark. He was making

Test cricket look more like a game of fun and consequences rather than do or die. Perhaps his perspective is shaped by the seriousness of world events and the role that sport, even something as nationally sensitive as the Ashes, really plays."

Lawson added that unlike some recent captains—he didn't offer any clues as to who he had in mind—Cummins did not appear to want to "own" the team and create a legacy. "He just wants to play, and let others play, expressing their talent."

Cummins' respect for his teammates—for pretty much everyone, really—was amply demonstrated by an incident that took place immediately after the conclusion of the final Test in Hobart.

As he and the team gathered on the podium for the customary celebration, spraying champagne over themselves and anybody within reach, Usman Khawaja leapt away.

The Pakistani-born batsman, the first Muslim to play for Australia, wanted to avoid being doused with the alcohol, in accordance with his religious beliefs.

Cummins realised immediately what was happening and shut down the fizz-flinging and made sure Khawaja was able to re-join the celebration.

A small thing? Hardly—not in the greater scheme of things. It was certainly good optics when the two previous captains had been involved in thoughtless and damaging scandals.

For the Muslim community it was a poignant moment that attracted wide attention. "Every Muslim notices that stuff," said Rana Hussain, Cricket Australia's Diversity and Inclusion manager.

"At the end of big games you watch the Muslim players, 'what are they going to do, how are they going to feel?' and you relate so hard. I did see Usman running away and I thought, oh God, then I saw that they put the bottles away and Pat called him over and was insistent about it. I had a big smile on my face because I thought, 'OK, this is perfect.' There's a time when the sentiment would have been 'alright, well, you don't have to, you've got to miss out' and Pat clocked it—that in itself as amazing. As a Muslim myself it made me smile."

The social media response had been heart-warming, she said.

Khawaja had often spoken about how he had struggled as a young man to fit into the beer-drinking culture of Australian cricket dressing rooms.

The following day he posted the video of the incident with the comment: "If this doesn't show that my teammates have my back, what will? They stopped their celebrations and champagnes so I could join back in.

"Inclusivity in our game and our values as a sport are so important. I feel like we are trending in the right direction."

While Cummins was rightly praised, the footage also raised questions—the fun police are always on duty, of course—about Cricket Australia's decision to place champagne on the podium and why players needed to be reminded to put them down.

"It was great awareness from your teammates but it would have been fully inclusive to save the champagne popping for the rooms and let you be in ALL of the on-field photos and celebrations, would it not?" one fan asked.

Khawaja responded: "Baby steps."

After such an impressive start, what now for Captain Pat?

For starters, he has no ambitions to captain the white ball teams, the domain of Aaron Finch, although he will continue to play in them.

Where he hopes it will lead is to London in 2023 for the final of the World Test Championship, the inaugural edition of which was contested by New Zealand, the surprise winners, and India after the Australians shot themselves in the foot by being docked too many points for slow over rates a few months earlier.

"I absolutely want to be in the final," he said. "Winning away from home, that's a big challenge for any Test team. You can see England come here, it's foreign conditions for them. When Australian cricket is at its best, the Test side wins at home and have a really good record away. I feel like its building. We have a great squad of 15-20 guys we can pick from. We have options for anywhere in the world."

More personally, two other interesting predictions about his future have attracted a lot of comment.

One came from Dennis Lillee, who helped fix his back and who is a huge fan. The old champion, widely regarded as Australia's greatest fast bowler himself, predicted on the Fox documentary that his protege would become "the greatest bowler we've ever had, which probably means in the world as well."

"That's a big call," Cummins responded. "It's very kind of him, but I don't think about that. I just look at the game in front of me and try to do my best. I don't really think about the big picture of my whole career, to be honest."

And Robert Craddock, Australia's most experienced and informed cricket journalist, said early in the Ashes campaign that it was already evident that Cummins was set to become one of the most powerful captains in history.

"Within reason, he will get what he wants as Australian captain for a variety of reasons, not the least being that he is well-liked by both sides of the fence, players and Cricket Australia. Cummins' power is accentuated because he is his side's best player and also because Australia needs him more than he needs it in many different ways."

These included the shallowness of the leadership pool—"there is daylight between him and the next viable option"—and because he makes more money from other sources than from playing for Australia he is in a position of strength in any conflict with the administration.

That was never the case with other big-name captains such as the Chappells, Benaud, Allan Border and even Don Bradman. "Not even Bradman won every argument with his board," Craddock wrote. "Cummins' early style as a captain is a laid-back one of occasional smiles and stress relief. It's not a bad way to start. With the power Cummins holds, he can paint the canvas his own way. Great challenges and opportunities await him."

Postscript: Cummins' golden summer did not end with the Ashes. Just over a month later, he led his team on an historic tour of Pakistan—the first by Australia for 24 years—and emerged triumphant again, winning the three-match series 2-1.

On lifeless, rock-hard pitches, the first two matches were drawn but Cummins was determined to get a result in the third one in Lahore.

He did that by making a generous declaration late on the fourth day, setting Pakistan a potentially gettable 351 off 121 overs at a rate of under three an over. Despite a strong start—they still had 10 wickets in hand, needing 278 off 90 when the final day began—Pakistan were bowled out 151 short of their target. Again, Cummins' enterprising, confident captaincy had triumphed.

As well, the series—like the Ashes—was played out in great spirit, another Cummins trademark. "It was an amazing experience, a lot of fun," he said. "We are elated."

When the tour ended, the interim coach Andrew McDonald accepted the job on a full-time basis over all three formats for four years, having taken his time to fully engage with Cricket Australia on what was expected of him.

Meanwhile, the now-departed Justin Langer continued to make no decision on his future, with strong rumours that he was to be offered the same job with England, and was likely to accept, proving to be incorrect.

After losing 1-0 to the West Indies in the next assignment after the Ashes, Joe Root resigned the England captaincy, and was replaced by Ben Stokes.

EPILOGUE

The arrival of the English cricket team in Australia for the Ashes—and vice versa—always creates a frisson of enthusiasm and interest that is unique and sets it apart from the many international sporting occasions that are synonymous with both countries. Which is not to say that it is automatically the chart-topper, only that it has an appeal and an identity and an importance—a mystique—all of its own. And it is timeless, or at least has been up until now.

Long may it stay that way.

But well into the third decade of the 21st century there is fierce competition for occupation of the high ground in the mainstream, professional sports landscape—and cricket is well aware that it cannot afford to take its eye off the ball in any shape or form.

The quality of the offering must never be compromised, even if the natural ebb and flow of rivalries and talent streams do mean that the edge is sometimes taken off the contest.

That's why there were some mixed feelings about how the latest battle for the old urn—which dates back to 1882—played out, with Australia winning 4-0 by huge margins and England never getting close to landing a punch in return.

The Ashes were decided in 12 of the 25 scheduled playing days and with one match complete an hour into the third day, another in three days and another in four, 14 sessions went unplayed—virtually an entire match lost.

If you consider that to be the definition of being short-changed, you probably have a valid argument.

On the other hand, Australian sports fans always enjoy a bit of Pom-bashing on the field of play in any given sport, cricket more than any other, and the same goes in reverse when the shoe is on the other foot. Winners are grinners.

So from that perspective, it was highly entertaining—and constantly dramatic, with enough major talking points on and off the field to keep the media well-stocked with headlines just about every day.

What it did lack, of course, was the constant, hard competitive edge that is crucial to all elite sport.

Australia's winning margins were nine wickets in Brisbane, 275 runs in Adelaide, an innings and 14 in Melbourne and 146 runs in Hobart, and it would have been well into three figures again if they had taken the final wicket in Sydney.

There were fleeting periods in all games when the hapless tourists looked to be in with some sort of chance of turning things around, but they always ended up being stomped into the turf, usually with plenty of time to spare.

England's modern-day record in Australia is appalling and showing no signs of getting any better, so they certainly need to find a way of improving it.

In six visits from 2002–03, from 30 Tests they have lost 23 and won four with three draws. Three of the four wins were in the one series they won, in 2010–11, so in five others they have won only once, and that was 20 years ago. Go further back, over 30 years the scoreline is 32 to six.

Are Australian fans expected to keep on turning up and tuning in to this without demur?

Well, cricket is still what it has always been—Australia's No. 1 international sport.

So yes, they—we—do keep the faith, according to Cricket Australia.

This time, despite the various discouragements, legal and social, presented by the covid pandemic, almost half a million people attended the 20 days of play and TV viewing figures "were among the highest in cricket history," CEO Nick Hockley said in a media release.

"Almost" and "among" are rubbery terms, of course, but until someone who would know suggests otherwise, the series has to be considered successful in more ways than one.

Perhaps one prevailing sentiment was neatly captured by one of Australia's best and most experienced cricket writers Malcolm Conn, whose viewpoints have been influenced by a recent stint as a communications executive with Cricket Australia.

Now back with the *Sydney Morning Herald* and *The Age*, he wrote a column after just two Tests headed "Don't pity the tourists, let's enjoy the Ashes".

"However bad England may be, Ashes victories are precious," he wrote. "This cavalcade of success in Australia won't last forever and the alternatives doesn't bear thinking about. Too often Australia's dominance at home is written off as weak opposition ruining summers with a lack of competition."

He pointed out that Australia had won just three of the nine series before this one, all at home, so it wasn't as if they had a stranglehold on the urn wherever it was contested, as did the teams led by Allan Border, Mark Taylor and Steve Waugh during the nineties and early 2000s.

There was also a lot to like in the success Australia was having in finding and developing good young players, notably Cameron Green—"so there has been a lot to celebrate."

A month later, there was a lot more.

I agree with Conn—no surprise there, perhaps; we are long-time mates and colleagues after all—but I've been hooked on cricket in general, and the Ashes in particular, all my longish life, a very large part of which has been spent writing about it professionally and watching it for pleasure.

Yes, of course I'd enjoy five lots of five days of hard-fought combat, ending 3-2 but you know what—such a scoreline has only ever occurred six times, and three of those date back almost 120 years.

So it doesn't necessarily have to be a nail-biter to be entertaining. There is always plenty of drama, memorable stories unfold, reputations are made and unmade, record books—and no sport so loves facts and figures more than cricket—are rewritten and expanded. Hopefully the preceding pages have provided some evidence of that.

Along with its great sense of history and tradition, one of the concept's powerful strengths—in my opinion, which is not universally shared—is that it is played over five matches, which is no longer the case in any other match-up with or between any other countries.

Whether it is taking place in England or Australia, that means there is ample scope for subtly different playing conditions to be explored, for strategies to be devised and tested, for players to work their way into and out of form, for new stars to emerge and fading ones to be farewelled, for a narrative to fully unfold, and for fans in almost every part of the country to get the chance to witness it in person.

In other ways cricket has embraced a "less is more" philosophy, which is why white ball formats, especially T20, have been so successful, certainly their World Cups—but it would be a mistake to translate that thinking to the Ashes.

There are always dissenters, of course.

The England team had barely boarded the plane home when sportswriter Tim Wigmore, of the London *Telegraph*, insisted that three matches was the way to go.

In a column also published in Australia, he pointed to the "terrific, oscillating series brimming with high-octane cricket between two well-matched sides whose ultimate outcome became clear only deep into the final innings of the series" between South Africa and India, which was played concurrently.

The contrast with "the abject spectacle of the Ashes" was stark, he wrote.

"Increasingly, the prestige, hype and mythology of the Ashes Down

Under is not enough to obscure an unpalatable truth: this does not look like elite sport, never mind the pinnacle of the Test game when one side are consistently so poor," he added.

"Indeed, among all the Australian delight about their emphatic triumph, it was possible to detect a certain strain of disappointment: that a series still hyped as offering an unrivalled test had so conspicuously failed to do so. Victory feels altogether less meaningful if it is not accompanied by the sense of having overcome a worthy foe."

Wigmore is of course entitled to his opinion and it is by no means invalid—but there is little in the way of available evidence that there is much support for it among the cricket fans, or the administrations, or the players, in either country.

And certainly not from me. Long live the Ashes. For all its flaws and imperfections, it is still among the best sporting theatre available in this or any other country.

FOR THE RECORD
ASHES SCOREBOARDS,
SUMMARIES AND AVERAGES

2021-22 ASHES SERIES—TEST BY TEST
Australia v England

Australia wins series 4–0.

The Teams
Australia: Pat Cummins (c), Steve Smith (vc), Alex Carey, Cameron Green, Josh Hazlewood, Marcus Harris, Travis Head, Usman Khawaja, Marnus Labuschagne, Nathan Lyon, Michael Neser, Jhye Richardson, Mitchell Starc, Mitchell Swepson, David Warner
England: Joe Root (c), James Anderson, Jonathan Bairstow, Dom Bess, Stuart Broad, Rory Burns, Jos Buttler, Zak Crawley, Haseeb Hameed, Dan Lawrence, Jack Leach, Dawid Malan, Craig Overton, Ollie Pope, Ollie Robinson, Ben Stokes, Chris Woakes, Mark Wood

Australia 4th ranked Test team, England 5th ranked Test team.

FIRST TEST, December 8–12 (red ball). The Gabba Brisbane

Australia wins by 9 wickets.

Teams

Australia: David Warner, Marcus Harris, Marnus Labuschagne, Steve Smith, Travis Head, Cameron Green, Alex Carey (wk), Pat Cummins (c), Mitchell Starc, Nathan Lyon, Josh Hazlewood.

England: Rory Burns, Haseeb Hameed, Dawid Malan, Joe Root (c), Ben Stokes, Ollie Pope, Jos Buttler (wk), Chris Woakes, Ollie Robinson, Mark Wood, Jack Leach.

Match Summary:

England captain Joe Root won the toss and elected to bat.

Strangely, England's most experienced bowlers, Broad and Anderson, were omitted.

England First innings: All out 147 (Buttler 39, Pope 35, Hameed 25, Woakes 21); Bowling: Cummins 5-38, Starc 2-35, Hazlewood 2-42, Green 1-6.

Australia first innings: All out 425 (Head 152, Warner 94, Labuschagne 74, Starc 35). Bowling: Robinson 3-58, Wood 3-85, Woakes 2-76.

England second innings: All out 297 (Root 89, Malan 82, Hameed 27, Buttler 23). Bowling: Lyon 4-91, Green 2-23, Cummins 2-51.

Australia second innings: 1 for 20 (Carey 9, Harris n.o. 9). Bowling: Robinson 1-13.

England didn't get any favours batting first, the Australian skipper showing why he is No. 1 bowler in Test cricket by taking five England wickets as the visitors were bundled out for 147. Only four batters made it into double figures, eight wickets down for 74 runs in the morning session.

Head led Australia's reply with a breezy 152 from 148 balls after Warner made 94. England spinner Leach bore the brunt of the attack, conceding 102 runs for a lone wicket, the prized scalp of No. 1 ranked batter Labuschagne.

England made a better fist of their second innings, with skipper Root making 89 and Malan 82. But the total of 297 left Australia with only 20 runs to get to go one-up. They managed that with loss of just one wicket.

Australia won by 9 wickets inside 4 days (Day 2 final session abandoned due to weather).

Umpires: Paul Reiffel and Rod Tucker; Paul Wilson (TV). Match referee: David Boon.

Notable: Carey took 8 catches in the match, the most by a debutant wicketkeeper. Head was the first to score 100 in a session of a Test at the Gabba.

Lyon completed 400 Test wickets, the third Australian to achieve the feat, after Shane Warne and Glenn McGrath.

England captain Root broke former captain Michael Vaughan's record (1,481) for most runs in a calendar year by an English batsman. It was Root's 25th half century for 2021.

Man of the Match: Head.

Pat Cummins: 7 wickets for 89 for the match (33.1 overs – 9 maidens, 155 dot balls). 12 runs in the first innings, did not bat in second innings. He was the first Australian to take a five-wicket haul in their first Test as captain since George Giffen in 1895.

Other records: First captain since England's Bob Willis (1982) to get a five-wicket haul (5-38 off 13 overs) in an Ashes Test; first Australian captain to take a five-wicket haul since Michael Clarke in 2012; only the 11th bowler to take five wickets in a first innings as captain, and the only Australian to achieve that.

Australia v England
SECOND TEST, December 16–20, Adelaide Oval (D/N, pink ball)

Australia wins by 275 runs.

Australian captain Cummins was ruled out of the match after being a close contact at dinner on match eve with a person who tested positive to Covid-19. Josh Hazlewood was rested because of injury.

They were replaced by Neser and Richardson. Vice-captain Smith took over as captain. England omitted Leach and Wood. They were replaced by Broad and Anderson.

Teams
Australia: David Warner, Marcus Harris, Marnus Labuschagne, Steven Smith (c), Travis Head, Cameron Green, Alex Carey (wk), Michael Neser, Mitchell Starc, Jhye Richardson, Nathan Lyon
England: Rory Burns, Haseeb Hameed, Dawid Malan, Joe Root (c), Ben Stokes, Ollie Pope, Jos Buttler (wk), Chris Woakes, Ollie Robinson, Stuart Broad, James Anderson

Match summary:
Smith won the toss and elected to bat.
Australia first innings: 9 decl 473 (Labuschagne 103, Warner 95, Smith 93, Carey, 51). Bowling: Stokes 3-113, Anderson 2-58.
England first innings: All out 236, trailling by 237 (Malan 80, Root 62, Stokes 34, Woakes 24). Bowling: Starc 4-37, Green 2-24, Lyon 3- 58.
Follow-on not enforced, Australia second innings: 9 decl 230 (Labuschagne 51, Head 51, Green n.o. 33). Bowling: Root 2-27, Malan 2-33, Robinson 2-54.
England second innings: All out 192 (Woakes 44, Burns 34, Buttler 26, Root 24). Bowling: Richardson 5-42, Starc 2-43, Lyon 2-55.

England's second innings 192 total was the 11th time they had failed to make 200 in an innings in 2021.

Again, Australia's top order set a solid foundation, 291 runs coming from the bats of Labaschagne (103), Warner and Smith. Opener Harris again failed to get among the runs.

England wicketkeeper Buttler had a mixed match—three dropped catches matched by three spectacular catches. He twice dropped Labuschagne in Australia's first innings, on 21 and 95, making it 14 times the Australian had been dropped in Test matches.

By the time Australia's second innings began, England in the first six days of the Ashes series had missed 17 chances to take wickets (catches and runouts) at the cost of 235 runs. Buttler held out steadfastly as England tried to stave off defeat, facing 207 balls for his 26 runs before he was out, hit wicket when he trod on his stumps.

Umpires: Paul Wilson, Rod Tucker, Paul Reiffel (TV). Match Referee: David Boon.

Notable: Neser's debut in Adelaide made him Australia's 462nd Australian men's Test cricketer. Until then, the 31-year-old Queenslander had been part of the Australian squad for 17 Tests without ever getting a "baggy green" cap. He had been named in five different Test squads— two tours of the UAE and England and home series against Pakistan, New Zealand and India. He grabbed his first Test wicket with his second Test delivery.

Replacement Australian skipper Smith claimed six catches for the match.

England captain Root was unable to take the field for the morning session of the fourth day after suffering an injury during warm-up. The injury was said to have affected his lower abdomen with one commentator revealing it was an area that would usually be covered by a protector. Apparently a protector wasn't in use. Root was able to take his place on the field later in the day but nearing the end of his innings copped a rocket ball from Starc in a similar area and was in great discomfort when dismissed just short of the end of the day's play. It was unlikely the England captain would be sending photos of the affected area to anyone.

The morning didn't start well for commentators either—two media people tested positive to Covid overnight forcing the BBC and Australia's ABC to abandon their broadcast box for testing and cleaning.

Anderson posted his 100th not out with the bat in England's first innings, the first Test player to reach that milestone.

Australia's record in Ashes Tests at Adelaide became 19 wins, 9 losses.

Man of the Match: Labuschagne, whose performance saw him overtake Root as No. 1. In the world batting rankings.

Pat Cummins: Ruled out of the match just hours before play, tweeted: "Gutted to miss this Test but really excited to see Neser finally get his chance in the baggy green. He has done the hard yards and is a seriously skilful player. Super frustrating but covid has thrown us all some curve balls over the last couple of years. Will be cheering along!"

He was clear to play in the Third Test.

Australia v England
THIRD TEST, December 26–30, Melbourne Cricket Ground (The Boxing Day Test, red ball)

Australia wins by an innings and 14 runs.

Australia needed only a draw to retain the Ashes, leading the five-Test series 2-0 as the Third Test began. England had never managed to come from 2-0 down to win an Ashes series.

Both teams made changes for the Third Test, the last of 2021. Cummins returned to lead the Australians. Fast bowlers Hazlewood,

Neser and Richardson were rested to ensure recovery from their bowling efforts in the earlier Tests. Boland was called up for his first Test. England omitted Burns, Pope, Woakes and Broad, replacing them with Crawley, Bairstow, Wood and Leach.

The start of play on Day 2 was delayed for half an hour because of a covid scare in the English camp. Play went ahead when all players returned a negative test.

Teams
Australia: David Warner, Marcus Harris, Marnus Labuschagne, Steve Smith, Travis Head, Cameron Green, Alex Carey (wk), Pat Cummins (c), Mitchell Starc, Nathan Lyon, Scott Boland
England: Haseeb Hameed, Zac Crawley, Dawid Malan, Joe Root (c), Ben Stokes, Jonny Bairstow, Jos Buttler (wk), Mark Wood, Ollie Robinson, Jack Leach, Jimmy Anderson.

Match summary:
Cummins won the toss and elected to bowl. In their previous 19 home Tests Australia had opted to bat first after winning the toss; electing to bowl was something new.
England first innings: All out 185 (Root 50, Bairstow 35, Stokes 25, Robinson 22). Bowling: Cummins 3-36, Lyon 3- 36, Starc 2-54.
Australia first innings: 267 all out (Harris 76, Warner 38, Head 27). Bowling: Anderson 4-33, Robinson 2-64, Wood 2-71.
England second innings: All out 68 (Root 28, Stokes 11). Bowling: Boland 6-7, Starc 3-29.

Johnny Mullagh Medal for Man of the match: Boland. The Medal commemorates trailblazing Aboriginal cricketer Johnny Mullagh, who toured England with an indigenous Australian team in 1868. Mullagh was inducted into the Australian cricket hall of fame in 2020.

Australia secured the Ashes emphatically (by an innings and 14 runs on day three) inside 12 days of play in a scheduled 25 days of play over five Tests.

The decision to bowl paid off for Cummins, leading the charge himself with three top-order wickets in the first session. Skipper Root offered most resistance with 50. Lyon also claimed three wickets including the threatening Stokes.

Boland claimed his first Test scalp in a steady 1-48 return from his 13 overs without much indication of the havoc he would wreak in England's second innings.

Anderson justified his recall with four wickets, including Australia's openers.

Few would have tipped what was to come when England batted again, all out for just 68. Boland became an instant cult figure for the Melbourne crowd when he ripped into the England line-up. His figures were an unimaginable 6-7, collecting wickets throughout the batting order from opener Hameed to tail-ender Robinson.

Australia didn't have to bat again.

Umpires: Paul Reiffel, Paul Wilson. Rod Tucker (TV). Match Referee: David Boon.

Notable: Boland took 6 wickets for 7 runs off 4 overs (one maiden) in the second innings. His match figures of 7-55 from 17 overs were the fifth ever best for a Test bowler on debut. But there was a question about his future—if Josh Hazlewood was fit, would Boland retain his place for the Sydney test in January?

Boland became the second man of Aboriginal descent to play for Australia in 144 years, Jason Gillespie preceding him 15 years earlier. He was the 463rd recipient of a Baggy Green cap and claimed his first Test wicket with the fifth ball of his 12th over in England's first innings. He also took two outfield catches. He grabbed two England wickets late on the second day and was instrumental in wrapping up the match and the series on the morning of the third day with five more wickets.

Battered, they were. England's batters were out-bowled as Australia took an unassailable 3-0 lead in the series, with two Tests remaining. England's batters had not managed an innings of 300 runs in half a dozen trips to the wicket—their totals were 147, 297, 236, 192, 185 and 68. There were no centuries, and only two batters made 50s—Malan and Root, three times each. The total was only one run better than their capitulation against Australia at Leeds in 2019.

The dismissal of opener Hameed on the first morning was England's 50th duck of the year and 14th Test duck for an England opener in 2021—the previous record was seven. There were four ducks in England's second innings.

Root was dismissed in the first innings for 50, his ninth half-century in Australia without scoring a century. That innings and his 28 in the second gave him 1,685 Test runs in 2021—the third-highest tally of any Test player in a calendar year.

England's woes were year-long. Their top run-scorers in all Tests for 2021: Root 1,708, Burns 530, Extras 412, Bairstow 391, Pope 368.

The Boxing Day test boasted the top three batsmen in world rankings—Labuschagne, Root and Smith, and three of the top 10 bowlers—Cummins, Anderson (8) and Starc (9). Labuschagne and Smith contributed only 17 runs between them, Labuschagne's one run was his first dismissal for less than 47 in the first innings of his last 15 Test matches.

At the end of the Third Test, Four Australians boasted a better batting average than England's best batsmen, including fast bowler Starc: Head 62.0, Warner 60.0, Starc 58.50, Labuschagne 57.25, Root 42.16. The bowling averages showed only Anderson figuring prominently for England at 14.14. He trailed Australians Boland 7.85 and Green 11.0 and just ahead of Cummins, 14.40. Starc was the leading wicket-taker, with 14 scalps at 19.6.

The runs aggregate between the two sides of 520 runs was also a record low for MCG Tests between the two countries, breaking a 118-year-old record of 542 from 1903-1904.

Man of the Match: Boland.

Pat Cummins: If a century by a captain is an exceptional captain's knock, Pat Cummins' three wickets before lunch on the first day would be the bowling equivalent.

The skipper, returning after missing the Adelaide Test, made his presence felt almost immediately. Starc opened the bowling, but it was Cummins who drew first blood in the second over of the match, dismissing opener Hameed with his fifth ball, his 100th Test wicket in Australia. Cummins struck again with the second ball of the eighth over of the day, Crawley caught in the gully by Green. Then to bring the lunch break forward, he snared his third victim - Malan, caught by Warner off an edge. Cummins bowled 10 of the 27 overs in the first session. At his turn to bat when the Australians needed the tail to wag to establish significant a first innings lead, he made 21 runs that contributed to his team's 82-runs lead on the first innings.

Cummins bowled 10 overs for 19 runs but without a wicket in England's second innings.

Australia v England
FOURTH TEST, January 5—9. Sydney Cricket Ground (red ball)

Match drawn.

Sydney's traditional New Year's Test had everything.
The Covid-19 pandemic still loomed large as the Ashes combatants moved to the SCG for the Pink Test supporting the McGrath Foundation. The epidemic had already wreaked havoc on Australia's domestic Big Bash competition.

The Test didn't escape unscathed.

Former Australia fast bowler Glen McGrath and his late wife Jane helped set up the Pink Test theme in 2007 to raise awareness and funds to help fight breast cancer. But McGrath himself fell victim to a covid positive test and could not make it to the SCG for Jane McGrath Day on Day Three.

Test batsman Head and some English support staff also were in quarantine as the Test began. A positive Covid test result ruled Head out. To that point he was Australia's leading run-scorer in the series, with 248 at an average of 62.

Preparing for the worst, Australia added three standby players to the squad, Nic Maddinson, Josh Inglis and Mitchell Marsh. The good news was that all other Australian players and support staff had negative PCR results and the "emergencies" were not required.

Opener Harris, who had dined with Head, had to await test results before he was able to travel to Sydney, the delay meaning he couldn't fly with teammates and had to drive himself there after testing negative. Starc and Lyon also opted for a road trip as a precaution.

The virus didn't miss the England squad: coach Chris Silverwood and three of his assistants went into isolation in Melbourne after positive tests and were ruled out of the Sydney action.

Match referee David Boon also was sent into isolation after a positive test, he too missing the Sydney match.

With Hazlewood still on the injured list Boland retained his place in the Australian side—it would have been hard to overlook him - with Usman Khwaja replacing Head for his first Test match since the 2019 Ashes.

England made one change, Broad in for his 151st Test, replacing Robinson.

Teams

Australia: Marcus Harris, David Warner, Marnus Labuschagne, Steve Smith, Usman Khawaja, Cameron Green, Alex Carey (wk), Pat Cummins (c), Mitchell Starc, Nathan Lyon, Scott Boland.

England: Haseem Hameed, Zak Crowley, Dawid Malan, Joe Root (C), Ben Stokes, Jonny Bairstow, Jos Buttler (wk), Mark Wood, Jack Leach, Stuart Broad, James Anderson.

Match summary:

Cummins won the toss and elected to bat.

Australia First Innings: 8 dec 416 (Khawaja 137, Smith 67, Harris 38, Starc n.o. 34). Bowling: Broad 5-101, Anderson 1-54, Wood 1-76, Root 1-36.

England First Innings: 294 all out (Bairstow 113, Stokes 66, Wood 39). Bowling: Boland 4-36, Cummins 2-68, Lyon 2-88.

Australia second innings: 6 decl 265 (Khawaja 101 n.o, Green 74). Bowling: Leach 4-84, Wood 2-65.

England second innings: 9 for 270 (Crawley 77, Stokes 60, Bairstow 41). Bowling: Boland 3-30, Lyon 2-28, Cummins 2-80.

Recalled to the Test line-up after nearly three years after being dropped, Khawaja's back-to-back centuries gave Australia a decided edge.

Batting at No. 5, his 137 in the first innings helped Australia declare at 8-416. He had a life on 4 when dropped by Root. Khawaja followed up in the second innings with another century, unbeaten on 101 as Australia declared at 6-265.

Khawaja was ably supported by Green who made 74. That left England chasing 388 runs to win, not a realistic prospect given they had struggled to post an innings of 300 runs. Rain intervention along with holding out for a draw were the only options.

And hold out they did—the match came down to the last over, bowled by vice-captain Smith in fading light that ruled out a pace attack, as Australia sought to take the last English wicket for victory. The wicket didn't come and the visitors were relieved to salvage the draw.

Boland entered the bowling attack in the afternoon session of the third day with immediate success. He grabbed two wickets without conceding a run, at that stage boasting the figures of 8-7 after his six-wicket haul in Melbourne. He took a further two wickets on the fourth day as England was all out for 294, still 122 runs behind.

Bairstow provided England's tour highlight with a fighting 113, out early on the morning of the fourth day but giving the tourists some hope of staving off defeat.

The England side copped a battering at the crease and had to field substitute players in Australia's second innings. Keeper Buttler, Stokes and Bairstow all suffered injuries. Bairstow overcame a nasty thumb injury to post the first England century of the series. Buttler (injured finger and to return home) was replaced behind the stumps by Pope (not in the original 11 but allowed to keep wickets under a 2017 rule change allowing a substitute to don the gloves) who claimed four catches. Bairstow who would have otherwise been keeping as tour reserve keeper was not able to do so after his thumb injury. Stokes, England's most consistent player to that point suffered a side strain that restricted his movement and took him out of the bowling attack in Australia's second innings.

The return of Stuart Christopher John Broad, MBE, to the England side for only his second appearance of the tour, paid off from the get-go, the in-and-out of the team fast bowler knocking over Warner before a long rain delay on Day One. Broad dismissed Warner seven times in 10 innings of the 2019 Ashes series in England and this was the 13th time overall that Broad had dismissed Warner, more than any other bowler in Tests. Broad went on to take 5-101 from 29 overs in Australia's first innings, his 20th "fifer" in Test cricket and eighth in Australia.

Bairstow and Stokes mounted a decent rescue attempt with a 128-run partnership that put England on the way to avoiding the follow-on which probably seemed inevitable at 4-36. In the afternoon of the Third Day, Bairstow copped a searing Cummins delivery on the thumb. After treatment, he battled on gamely to remain not out on 103. His century was his 7th in 141 Test innings and his second in Australia after Perth (119) in December 2017. He added only another 10 runs on the fourth day, out to Boland.

On Day Five England's batsman showed their most resolve of the tour to make an Australian victory seem unlikely. Yet the English wickets fell but in shades of the India upset 12 months previously, a fielding lapse proved costly when Smith dropped Bairstow off Starc; his wicket would have meant only bowlers were left to face up with plenty of time and overs remaining.

If England had a hero it was the injured Bairstow who offered stout resistance for 156 minutes and 105 balls as Australia tried to wrap up the England second innings for victory. His 41 runs were inconsequential compared to the time he spent fending off the bowlers, finally falling to a bat-pad chance off Boland.

With three overs remaining, bad light forced the Australians to finish with spin. Smith obliged with his first Test wicket since 2016. England had two overs to face and Australia had one wicket to get. Fielders crowded Broad and Anderson hoping for a defensive lapse.

It came down to the last ball, bowled by Smith to Anderson who kept his wicket intact as England held out.

Umpires: Rod Tucker, Paul Reiffel. Paul Wilson (TV). Match referee: Steve Bernard (Australia)

Notable: Khawaja trivia: He and Bradman are the only two Australians aged 35 or over to score two centuries in a Test; he joins Doug Walters and Ricky Ponting in having scored two centuries at the SCG; first Australian to score twin centuries in a test batting at No 5 since Steve Waugh (108 and 116) at Old Trafford in 1997. In 140 years of Ashes cricket six Australians have scored 100 in each innings of a Test: Warren Bardsley, Arthur Morris, Steve Waugh, Matthew Hayden, Smith and Khawaja.

In the ICC ratings updated after the Third Test, Starc moved up to No 5 in the all-rounder category, replacing Stokes who dropped to 6.

Root led England on to the SCG as England's longest-serving Test captain, for 60 Test matches.

England's Anderson was selected for his 169th Test match, second only to Indian Sachin Tendulkar and passing Australians Ricky Ponting and Steve Waugh for most appearances.

Green thought he had the wicket of Stokes. So did umpire Reiffel.

Replays revealed the ball hit the leg stump without dislodging the bails before deviating away. Green at that stage had 1-0 after claiming Malan's wicket. The umpires had asked the grounds staff to make the stumps a little firmer; they did by using mud to make sure they stuck fast.

The umpires had an issue with Head's appearance on the field and he was sent off. It was nothing to do with his quarantine; he had gone on as a substitute fielder without his name appearing on the team sheet.

With England's wicket-keeping stocks exhausted and with an eye to the final Test in Hobart just under a week away, an SOS was sent to Sam Billings who was in Queensland playing for the Sydney Thunder in the Big Bash. Billings, along with several other England players taking part in BBL 11, were called home early to prepare for the England short-form tour to the West Indies. Billings was due to fly out of Australia on the third day of the Sydney Test but instead found himself in a rented ute driving to Sydney, to avoid flight and covid complications. He spent a night in Coffs Harbour before arriving in Sydney late on Day Four of the Test, joining the squad that would head to Tasmania.

Green made his second-highest Test score of 74 and put on the highest partnership of the series with Khawaja, 179,

Boland's Test career bowling figures (two Tests): 55.1 overs, 14 wickets for 121 runs at an average of 8.64. Of all bowlers in history with at least 10 Test wickets, Boland's average was the lowest.

Man of the match: Khawaja.

Pat Cummins: Cummins hit four 4s in his first innings score of 24 as he backed up Khawaja who was on the way to a century. He had two catches dropped from his bowling including a difficult caught and bowled chance. He claimed 2-68 off 30 overs in England's first innings and a further 2-80 from 22 overs in the second innings, one of his missiles catching Bairstow. Questions were asked about how long Cummins chose to bat on before his second innings declaration. But it was also noted that some early declarations had cost Australia dearly in previous matches, including just 12 months previously when India scored a famous victory chasing down 328 while the Australians needed to bowl them out on the last day of the final game at the Gabba, India winning the series 2-1.

Australia v England
FIFTH TEST, January 14–18, Blundstone Arena, Hobart (Day/Night, pink ball)

Australia wins by 146 runs. Australian wins the Ashes series 4–0 (one draw).

Australia had sealed the Ashes by the time the series arrived in Hobart for the last Test. After hanging on for a draw in Sydney and making Australia struggle in both innings in Hobart, England rekindled hopes for a victory in Australia for the first time in a decade.

But it wasn't to be. Chasing a modest 271 with more than two days play remaining in their final dig, England began confidently. Call it a collapse, call it capitulation, but the result was that England fell short by 146 runs under lights on the third day of play.

Hobart hosted the fifth Test in place of Western Australia due to strict Covid pandemic border restrictions on inward travellers.

It was the first Test played in Tasmania in more than five years when Australia was thrashed by an innings by South Africa in November 2016. It was the first Ashes tested hosted by Blundstone Oval.

England rang the selection changes to try to salvage a win out of the five-Test series.

Five changes were made to the team from Sydney, the most notable being the omission of Bairstow, a century-maker in Sydney, whose thumb injury was serious enough to force him out. Billings replaced the injured Buttler to become England's 700th Test player.

Also in: Burns, Pope, Woakes and Robinson, with Hameed, Anderson and Leach also omitted. The surprise was the omission of Anderson for a match that was to start on a pitch with a green tinge. Stokes stayed in the team despite an injury in Sydney

Australia made the obvious change of returning Head to the line-up in the middle order at the expense of opener Harris with Khawaja elevated to open with childhood teammate Warner. Harris made 179 runs at 29.83 for the series, the lowest among Australia's specialist batsmen.

Hazlewood was again rested, still recovering from injury. Boland was the obvious choice to take his place, boasting a record of 2 Tests, 14 wickets at an average of 8.64, a strike rate of 23.6 and an economy rate of 2.19. Boland had been under an injury cloud from Sydney when he fell awkwardly with his elbow impacting his ribs but he was declared ready to go on the morning of the first day.

Teams

Australia: David Warner, Usman Khawaja, Marnus Labuschagne, Steve Smith, Travis Head, Cameron Green, Alex Carey, Pat Cummins, Mitchell Starc, Nathan Lyon, Scott Boland.

England: Zak Crawley, Rory Burns, Dawid Malan, Joe Root, Ben Stokes, Ollie Pope, Sam Billings, Chris Woakes, Mark Wood, Ollie Robinson, Stuart Broad.

Match summary:

Root won the toss and elected to bowl.

Australia first innings: 303 all out (Head 101, Green 74, Labuschagne 44, Lyon 31, Carey 24). Bowling: Broad 3-59, Wood 3-115, Robinson 2-24, Woakes 2-64.

England first innings: 188 all out (Woakes 36, Root 34, Billings 29, Malan 25). Bowling: Cummins 4-45, Starc 3-53.

Australia second innings: 155 all out (Carey 49, Smith 27, Green 23). Bowling: Wood 6-37, Broad 3-51).

England second innings: 124 all out (Crawley 36, Burns 26). Bowling: Boland 3-18, Green 3-21, Cummins 3-42.

England faced a huge task to salvage something from the final Test of the series and were given hope by some erratic batting performances by Australia's premier batsmen.

As legendary American baseballer Yogi Berra would have said, it was "deja vu all over again" for Australia's top order—disaster in the top order of the first innings followed by another disaster at the start of the second innings.

While pre-match speculation centred on who would open the batting with Warner, it turned out that Warner wasn't the rock Australia was hoping for, managing a pair of ducks on his two trips to the wicket, the second "pair" of his career.

He fell to Robinson in the first innings and to Broad in the second innings without troubling the scorers. It was the 14th time Broad had dismissed Warner, more than any other batsmen in his Test career.

The failure of Warner, Khawaja and Smith in the first innings was compounded by the failure of Warner, Labuschagne (both without scoring) and Khawaja in the second innings.

The England bowlers made use of the favourable conditions in the first hour of play on Day One and again in the night session on Day Two.

The wicket had a greenish tinge and as Broad found out early, it was a bit slippery, landing flat on his face during his first over.

Australia faced first innings oblivion after being sent in and only reached 3-12 in the first hour. It could have been worse as Crawley dropped Labuschagne before he had scored.

Labuschagne went on to make 44 before being dismissed in comical fashion, slipping over as he pushed forward only to see his stumps rattled. Australia managed to get to 6-241 at stumps.

Broad and Robinson (two wickets apiece) had the ball seaming around menacingly.

Root put five slips in place for the edges that inevitably flew.

After the early departure of three top order batsmen, Head and Labuschagne put on 71 then Head and Green added 121 to take control of the bowling and resurrect the Australian scorecard. The tail also contributed; Lyon made 31 including a towering six out of the ground and into a neighbouring property.

Robinson suffered a back spasm and was restricted to 8 overs.

England's first innings was also disastrous—Openers Burns and Crawley were gone before the total was 30, and the side was all out for 188 with 36 by Woakes the best.

Predictions that the pitch would flatten out on Day Two after seaming viciously on Day One appeared unfounded, 17 wickets falling on the second day. Cummins and Starc collected seven between them.

The English bowlers were menacing again in the night session; Boland wore several nasty deliveries on his hands as he stood firm as night-watchman at the end of the day to see Australia to 3-37 after 19 overs of hostile England bowling under lights, and a lead of 152.

The bowlers, particularly Wood, came out fired up in the first session of the Day Three. Wood added three scalps—Boland, Head and Smith—as Australia struggled to put runs on the board and give England a sizeable total to chase.

Things got worse in the second session with Wood's short-pitched barrage earning him another three wickets; his figures of 6-37 were a career best and taking his overall Test record to 17 wickets at 26.64. Broad picked up three as Australia crumbled to all out 155 (Carey best with 49).

That left England more than two days to get 271 runs for victory. At 0-68 England gave the impression they could pull off an upset. The recalled Burns with Crawley were scoring at four runs an over.

Green was brought into the attack just on tea with immediate success, dismissing Burns. It was downhill from there, England losing 10 wickets for 56 runs in 22.5 overs. Green, Cummins and Boland each claimed three wickets as Australia cleaned up the innings for a 146-runs victory inside three days.

Umpires: Paul Wilson and Rod Tucker. Paul Reiffel (TV). Match referee: David Boon

Notable: Australia lost their third wicket for 12 runs (Warner 0, Khawaja 6, Smith 0) in 10 overs on Day One. In the first innings of the previous Hobart Test, in 2016 against South Africa, they lost their fourth wicket for a total of 8 runs (Warner 1, Burns 1, Khawaja 4, Voges 0) and their first innings was wrapped up for only 85. South Africa won the toss and bowled and went on to win by an innings and 80 runs.

Irony: Adam Voges, Callum Ferguson and Peter Nevill did not play another Test after the Hobart disaster in 2016. Only three batters of the top seven in Australia's line-up remained for the 2022 Test—Warner, Smith and Khawaja. Six years later they were the first three out.

With the wicket of Warner, Broad became the highest wicket taker for England in Ashes Tests at 129, one more than Sir Ian Botham. Botham has more wickets against Australia but some came in the era when the Ashes weren't contested under Mike Brearley's leadership after World Series Cricket.

Fielding lapses were not uncommon through the series; by the end of Day 2 Australia had dropped 13 catches (including two off Boland in England's first innings) and England 17. Australia actually held two catches that were given not out and not reviewed.

Carey, who was given two lives by the review system, on 19 and 30, gave Australia's second innings respectability, falling short of a half century.

Fast bowling dominated in Hobart with the quicks taking 39 wickets, the most wickets picked up by pace bowlers in an Ashes Test, passing 38 in Leeds in 1981 and Perth in 2010.

Nathan Lyon wasn't required to bowl at all in the Hobart Test and once in the Melbourne Test; only four times in 104 Tests has that been the case in a completed innings. Lyon's main contributions on the second day in Hobart were three hooked sixes while batting and a stunning catch at point.

Player of the Match: Head.

Player of the series (Compton Miller Medal): Head.

Pat Cummins: Cummins was on target in England's first innings, trapping opposing skipper Root LBW. He also claimed the wickets of Crawley, Malan and Wood in a 4-45 result from 13.4 overs.

In England's first innings, Australia passed up the review options twice, replays showing they would have been successful in taking wickets both times. There were times, too, when chances were missed; in one case the slips fielders appeared to get in each other's way in their tight formation.

In England's second innings, Cummins claimed the wickets of Pope, Wood and last man Robinson to finish as the leading wicket-taker for the series with 21 at an average of 18.04.

Cummins picked up four wickets in a match for the 14th time since 2017, more than any other bowler in world cricket.

Cummins made 2 and 13 in his two visits to the batting crease, finishing the series with 72 runs at an average of 14.4 (he did not play in the Second Test).

His Test bowling record stood at 174 wickets from 36 Tests at an average of 21.18. That included six 5-wicket hauls.

His all-time Ashes record stood at 62 wickets across three Ashes series at an average of 20.64 (economy rate: 2.74).

Series round-up
1st Test, Brisbane: Australia won by 9 wickets
2nd Test, Adelaide: Australia won by 275 runs
3rd Test, Melbourne: Australia won by an innings and 14 runs
4th Test, Sydney: Draw
5th Test, Hobart: Australia won by 146 runs

At a glance

- It was Australia's 34th series win against England. England have won 32 in 72 Ashes series. Six were drawn.
- England's batting average was 19.18, the lowest for any team in a five-match Test series since 2001. It was also England's worst batting average in an Ashes series since 1890, when they averaged 15.74 over the two matches.
- Six times in 10 innings England failed to pass 200 and not once managed 300.
- Only one wicket in Sydney stood between England and the ignominy of a third 5–0 series whitewash in 15 years.
- Australia have won all the ten day-night Tests they have played. They have played three day-night Tests against England, including two in the 2021-22 Ashes series. Australian batsmen averaged 33.87 and the bowlers averaged 20.83 in those 10 Tests.
- The Hobart result marked 15 Consecutive Tests for England in Australia without a win, the shared second longest streak without a Test win for any team in Australia. New Zealand played 18 Tests between their victories in 1985 and 2011. Sri Lanka have played 15 Tests in Australia without a win.
- Joe Root as skipper has lost 10 Tests. Only Archie McLaren with 11 has lost more. Eight of Root's 10 losses have been in Australia. West Indies skipper Brian Lara lost eight Tests in South Africa.
- Scott Boland's bowling average in the Ashes series was 9.55. Only two players with 15-plus wickets in their debut Test series had a better bowling average than Boland; 8.50 by Narendra Hirwani and 9.47 by Charlie Turner.
- Three times England wickets were overturned by a no-ball ruling. Alex Carey was reprieved after Chris Woakes overstepped in Hobart; Ben Stokes did so against David Warner and Ollie Robinson against Marnus Labuschagne in Brisbane.

Joe Root stepped down as England Captain in April 2022, saying the job had taken a heavy toll on him after dispiriting tours of Australia and the Caribbean and a string of poor results. Root became England's second-highest test run-scorer of all time, behind Alastair Cook. His tally of 5,295 runs as skipper is the highest by an England captain.

Captain Pat's Ashes 2021–22

BOWLING					BATTING			
Wkts	Runs	Av	Econ	Bat 1	Bat 2	Runs	Av	Ct
First test Gabba								
7	89	12.7	2.7	DNB	12	12	12	
Second Test Adelaide*								
–	–	–	–	–	–	–	–	
Third Test MCG								
3	55	18.3	2.15	21	DNB	21	21	
Fourth Test SCG								
4	148	37	3.5	DNB	24	24	24	1
Fifth Test Hobart								
7	87	12.4	3.32	2	13	15	7.5	1
Ashes Series								
21	379	18.04	2.99			72	14.4	2

Best bowling: Inns 5-38   Match 7-87.   Overs: 126.4

*Did not play in Adelaide Test, Covid contact isolation.

TEST CAREER BOWLING (AFTER ASHES SERIES)

Mat	Inns	Overs	Mdns	Runs	WKTS	BBM	AV	Econ	SR	5W	10W
38	73	1415.4	349	3921	185	10-62	21.19	2.76	45.9	6	1

TEST CAREER BATTING

Mat	Inns	NO	Runs	HS	Av	SR	50s	0s	4s	6s	
38	55	7	780	63	16.25	38.19	2	9	80	11	

TEST CAREER BOWLING (AFTER PAKISTAN SERIES, MARCH 2022. AUSTRALIA WON 3-TEST SERIES 1-0)

Mat	Inns	Overs	Mdns	Runs	WKTS	BBM	AV	Econ	SR	5W	10W
41	79	1525.5	376	4191	197	10-62	21.27	2.75	46.47	7	1

TEST CAREER BATTING

Mat	Inns	NO	Runs	HS	Av	SR	50s	0s	4s	6s	
41	58	9	833	63	17.00	39.40	2	9	84	14	

Test Catches: 22

Pat Cummins remained the ICC top-ranked bowler in Test cricket, having held the position since the 2019 Ashes. However, he was omitted from the ICC's Test team of the year, apparently because of the limited number of Tests played by Australia (five for the year). Marnus Labuschagne was the only Australian included in the ICC team of the year. Joe Root was named ICC Player of the Year.

The Ashes 2021–2022 Scorecards

England First Innings		Runs	Mins	Balls	4s	6s	SR
Total	(50.1 overs)	147 all out					
Burns	b Starc	0	3	1	0	0	0
Hameed	c Smith b Cummins	25	124	75	3	0	33.3
Malan	c Carey b Hazlewood	6	18	9	1	0	66.7
Root (c)	c Warner b Hazlewood	0	13	9	0	0	0
Stokes	c Labuschagne b Cummins	5	37	21	1	0	23.8
Pope	c Hazlewood b Green	35	136	79	2	0	44.3
Buttler (w)	c Carey b Starc	39	64	58	5	0	67.2
Woakes	c Hazlewood b Cummins	21	50	24	4	0	87.5
Robinson	c Carey b Cummins	0	7	3	0	0	0
Wood	c Harris b Cummins	8	22	15	1	0	53.3
Leach	not out	2	10	7	0	0	28.6
Extras	1w, 5lb	6					

First Test, The Gabba, Brisbane, December 8–12 2021

Bowling	O	M	R	W	Econ	0s	nb	w
Starc	12	2	35	2	2.9	57	0	0
Hazlewood	13	4	42	2	3.2	60	0	0
Cummins	13.1	3	38	5	2.9	61	0	1
Lyon	9	2	21	0	2.3	42	0	0
Green	3	1	6	1	2.0	16	0	0

Fall of wickets: 0 (Burns), 11 (Malan), 11 (Root), 29 (Stokes), 60 (Hameed), 112 (Buttler), 118 (Pope), 122 (Robinson), 144 (Wood), 146 (Woakes).

Australia First Innings		Runs	Mins	Balls	4s	6s	SR
Total	(104.3 overs)	425 all out					
Warner	c Stokes b Robinson	94	278	176	11	2	53.4
Harris	c Malan b Robinson	3	24	17	0	0	17.6
Labuschagne	c Wood b Leach	74	212	117	6	2	63.2
Smith	c Buttler b Wood	12	30	19	2	0	63.2
Head	b Wood	152	258	148	14	4	102.7
Green	b Robinson	0	2	1	0	0	0
Carey (w)	c Pope b Woakes	12	45	32	1	0	37.5
Cummins (c)	c Hameed b Root	12	57	27	0	0	44.4
Starc	c Burns b Woakes	35	98	64	5	0	54.7
Lyon	c Robinson b Wood	15	37	24	2	0	62.5

Australia First Innings		Runs	Mins	Balls	4s	6s	SR
Hazlewood	not out	0	11	6	0	0	0
Extras	4nb, 4b, 2w, 6lb	16					

Bowling	O	M	R	W	Econ	0s	nb	w
Woakes	25	8	76	2	3.0	115	0	0
Robinson	23	8	58	3	2.5	114	0	0
Wood	25.3	4	85	3	3.3	116	1	1
Stokes	12	0	65	0	5.4	46	3	1
Leach	13	0	102	1	7.8	39	0	0
Root	6	0	29	1	4.8	22	0	0

Fall of wickets: 10 (Harris), 166 (Labuschagne), 189 (Smith), 195 (Warner), 195 (Green), 236 (Carey), 306 (Cummins), 391 (Starc), 425 (Lyon), 425 (Head).

England Second Innings		Runs	Mins	Balls	4s	6s	SR
Total	(103 overs)	297 all out					
Hameed	c Carey b Starc	27	92	58	4	0	46.6
Burns	c Carey b Cummins	13	44	27	2	0	48.1
Malan	c Labuschagne b Lyon	82	281	195	10	0	42.1
Root (c)	c Carey b Green	89	246	165	10	0	53.9
Stokes	c Green b Cummins	14	74	49	3	0	28.6
Pope	c Smith b Lyon	4	9	6	1	0	66.7
Buttler (w)	c Carey b Hazlewood	23	69	39	4	0	59
Woakes	Carey b Green	16	65	47	2	0	34

England Second Innings		Runs	Mins	Balls	4s	6s	SR
Robinson	c Head b Lyon	8	31	17	0	0	47.1
Wood	b Lyon	6	14	13	1	0	46.2
Leach	not out	0	8	2	0	0	0
Extras	4b, 6w, 5lb	15					

Bowling	O	M	R	W	Econ	0s	nb	w
Starc	20	3	77	1	3.9	86	0	0
Hazlewood	14	6	32	1	2.3	72	0	0
Cummins	20	6	51	2	2.5	94	0	1
Lyon	34	5	91	4	2.7	154	0	0
Green	12	3	23	2	1.9	60	0	1
Labuschagne	3	0	14	0	4.7	7	0	0

Fall of wickets: 23 (Burns), 61 (Hameed), 223 (Malan), 229 (Root), 234 (Pope), 266 (Stokes), 268 (Buttler), 286 (Robinson), 296 (Wood), 297 (Woakes).

Australia Second Innings		Runs	Mins	Balls	4s	6s	SR
Total	(5.1 overs)	20 for 1					
Carey (w)	c Buttler b Robinson	9	24	23	0	0	39.1
Harris	not out	9	25	10	1	0	90
Labuschagne not out		0	2	0	0	0	–
Extras	2nb	2					

Bowling	O	M	R	W	Econ	0s	nb	w
Robinson	3	0	13	1	4.3	11	2	0
Woakes	2	0	3	0	1.5	10	0	0
Wood	0.1	0	4	0	24.0	0	0	0

Fall of wickets: 16
(Carey).
Australia won by 9 wickets.

Second Test, Adelaide Oval, December 16–20, 2021

Australia First Innings		Runs	Mins	Balls	4s	6s	SR
Total	(150.4 overs)	473 for 9 dec					
Harris	c Buttler b Broad	3	35	28	0	0	10.7
Warner	c Broad b Stokes	95	295	167	11	0	56.9
Labuschagne	lbw Robinson	103	405	305	8	0	33.8
Smith (c)	lbw Anderson	93	327	201	12	1	46.3
Head	b Root	18	59	36	3	0	50
Green	b Stokes	2	6	5	0	0	40
Carey (w)	c Hameed b Anderson	51	128	107	5	0	47.7
Starc	not out	39	62	39	5	0	100
Neser	c Broad b Stokes	35	44	24	5	1	145.8
Richardson	c Buttler b Woakes	9	9	3	0	1	300
Extras	11nb, 5w, 9lb	25					

England Bowling	O	M	R	W	Econ	0s	nb	w
Anderson	29	10	58	2	2.0	144	0	0
Broad	26	6	73	1	2.8	127	2	0
Woakes	23.4	6	103	1	4.4	106	2	2
Robinson	27	13	45	1	1.7	145	4	0
Stokes	25	2	113	3	4.5	101	3	3
Root	20	2	72	1	3.6	70	0	0

Fall of wickets: (Harris), 176 (Warner), 241 (Labuschagne), 291 (Head), 294 (Green), 385 (Smith), 390 (Carey), 448 (Neser), 473 (Richardson)

England First Innings		Runs	Mins	Balls	4s	6s	SR
Total	(84.1 overs)	236 all out					
Hameed	c Starc b Neser	6	34	21	0	0	28.6
Burns	c Smith b Starc	4	12	3	1	0	133.3
Malan	c Smith b Starc	80	214	157	10	0	51
Root (c)	c Smith b Green	62	169	116	7	0	53.4
Stokes	b Green	34	145	98	3	1	34.7
Pope	c Labuschagne b Lyon	5	22	19	1	0	26.3
Buttler (w)	c Warner b Starc	0	20	15	0	0	0
Woakes	b Lyon	24	51	40	5	0	60
Robinson	lbw Lyon	0	11	7	0	0	0
Broad	c Head b Starc	9	44	17	0	1	52.9
Anderson	not out	5	29	13	1	0	38.5
Extras	1nb, 6lb	7					

Australian Bowling	O	M	R	W	Econ	0s	nb	w
Starc	16.1	6	37	4	2.3	82	0	0
Richardson	19	4	78	0	4.1	80	1	0
Neser	11	0	33	1	3.0	48	0	0
Lyon	28	11	58	3	2.1	138	0	0
Green	10	3	24	2	2.4	46	0	0

Fall of wickets: 7 (Burns), 12 (Hameed), 150 (Root), 157 (Malan), 164 (Pope 164), 169 (Buttler), 202 (Woakes), 204 (Robinson), 220 (Stokes), 236 (Broad).

Australia Second Innings		Runs	Mins	Balls	4s	6s	SR
Total	(61 overs)	230 for 9 dec					
Warner	run out (Broad)	13	56	38	1	0	34.2
Harris	c Buttler b Broad	23	81	66	3	0	34.8
Neser	b Anderson	3	23	13	0	0	23.1
Labuschagne	c Stokes b Malan	51	151	96	6	0	53.1
Smith (c)	c Buttler b Robinson	6	43	31	1	0	19.4
Head	c Stokes b Robinson	51	79	54	7	0	94.4
Green	not out	33	60	43	0	0	76.7
Carey (w)	b Root	6	7	6	1	0	100
Starc	c Pope b Root	19	23	20	0	1	95
Richardson	c Buttler b Malan	8	5	4	0	1	200
Extras	5nb, 3b, 1w, 8lb	17					

England Bowling	O	M	R	W	Econ	0s	nb	w
Anderson	10	6	8	1	0.8	55	0	0
Broad	10	3	27	1	2.7	48	0	0
Robinson	15	2	54	2	3.6	59	2	0
Woakes	12	3	46	0	12.0	4	3	1
Root	6	1	27	2	4.5	21	0	0
Stokes	2	0	24	0	12.0	4	3	1
Malan	6	0	33	2	5.5	13	0	0

Fall of wickets: 41 (Warner) 48 (Neser). 48 (Harris) 55 (Smith), 144 (Head), 173 (Labuschagne), 180 (Carey), 216 Starc), 230 (Richardson).

CAPTAIN PAT

England Second Innings		Runs	Mins	Balls	4s	6s	SR
Total	(113.1 overs)	192 all out					
Burns	c Smith b Richardson	34	134	95	5	0	35.8
Hameed	c Carey b Richardson	0	10	6	0	0	0
Malan	lbw Neser	20	81	52	4	0	38.5
Root (c)	c Carey b Starc	24	99	67	1	0	35.8
Stokes	lbw Lyon	12	110	77	1	0	15.6
Pope	c Smith b Starc	4	10	7	1	0	57.1
Buttler (w)	Hit wkt b Richardson	26	258	207	2	0	12.6
Woakes	b Richardson	44	119	97	7	0	45.4
Robinson	c Smith b Lyon	8	61	39	1	0	20.5
Broad	not out	9	48	31	1	0	29
Anderson	c Green b Richardson	2	17	5	0	0	40
Extras	4nb, 2b, 3lb	9					

Australian Bowling	O	M	R	W	Econ	0s	nb	w
Starc	27	10	43	2	1.6	140	1	0
Richardson	19.1	9	42	5	2.2	100	2	0
Lyon	39	16	55	2	1.4	202	0	0
Neser	13	5	28	1	2.2	67	0	0
Green	9	5	9	0	1.0	50	1	0
Labuschagne	4	2	10	0	2.5	21	0	0
Smith	1	1	0	0	0.0	6	0	0
Head	1	1	0	0	0.0	6	0	0

Fall of wickets: 4 (Hameed), 48 (Malan), 70 (Burns), 82 (Root), 86 (Pope), 105 (Stokes), 166 (Woakes), 178 (Robinson), 182 (Buttler), 192 (Anderson).
Australia won by 275 runs.

Third Test, MCG, December 26–30, 2021

England First innings		Runs	Mins	Balls	4s	6s	SR
Total	(65.1 overs)	185 all out					
Hameed	c Carey b Cummins	0	10	10	0	0	0
Crawley	c Green b Cummins	12	37	25	0	0	48
Malan	c Warner b Cummins	14	110	66	1	0	21.2
Root (c)	c Carey b Starc	50	115	82	4	0	61
Stokes	c Lyon b Green	25	90	60	2	1	41.7
Bairstow	c Green b Starc	35	126	75	3	0	46.7
Buttler (w)	c Boland b Lyon	3	29	11	0	0	27.3
Wood	lbw Boland	6	22	15	0	0	40
Robinson	c Boland b Lyon	22	46	26	3	0	84.6
Leach	c Smith b Lyon	13	21	18	0	1	72.2
Anderson	not out	0	9	4	0	0	0
Extras	1nb, 4lb	5					

Bowling	O	M	R	W	Econ	0s	nb	w
Starc	15	3	54	2	3.6	70	1	0
Cummins	15	2	36	3	2.4	70	0	0
Boland	13	2	48	1	3.7	55	0	0
Green	8	4	7	1	0.9	43	0	0
Lyon	14.1	3	36	3	2.5	66	0	0

Fall of wickets: 4 (Hameed), 13 (Crawley), 61 (Malan), 82 (Root), 115 (Stokes), 128 (Buttler), 141 (Wood), 159 (Bairstow), 176 (Leach), 185 (Robinson).

CAPTAIN PAT

Australia First innings		Runs	Mins	Balls	4s	6s	SR
Total	(87.5 overs)	267 all out					
Harris	c Root b Anderson	76	269	189	7	0	40.2
Warner	c Crawley b Anderson	38	62	42	5	0	90.5
Lyon	c Buttler b Robinson	10	28	22	2	0	45.5
Labuschagne	c Root b Wood	1	24	14	0	0	7.1
Smith	b Anderson	16	52	31	1	0	51.6
Head	c Root b Robinson	27	82	48	2	0	56.3
Green	lbw Leach	17	77	63	2	0	27
Carey (w)	c Buttler b Stokes	19	66	43	0	0	44.2
Cummins (c)	c Hameed b Anderson	21	53	32	2	0	65.6
Starc	not out	24	61	37	1	0	64.9
Boland	c Crawley b Wood	6	20	11	0	0	54.5
Extras	5nb, 2b, 1w, 4lb	12					

Bowling	O	M	R	W	Econ	0s	nb	w
Anderson	23	10	33	4	1.4	116	0	0
Robinson	19.2	4	64	2	3.3	89	4	0
Wood	19.5	2	71	2	3.6	84	0	0
Stokes	10.4	1	47	1	4.4	43	1	1
Leach	15	0	46	1	3.1	58	0	0

Fall of wickets: 57 (Warner), 76 (Lyon), 84 (Labuschagne), 110 (Smith), 171 (Head), 180 (Harris), 207 (Green), 219 (Carey), 253 (Cummins), 267 (Boland).

England Second Innings		Runs	Mins	Balls	4s	6s	SR
Total	(27.4 overs)	68 all out					
Hameed	c Carey b Boland	7	52	31	1	0	22.6
Crawley	c Carey b Starc	5	21	16	1	0	31.3
Malan	lbw Starc	0	3	1	0	0	0
Root (c)	c Warner b Boland	28	101	59	4	0	47.5
Leach	b Boland	0	3	2	0	0	0
Stokes	b Starc	11	30	16	2	0	68.8
Bairstow	lbw Boland	5	31	18	0	0	27.8
Buttler (w)	not out	5	26	14	1	0	35.7
Wood	c & b Boland	0	7	3	0	0	0
Robinson	c Labuschagne b Boland	0	3	2	0	0	0
Anderson	b Green	2	7	4	0	0	50
Extras	5lb	5					

England Bowling	O	M	R	W	Econ	0s	nb	w
Starc	10	3	29	3	2.9	50	0	0
Cummins	10	4	19	0	1.9	50	0	0
Boland	4	1	7	6	1.8	20	0	0
Green	3.4	0	8	1	2.2	17	0	0

Fall of wickets: 7 (Crawley), 7 (Malan), 22 (Hameed), 22 (Leach), 46 (Stokes), 60 (Bairstow), 61 (Root), 65 (Wood), 65 (Robinson) 68 (Anderson).

Australia won by an innings and 14 runs.

Fourth Test, SCG, January 5–9, 2022

Australia First Innings		Runs	Mins	Balls	4s	6s	SR
Total	(134 overs)	416 for 8 dec					
Warner	c Crawley b Broad	30	95	72	6	0	41.7
Harris	c Root b Anderson	38	185	109	4	0	34.9
Labuschagne	c Buttler b Wood	28	99	59	4	0	47.5
Smith	c Buttler b Broad	67	192	141	5	0	47.5
Khawaja	b Broad	137	410	260	13	0	52.7
Green	c Crawley b Broad	5	18	14	1	0	35.7
Carey (w)	c Bairstow b Root	13	71	39	2	0	33.3
Cummins (c)	c Buttler b Broad	24	51	47	4	0	51.1
Starc	not out	34	99	60	3	0	56.7
Lyon	not out	16	12	7	2	1	228.6
Extras	4nb, 12w, 8lb	24					

Bowling	O	M	R	W	Econ	0s	nb	w
Anderson	30	9	54	1	1.8	148	0	0
Broad	29	5	101	5	3.5	129	1	0
Stokes	13.5	3	37	0	2.7	69	3	2
Wood	26.1	6	76	1	2.9	126	0	2
Leach	24	2	89	0	3.7	87	0	0
Malan	3	0	15	0	5.0	9	0	0
Root	8	0	36	1	4.5	29	0	0

Fall of wickets: 51 (Warner), 111 (Harris), 117 (Labuschagne), 232 (Smith), 242 (Green), 285 (Carey), 331 (Cummins), 398 (Khawaja).

England First Innings		Runs	Mins	Balls	4s	6s	SR
Total	(79.1 overs)	294 all out					
Hameed	b Starc	6	43	26	1	0	23.1
Crawley	b Boland	18	82	55	2	0	32.7
Malan	c Khawaja b Green	3	63	39	0	0	7.7
Root (c)	c Smith b Boland	0	14	7	0	0	0
Stokes	lbw Lyon	66	150	91	9	1	72.5
Bairstow	c Carey b Boland	113	278	158	8	3	71.5
Buttler (w)	c Khawaja b Cummins	0	17	8	0	0	0
Wood	c Lyon b Cummins	39	63	41	2	3	95.1
Leach	c Cummins b Lyon	10	31	29	2	0	34.5
Broad	c Carey b Boland	15	31	19	1	0	78.9
Anderson	not out	4	7	4	1	0	100
Extras	2nb, 9b, 3w, 6lb	20					

Bowling	O	M	R	W	Econ	0s	nb	w
Cummins	20	6	68	2	3.4	95	1	2
Starc	16	2	56	1	3.5	72	1	0
Boland	14.1	6	36	4	2.5	69	0	0
Green	9	4	24	1	2.7	46	0	1
Lyon	17	0	88	2	5.2	63	0	0
Labuschagne	3	0	7	0	2.3	13	0	0

Fall of wickets: 22 (Hameed), 36 (Crawley), 36 (Root), 36 (Malan), 164 (Stokes), 173 (Buttler), 245 (Wood), 266 (Leach), 289 (Bairstow), 294 (Broad).

Australia Second Innings		Runs	Mins	Balls	4s	6s	SR
Total	(68.5 overs)	265 for 6 dec					
Harris	c (Sub) b Leach	27	84	61	3	0	44.3
Warner	c (Sub) b Wood	3	27	18	0	0	16.7
Labuschagne	c (Sub) b Wood	29	76	42	1	0	69
Smith	b Leach	23	53	31	2	1	74.2
Khawaja	not out	101	206	138	10	2	73.2
Green	c Root b Leach	74	167	122	7	1	60.7
Carey (w)	c (Sub) b Leach	0	5	1	0	0	0
Extras	5w, 3lb	8					

Bowling	O	M	R	W	Econ	0s	nb	w
Anderson	12	1	34	0	2.8	57	0	0
Broad	11	3	31	0	2.8	52	0	0
Wood	15	0	65	2	4.3	59	0	1
Leach	21.5	1	84	4	3.8	81	0	0
Root	7	0	35	0	5.0	23	0	0
Malan	2	0	13	0	6.5	3	0	0

Fall of wickets: 12 (Warner), 52 (Harris), 68 (Labuschagne), 86 (Smith), 265 (Green), 265 (Carey).

England Second Innings		Runs	Mins	Balls	4s	6s	SR
Total	(102 overs)	270 for 9					
Crawley	lbw Green	77	154	100	13	0	77
Hameed	c Carey b Boland	9	88	58	0	0	15.5
Malan	b Lyon	4	39	29	0	0	13.8
Root (c)	c Carey b Boland	24	131	85	3	0	28.2
Stokes	c Smith b Lyon	60	174	123	10	1	48.8
Bairstow	c Labuschagne b Boland	41	156	105	3	0	39
Buttler (w)	lbw Cummins	11	45	38	0	0	28.9
Wood	lbw Cummins	0	4	2	0	0	0
Leach	c Warner b Smith	26	77	34	2	0	76.5
Broad	not out	8	47	35	0	0	22.9
Anderson	not out	0	8	6	0	0	0
Extras	3nb, 7lb	10					

Bowling	O	M	R	W	Econ	0s	nb	w
Starc	18	2	68	0	3.8	74	0	0
Cummins	22	5	80	2	3.6	99	3	0
Boland	24	11	30	3	1.3	128	0	0
Lyon	22	10	28	2	1.3	117	0	0
Green	10	1	38	1	3.8	45	0	0
Labuschagne	2	0	9	0	4.5	6	0	0
Smith	4	1	10	1	2.5	19	0	0

Fall of wickets: 46 (Hameed), 74 (Malan), 96 (Crawley), 156 (Root), 218 (Buttler), 218 (Wood), 237 (Bairstow), 270 (Leach).
Match drawn.

Fifth Test, Hobart, January 14–18, 2022

Australia First Innings		Runs	Mins	Balls	4s	6s	SR
Total	(75.4 overs)	303 all out					
Warner	c Crawley b Broad	0	27	22	0	0	0
Khawaja	c Root b Broad	6	41	26	0	0	23.1
Labuschagne	b Broad	44	86	53	9	0	83
Smith	c Crawley b Robinson	0	5	2	0	0	0
Head	c Robinson b Woakes	101	185	113	12	0	89.4
Green	c Crawley b Wood	74	157	109	8	0	67.9
Carey (w)	b Woakes	24	105	60	2	0	40
Starc	c Burns b Wood	3	29	17	0	0	17.6
Cummins (c)	c Crawley b Wood	2	20	12	0	0	16.7
Lyon	b Broad	31	45	27	1	3	114.8
Boland	not out	10	28	13	2	0	76.9
Extras	3b, 2w, 3lb	8	28	13	2	0	76.9

Bowling	O	M	R	W	Econ	0s	nb	w
Broad	24.4	4	59	3	2.4	115	0	1
Robinson	8	3	24	2	3.0	39	0	0
Wood	18	1	115	3	6.4	59	0	0
Woakes	15	2	64	2	4.3	65	0	1
Root	10	1	35	0	3.5	35	0	0

Fall of wickets: 3 (Warner), 7 (Khawaja), 12 (Smith), 83 (Labuschagne), 204 (Head) 238 (Green), 246 (Starc) 252 (Cummins), 280 (Carey), 303 (Lyon).

England First Innings		Runs	Mins	Balls	4s	6s	SR
Total	(47.4 overs)	3188 all out					
Burns	run out (Labuschagne)	0	11	6	0	0	0
Crawley	c Head b Cummins	18	40	21	3	0	85.7
Malan	c Carey b Cummins	25	92	64	5	0	39.1
Root (c)	lbw Cummins	34	74	46	3	0	73.9
Stokes	c Lyon b Starc	4	20	11	1	0	36.4
Pope	c Carey b Boland	14	39	23	3	0	60.9
Billings (w)	c Boland b Green	29	80	48	6	0	60.4
Woakes	c Carey b Starc	36	74	48	5	1	75
Wood	b Cummins	16	33	15	2	0	106.7
Broad	b Starc	0	4	4	0	0	0
Robinson	not out	0	4	0	0	0	–
Extras	4b, 8lb	12					

Bowling	O	M	R	W	Econ	0s	nb	w
Starc	10	1	53	3	5.3	41	0	0
Cummins	13.4	2	45	4	3.3	62	0	0
Boland	14	6	33	1	2.4	71	0	0
Green	10	0	45	1	4.5	44	0	0

Fall of wickets: 2 (Burns), 29 (Crawley), 78 (Malan), 81 (Root), 85 (Stokes), 110 (Pope), 152 (Billings), 183 (Woakes), 182 (Broad) 188 (Wood).

Australia Second innings		Runs	Mins	Balls	4s	6s	SR
Total	(56.3 overs)	155 all out					
Warner	c Pope b Broad	0	3	3	0	0	0
Khawaja	c Billings b Wood	11	63	38	2	0	28.9
Labuschagne	c Billings b Woakes	5	14	11	0	0	45.5
Smith	c Malan b Wood	27	115	62	4	0	43.5
Boland	c Billings b Wood	8	39	33	0	0	24.2
Head	c Billings b Wood	8	20	16	1	0	50
Green	lbw Broad	23	81	47	3	0	48.9
Carey (w)	c Billings b Broad	49	126	88	4	0	55.7
Starc	c Pope b Wood	1	14	4	0	0	25
Cummins (c)	b Wood	13	50	33	1	0	39.4
Lyon	not out	4	7	5	0	0	80
Extras	1nb, 1b, 1w, 3lb	6					

Bowling	O	M	R	W	Econ	0s	nb	w
Broad	18	2	51	3	2.8	79	0	0
Woakes	11	3	40	1	3.6	50	1	0
Robinson	11	4	23	0	2.1	53	0	0
Wood	16.3	2	37	6	2.2	77	0	1

Fall of wickets: 0 (Warner), 5 (Labuschagne), 33 (Khawaja), 47 (Boland), 59 (Head), 63 (Smith), 112 (Green), 121 (Starc), 151 (Carey), 155 Cummins.

England second innings		Runs	Mins	Balls	4s	6s	SR
Total	(38.5 overs)	124 all out					
Burns	b Green	26	78	46	4	0	56.5
Crawley	c Carey b Green	36	112	66	7	0	54.5
Malan	b Green	10	26	20	2	0	50
Root (c)	b Boland	11	57	31	1	0	35.5
Stokes	c Lyon b Starc	5	26	15	0	0	33.3
Pope	b Cummins	5	45	26	0	0	19.2
Billings (w)	c Cummins b Boland	1	18	9	0	0	11.1
Woakes	c Carey b Boland	5	15	11	1	0	45.5
Wood	b Cummins	11	11	7	2	0	157.1
Robinson	b Cummins	0	7	1	0	0	0
Broad	not out	1	3	1	0	0	100
Extras	13lb	13					

Bowling	O	M	R	W	Econ	0s	nb	w
Starc	8	0	30	1	3.8	34	0	0
Cummins	12.5	3	42	3	3.3	57	0	0
Boland	12	5	18	3	1.5	64	0	0
Green	6	1	21	3	3.5	27	0	0

Fall of wickets: 68 (Burns), 82 (Malan), 83 (Crawley), (92 Stokes), 101 (Root), 107 (Billings), 107 (Pope), 115 (Woakes), 123 (Wood) 124.7 (Robinson).
Australia won by 146 runs.

ASHES 2021—22 in Australia: The Stats

Australia batting averages

Player	Mat	Inns	NO	Runs	HS	Ave	BF	SR	100	50	0	4s	6s
UT Khawaja	2	4	1	255	137	85.00	462	55.19	2	0	0	25	2
TM Head	4	6	0	357	152	59.50	415	86.02	2	1	0	39	4
M Labuschagne	5	9	1	335	103	41.87	697	48.06	1	2	0	34	2
MA Starc	5	7	3	155	39*	38.75	241	64.31	0	0	0	14	1
DA Warner	5	8	0	273	95	34.12	538	50.74	0	2	2	34	2
C Green	5	8	1	228	74	32.57	404	56.43	0	2	1	21	1
SPD Smith	5	8	0	244	93	30.50	518	47.10	0	2	1	27	2
MS Harris	4	7	1	179	76	29.83	480	37.29	0	1	0	18	0
NM Lyon	5	5	2	76	31	25.33	85	89.41	0	0	0	7	4
AT Carey	5	9	0	183	51	20.33	399	45.86	0	1	1	15	0
MG Neser	1	2	0	38	35	19.00	37	102.70	0	0	0	5	1
PJ Cummins	4	5	0	72	24	14.40	151	47.68	0	0	0	7	0
SM Boland	3	3	1	24	10*	12.00	57	42.10	0	0	0	2	0
JA Richardson	1	2	0	17	9	8.50	7	242.85	0	0	0	0	2
JR Hazlewood	1	1	1	0	0*	-	6	0.00	0	0	0	0	0

Australia bowling averages

Player	Mat	Inns	Overs	Mdns	Runs	Wkts	BBI	BBM	Ave	Econ	SR	5	10	CT	ST
SM Boland	3	6	81.1	31	172	18	6/7	7/55	9.55	2.11	27.0	1	0	4	0
SPD Smith	5	2	5.0	2	10	1	1/10	1/10	10.00	2.00	30.0	0	0	11	0
C Green	5	10	80.4	22	205	13	3/21	4/66	15.76	2.54	37.2	0	0	4	0
PJ Cummins	4	8	126.4	31	379	21	5/38	7/87	18.04	2.99	36.1	1	0	2	0
NM Lyon	5	7	163.1	47	377	16	4/91	5/113	23.56	2.31	61.1	0	0	4	0
JA Richardson	1	2	38.1	13	120	5	5/42	5/120	24.00	3.14	45.8	1	0	0	0
JR Hazlewood	1	2	27.0	10	74	3	2/42	3/74	24.66	2.74	54.0	0	0	2	0
MA Starc	5	10	152.1	32	482	19	4/37	6/80	25.36	3.16	48.0	0	0	1	0
MG Neser	1	2	24.0	5	61	2	1/28	2/61	30.50	2.54	72.0	0	0	0	0
TM Head	4	1	1.0	1	0	0	-	-	-	0.00	-	0	0	3	0
M Labuschagne	5	4	12.0	2	40	0	-	-	-	3.33	-	0	0	5	0
AT Carey	5	-	-	-	-	-	-	-	-	-	-	-	-	23	0
MS Harris	4	-	-	-	-	-	-	-	-	-	-	-	-	1	0
UT Khawaja	2	-	-	-	-	-	-	-	-	-	-	-	-	2	0
DA Warner	5	-	-	-	-	-	-	-	-	-	-	-	-	5	0

England batting averages

Player	Mat	Inns	NO	Runs	HS	Ave	BF	SR	100	50	0	4s	6s
JM Bairstow	2	4	10	194	113	48.50	356	54.49	1	0	0	14	3
JE Root	5	10	0	322	89	32.20	667	48.27	0	3	2	33	0
Z Crawley	3	6	0	166	77	27.66	283	58.65	0	1	0	26	0
DJ Malan	5	10	0	244	82	24.40	632	38.60	0	2	1	33	0
CR Woakes	3	6	0	146	44	24.33	267	54.68	0	0	0	24	1
BA Stokes	5	10	0	236	66	23.60	561	42.06	0	2	0	32	4
JC Buttler	4	8	1	107	39	15.28	390	27.43	0	0	2	12	0
SW Billings	1	2	0	30	29	15.00	57	52.63	0	0	0	6	0
SCJ Broad	3	6	3	42	15	14.00	107	39.25	0	0	1	2	1
RJ Burns	3	6	0	77	34	12.83	178	43.25	0	0	2	12	0
MJ Leach	3	6	2	51	26	12.75	92	55.43	0	0	1	4	1
OJ Pope	3	6	0	67	35	11.16	160	41.87	0	0	0	8	0
MA Wood	4	8	0	86	39	10.75	111	77.47	0	0	2	8	3
H Hameed	4	8	0	80	27	10.00	285	28.07	0	0	2	9	0
JM Anderson	3	6	4	13	5*	6.50	36	36.11	0	0	0	2	0
OE Robinson	4	8	1	38	22	5.42	95	40.00	0	0	4	4	0

England bowling averages

Player	Mat	Inns	Overs	Mdns	Runs	Wkts	BBI	BBM	Ave	Econ	SR	5	10	CT	ST
JM Anderson	3	5	104.0	36	187	8	4/33	4/33	23.37	1.79	78.0	0	0	0	0
OE Robinson	4	7	106.2	34	281	11	3/58	4/71	25.54	2.64	58.0	0	0	2	0
SCJ Broad	3	6	118.4	23	342	13	5/101	6/110	26.30	2.88	54.7	1	0	2	0
MA Wood	4	7	121.1	15	453	17	6/37	9/152	26.64	3.73	42.7	1	0	1	0
DJ Malan	5	3	11.0	0	61	2	2/33	2/33	30.50	5.54	33.0	0	0	2	0
JE Root	5	6	57.0	4	234	5	2/27	3/99	46.80	4.10	68.4	0	0	6	0
MJ Leach	3	4	73.5	3	321	6	4/84	4/173	53.50	4.34	73.8	0	0	0	0
CR Woakes	3	6	88.4	22	332	6	2/64	3/104	55.33	3.74	88.6	0	0	0	0
BA Stokes	5	5	63.3	6	286	4	3/113	3/137	71.50	4.50	95.2	0	0	3	0
JM Bairstow	2	-	-	-	-	-	-	-	-	-	-	-	-	1	0
SW Billings	1	-	-	-	-	-	-	-	-	-	-	-	-	5	0
RJ Burns	3	-	-	-	-	-	-	-	-	-	-	-	-	2	0
JC Buttler	4	-	-	-	-	-	-	-	-	-	-	-	-	12	0
Z Crawley	3	-	-	-	-	-	-	-	-	-	-	-	-	8	0
H Hameed	4	-	-	-	-	-	-	-	-	-	-	-	-	3	0
OJ Pope	3	-	-	-	-	-	-	-	-	-	-	-	-	4	0

THE ICC TEST CRICKET RANKINGS AFTER THE ASHES SERIES

Team rankings

1. Australia, 119 points
2. New Zealand, 117
3. India, 116
4. England, 101
5. South Africa, 99
6. Pakistan, 93
7. Sri Lanka, 83
8. West Indies, 75
9. Bangladesh, 53
10. Zimbabwe, 31

Batting rankings

1. Marnus Labuschagne AUS, 935 points
2. Joe Root ENG, 872
3. Kane Williamson NZ, 862
4. Steve Smith AUS, 845
5. Travis Head AUS, 773

Rohit Sharma IND , 773

Bowling rankings

1. Pat Cummins AUS, 898 points
2. Ravichandran Ahswin IND, 839
3. Kagiso Rabada SA, 828
4. Kyle Jamieson NZ, 825
5. Shaheen Afridi PAK, 822

ABOUT THE AUTHOR

Ron Reed is one of Australia's most experienced and acclaimed sports journalists, whose work over more than 50 years has earned numerous awards, including Sport Australia's Lifetime Achievement Award and Australian Sportswriter of the Year. Now a semi-retired freelance writer, he was twice Sports Editor of the *Melbourne Herald* evening paper, Editor of the old *Sporting Globe*, and Chief Sportswriter, columnist and feature writer for the *Herald Sun*, Australia's biggest selling daily paper. He has worked in more than 30 countries on every continent covering most of the world's major sports events multiple times, including nine Olympic Games, seven Commonwealth Games, several editions of cycling's Tour de France and the Giro d'Italia, numerous cricket tours, major tennis and golf tournaments, world championships in athletics, swimming, road and track cycling, triathlon, hockey and rowing as well as America's Cup sailing, horse racing and all of the football codes. *Captain Pat* is his eighth book.